COLLEGE READING SKILLS

COLLEGE READING SKILLS

Kathryn A. Blake

University of Georgia

Prentice-Hall, Inc., *Englewood Cliffs, New Jersey*

Library of Congress Cataloging in Publication Data

BLAKE, KATHRYN A.
  College reading skills.

  Includes bibliographical references.
  1. Reading (Higher education)   I. Title.
LB2395.B57   428.4'07'1173   72–7468
ISBN 0-13-150003-1

10 9 8 7 6 5 4 3

Printed in the United States of America.

PRENTICE-HALL INTERNATIONAL, INC., LONDON
PRENTICE-HALL OF AUSTRALIA, PTY. LTD., SYDNEY
PRENTICE-HALL OF CANADA, LTD., TORONTO
PRENTICE-HALL OF INDIA PRIVATE LIMITED, NEW DELHI
PRENTICE-HALL OF JAPAN, INC., TOKYO

Contents

Chapter

3 FINDING SUPPORTING IDEAS IN PARAGRAPHS 22

Chapter

4 FINDING MAIN IDEAS AND SUPPORTING IDEAS IN LONGER SELECTIONS 31

PART TWO: THE RAPID SEARCH SKILLS

PART THREE: THE EVALUATION SKILLS

Chapter
12 *SUMMARIZING AND NOTE-TAKING*   *179*

Chapter
13 *SYNTHESIZING*   *198*

PART FIVE: THE LOCATION SKILLS

Chapter
14 *USING A BOOK'S STRUCTURE*   *237*

PART SIX: THE VOCABULARY SKILLS

Preface

This book is for students interested in reading skills important to college work. Its coverage is comprehensive. My reason for seeking comprehensiveness is this. College students differ in their educational backgrounds and their current educational programs; consequently, they differ in the particular patterns of skills they have mastered and still need to master. The book's broad coverage makes it suitable as a source book. Particular chapters can be selected and tailored to particular characteristics of individuals and groups.

The chapters include three elements: illustration, description, and practice. The *illustration* serves as a model of the reading skill in use. The *description* presents some of the knowledge-base about the skill. The *practice* provides for some recitation in applying the knowledge-base. For many students, the practice exercises will not provide sufficient recitation for mastery. However, the formats are there and it is a straightforward procedure to add the number of additional practice sets appropriate for individuals.

One of the pleasures of projects like this is to acknowledge the people who contributed. The person who initiated events culminating in the book is Dr. Erskine Key, Vice-President for Instruction and Services at the Florida Junior College at Jacksonville. I am happy to thank Vice-President Key for getting me involved in reading instruction and for his kindness to me during my sojourn at the junior college.

Also, I am pleased to express appreciation to my co-workers at the University of Georgia and at other schools. At the University of Georgia, these people contributed: Dr. Ira E. Aaron, Head of the Reading Department; Mrs. Christine Burroughs, Circulation Librarian, University of

Georgia Libraries; and Dr. Mary Louise McBee, Associate Dean, Division of Student Affairs. Dr. Aaron evaluated the accuracy of the reading knowledge-base presented. Mrs. Burroughs read for accuracy of material on Location Skills; also, she remained gracious while I tied up source materials for a year. Dean McBee responded to the appropriateness of the material in terms of college students' characteristics and needs.

People at other schools who reacted to the work include: Dr. Harry J. Cowart, Director of the Reading Center, Clarke County (Georgia) Schools; Dr. John Paul Jones, The Fort Valley State College; Mrs. Abbie H. Jordon, Savannah State College; and Dr. Sarah Veal, DeKalb Junior College. And, of course, there are those four anonymous reviewers somewhere in the nation who gave such helpful feedback on the manuscript.

A number of students contributed by helping select materials used in the practice sets and by deepening my insight into the process of teaching reading to college students. These students include Janet Ashley, Ann Aspinwall, Mary Jane Bailey, Alvin Strong, Keith Taylor, Terry Taylor, and Dennis Williams, as well as the other students with whom I have worked in classes and individual tutorial sessions.

Producing a manuscript is always an arduous task and my appreciation gratefully goes to the following people. The typing and reproduction were dispatched by Mrs. Janet Edwards, Mrs. Sara Creamer, Mrs. Patricia Wimbush, Mrs. Judi Scott, and Mrs. Peggy Sorrells. Mrs. Jacqueline Tucker did copy-editing and proofreading.

These people all contributed to the strengths of the book and again they have my thanks. Of course, I, alone, am responsible for all errors of omission and commission.

KATHRYN BLAKE

COLLEGE READING SKILLS

1

You and Reading

320 Hill St.

Dear Sam:

I just got your letter. Thank you for asking me to come spend the weekend with you and the others out there. I could really use some time off.
Just skiing, and playing, and fishing, and, most of all, just sleeping. But
I can't make it. I don't think I'll even get all of my work done before the
term ends and exams start. No battle stories but would you believe: 375
pages to read for history, a term paper to write for psychology, two novels
to read and write about for English, and on top of all that, a test in
biology.

It seems hopeless—just hopeless. Still, maybe I'll get it all done if I sit
here long enough and keep at it. Anyway, I'd better try. Next time you
go out, let me know. I sure would like to go with you.

Thanks again,

Marian

Marian

Do you know how Marian feels? Have you ever been in that position? Are
you in it now? What can you do?

Most of us have been there. Had more to do than we could handle
without missing a lot of fun. And without wearing ourselves out too. Sitting there like Marian and keeping at it certainly will help. But working
hard is not enough. You need some skills. Like reading skills. Being a

better reader won't solve all your problems, but it will surely put you a long way down the road.

Do you need to be a better reader? You do if you are like most people. You have heard a great deal about reading in your first twelve years of school. Yet you need to learn much more if you hope to handle large amounts of difficult academic material in college. A lot of people share with you the need to learn more about reading. You would be surprised at how many college students are poor readers. And many students actually graduate with associate's, bachelor's, master's, and doctor's degrees still being very poor readers. If poor readers can graduate, why should you bother working on being a better reader? For two reasons. First, poor readers who manage to graduate pay a high price. They have to work longer and harder than they would if they were good readers. And, like Marian who wrote the letter cited above, they give up many other things to do that longer and harder work. In the long run, they would save time and work if they spent some effort on becoming better readers at the beginning. A second reason for being a better reader is that some poor readers don't graduate. They drop out when the time and work needed for their studies become too much or when all the time and work isn't enough for them to deal with their academic courses satisfactorily.

Can you be a better reader? Of course you can. Most people can. Reading is like a lot of things. You need to know what to do and then you need to practice until you get good at it. This book will help you be a better reader. How? It tells you what to do. Then it gives you practice materials. Let's start by looking at three things: your approach to reading, the structure of the book, and how you should study it.

APPROACHING READING

Your approach to reading should be active and thoughtful—the same as your approach to other things. You shouldn't just drift into a reading situation. At the outset, you should stand back and size up the situation. You should decide exactly what you want to do and how you can do it. Stated another way, you need to know exactly what your purpose is and how you will reach it. This story[1] shows well how wise it is to be active and thoughtful.

Once upon a time a Sea Horse gathered up his seven pieces of eight and

[1] Robert F. Mager, *Preparing Objectives for Programmed Instruction* (Palo Alto, California: Fearon, 1962), p. ix. Used with permission.

cantered out to find his fortune. Before he traveled very far he met an Eel, who said, "Psst. Hey bud, where ya going?"

"I'm going out to find my fortune," replied the Sea Horse proudly.

"You're in luck," said the Eel. "For four pieces of eight you can have this speedy flipper, and then you'll be able to get there a lot faster."

"Gee, that's swell," said the Sea Horse, and paid the money, put on the flipper, and slithered off at twice the speed. Soon he came upon a Sponge, who said, "Psst. Hey bud. Where ya going?"

"I'm going to find my fortune," replied the Sea Horse.

"You're in luck," said the Sponge. "For a small fee, I will let you have this jet-propelled scooter so that you will be able to travel a lot faster."

So the Sea Horse bought the scooter with his remaining money and went zooming through the sea five times as fast. Soon he came upon a Shark, who said, "Psst. Hey, bud, where ya going?"

"I'm going out to find my fortune," replied the Sea Horse.

"You're in luck. If you take this short cut," said the Shark, pointing to his open mouth, "you'll save yourself a lot of time."

"Gee, thanks," said the Horse and zoomed off into the inside of the Shark, there to be eaten.

What is the point of this story? The Sea Horse came to a sad end because he went along willy-nilly. He wasn't exact about his purpose and he didn't think through how he would reach it. So it is when you use reading. Be active, not passive. Know what you want to do and how to do it. Then do it.

You need to carry out several activities in order to take this active, thoughtful approach. In summary, these activities are: decide on your purposes, be flexible, gain a wide knowledge-base, understand the reading skills, get practice, and ignore false statements about reading. These activities are described in more detail below. They can make a difference in whether you control the reading situation or whether the reading situation controls you.

Decide on Your Purpose

Before you read something, you must decide exactly what you want to find out. Answer this question: "Exactly why am I reading this selection?" Do you need only a general notion about the writer's main ideas? Do you want to learn all of his supporting ideas so that you can use them on a test? Do you want to find out what he thinks about a problem like how to get a good buy on a car?

Deciding on purposes is very important for two reasons. First, it helps you pick the reading skills you should use. Second, it helps you know when you have gotten what you should from your reading. As you can see, deciding on your purposes saves you time and work and it may mean the difference between success or failure in using reading.

Be Flexible

Being flexible means picking the right reading skills and the right speeds to suit your purposes. The idea is that you should change your skills and speeds as you need to for doing different things. For example, you shouldn't read at the same speed all the time any more than you should always walk at the same speed. It all depends on what your purposes are. In the same way, you don't use the same reading skills all the time any more than you use the same skills in playing basketball and baseball. And so, in reading, be prepared to be flexible.

Gain a Wide Knowledge-Base

A knowledge-base is what you know about something. It is information that guides your actions. A wide knowledge-base is very important to good reading. It really helps you in figuring out what something says and what it means. You might be good in finding main ideas, in using context clues to word meanings, and at every other reading skill. But if you don't have a good knowledge-base, you'll have trouble getting the message. The old saying works here too: "Them as has, gits." The wider your knowledge-base is, the easier it is for you to learn and add to it.

How do you get a good knowledge-base? It comes as you live and learn. As you do more things. As you get to know more people. As you have more courses in school. And as you read more widely. The key here is this: move out; do things; think about your experiences and reading; figure out how they relate to other things. Don't give up easily. If you keep active, a wider knowledge-base will come to you. In turn, as your knowledge-base gets wider, your reading and studies will become much easier.

Understand the Reading Skills

Of course, when you're a good reader, you'll be able to use reading skills without thinking about what you are doing, just as now you can drive a car smoothly without thinking. But this book pays as much attention to your understanding of what you're doing as it does to your practicing. That is, it shows skills and situations in use and then tells about them—what they are, why they are valuable, and how you perform them. You might ask: "Why should I be able to describe a reading situation and a reading skill? Isn't it enough to be good at doing it?" The answer to both questions is "No." When you study psychology, you'll find out why you don't do as well when you learn things by rote—when you learn without understanding. Being able to tell what you are doing or what you should do helps you to do things more smoothly, to remember them better, and to use them better in new situations. Just remember how much time athletes spend in skull-practice looking at game films and analyzing and going over plays.

Get Practice

You need practice, too. Practice means taking what you learn about the skills and using it in new situations. It's not enough just to know about something. You have to practice doing it. You may know all about how to shoot baskets in basketball but you don't expect to be able to hit the basket most of the time unless you spend a lot of time practicing. So it is with reading. To be good at the reading skills, you need to learn about them and then do a lot of practicing.

There are practice materials in this book. And you should get further practice on your own. Why have this further, independent practice? For two reasons. First, you need more practice than there is room to give in the book. Second, you will like the practice more if the materials mean something special to you. The practice materials in the book were selected by people like you as being interesting to them. And they will be interesting to you. Still, although you share interests with your group, you also have your own individual interests for which you alone can pick material. Spend a lot of time practicing the reading skills with the materials in the book and with materials you choose for yourself.

Ignore False Statements About Reading

Many statements about reading are untrue. Following are some common misconceptions about reading.

If Something Is Published, It's Important. Not so. A lot of nonsense is published. Also, some things may be important to the writer and some readers, but may not be important for your purposes. Decide for yourself what's important for you.

If Something Is Published, It's True. Not so. Some writers deliberately write untrue or misleading material; some make honest mistakes. Others write material that is true when it is published but is disproved by later discoveries. Think for yourself and question what you read.

You Should Say the Words in Your Mind as You Read. Not so. Skip the "saying" stage and save yourself time. This is crucial for reading faster, because when you must say the words, you can't read any faster than you can talk. Learn to look and know as you do when you look at a picture.

People Simply Can't Learn to Read at Speeds Like 500 WPM. Sure they can. If they learn the skills and practice hard, they may reach faster speeds. Set your goals where you want to go and work to get there.

When People Read Fast, Their Comprehension Level Is Lower. Not so. A person who uses the right skills for speed reading keeps up his comprehension while building up his speed. Learn speed-reading skills.

People Can't Learn to Read Fast without Using Machines. Not so. Machines help because they make you go fast. They also show you how well you can do when you're reading fast. But you can get the same results without machines. Don't stop trying just because you can't get to a machine.

Knowing Word Meanings and Word-Analysis Skills Is Not Important for Good Comprehension. It all depends on the kind of material you want to read. If you want to stick to materials on your present reading level, then vocabulary doesn't matter much. But if you want to be able to read material at various difficulty levels, then a wide knowledge of vocabulary skills is important.

You Should Be Able to Read a Selection One Time and Be Through with It. Maybe so, maybe not. It depends on your purpose and the material. One reading may be enough if you only need a general idea and the material is simple and easy. More than one reading may be needed if the material is complex, if you want to get specific ideas, and if you want to remember what you read. Read a selection as often as you need to.

When You Are a Good Reader, You Have No More Trouble Understanding and Using Written Material. Not so. There is a lot more to understanding and using written material than just being able to read it. For example, you need a good knowledge-base. And to understand some materials, you need more knowledge than you do for other materials.

If You Can't Get the Writer's Message, It's Always Your Fault. Not so. Some writers lose control of their material, and don't know exactly what they want to say; some know what they want to say but cannot say it clearly. Writing clearly is very difficult.

STRUCTURE OF THE BOOK

Again, this book will help you become a better reader. But before you begin, stop a bit and look at the book's structure—its blueprint. Why? Because, as you will learn, you can deal with any written material better when you can see its structure—the parts that make it up and the relations among those parts.

The Parts

Parts One through Six are about specific reading skills; they deal with connected writing in paragraphs and longer selections. These are the *comprehension skills*, the *rapid search skills*, the *evaluation skills*, the *processing skills*, and the *location skills*. In addition, there are the skills for dealing with single words, the *vocabulary skills*.

Each skill gets a lot of attention. Why? Because the skills are the basic tools you need. A chapter is devoted to each skill, covering three topics: illustration, description, and practice.

Illustration. To start with, an example is given, showing you what the skill looks like in use with specific material. The illustration will make the general material in the description mean more to you.

Description. The description tells you what the skill is like in general—what the skill is like in the absence of any material and as it fits all material. In this general description, the skill is defined; its value is given; then the actual procedure is spelled out.

Practice. These are practice materials for you to use in learning the skill. They were picked out by people like you. Some came from magazines and tradebooks, some, from textbooks like those you use. Then, of course, there are the answers for you to use in checking your practice.

Relations Among Parts

The six parts of the book overlap in important ways. Generally, the relation among the parts is from simple to complex. Used this way, simple and complex mean how much a reading skill or situation uses other skills.

For example:
—The skills for dealing with connected writing are more complex than the vocabulary skills: in the vocabulary skills, you deal with single words;

in the connected-writing skills, you use your knowledge about vocabulary as you deal with long, highly organized sets of words.

—The evaluation skills are more complex than the comprehension skills. In the evaluation skills, you use the comprehension skills to see what the writer's message is. Then you use other skills to decide whether that message is true.

—The structural analysis skills are more complex than the phonetic analysis skills. In the structural analysis skills, you use the phonetic analysis skills to find and identify the parts of words. Then you use other structural analysis skills to figure out what those word-parts mean.

This all gets kind of knotty, doesn't it? Why is it important for you to know? For this very important reason. As you deal with the more complex skills and situations, you must remember and use the skills you learned earlier. If you do, you will learn the more complex skills more easily. Psychologists use the term *transfer of learning* to describe this remembering and using in a new situation what you learned in an earlier situation.

You need to switch around in the book as you work on the reading skills. Why? As you take on more complex skills, it may help you to turn back to skills you studied earlier. None of us remembers things perfectly. It will help you to do quick reviews as you need to.

I

COMPREHENSION SKILLS

Part One takes up the comprehension skills. These skills help you figure out the writer's message—what he is trying to tell you. Chapter 2, *finding main ideas in paragraphs*, concerns pinning down what a paragraph is about, a directly stated main idea or an implied one. Chapter 3, *finding supporting ideas in paragraphs*, is about looking for those ideas the writer uses to carry out his main idea. Chapter 4, *finding main ideas and supporting ideas in longer selections*, uses skills given in Chapters 2 and 3 with longer selections such as the chapter, the article, and the book.

2

Finding Main Ideas
in Paragraphs

In this paragraph, entitled *Fluster-Bluster*, the main idea is this: When people have an accident, they get flustered and say funny things. Note how this is the idea that all the other ideas carry out.

FLUSTER-BLUSTER[1]

People are funny. Especially if they're slightly flustered at the scene of an accident. Here are quotes from a collection of accident reports:

I left my car unattended for a minute when, by accident or design, it ran away.

I considered neither vehicle to blame. But if either were to blame it was the other one.

The claim form for the accidental killing of a cow read: Disposition of carcass. The answer? "Kind and gentle."

A pedestrian hit me and went under my car.

I thought the side window was down, but it was up, as I found when I put my head through it.

[1] *Fluster-Bluster,* in *Roof Lines* (Seattle, Washington: Safeco Insurance Company, April 1970). Used with permission.

11

I misjudged a lady crossing the street.

I unfortunately ran over a pedestrian, and the old gentleman was taken to the hospital, much regretting the circumstances.

A truck backed through my windshield into my wife's face.

DESCRIPTION

What Is a Main Idea? The main idea is the keynote of the paragraph. It is the topic which a writer carries out in the rest of the paragraph with supporting ideas. A writer may either directly state the main ideas or imply them. In either case, he relates his main ideas and supporting ideas together with guides to coherence.

Why Is Finding the Main Idea Valuable? Finding the main idea is important to understanding. It helps you pin down the writer's message quickly. It makes you better able to see the total picture—what he is saying and how he is saying it.

How Do You Use Guides to Coherence in Finding Main Ideas? You use guides to coherence to see links among ideas: among main ideas and supporting ideas and among supporting ideas. They are focal points in the various kinds of relations. Pinpoint the guides to coherence and you can locate main ideas and supporting ideas more easily. Look for these guides to coherence which writers use very often.

1. Transitional words and phrases (conjunctions)
   Writers use many conjunctions. For example:
   a. Joint relations: and, also, in addition, furthermore, moreover, in other words.
   b. Cause-effect relations: therefore, because, consequently, and so, thus, accordingly, as a result.
   c. Similarities: similarly, in the same way, in a like manner, likewise.
   d. Differences: however, nevertheless, on the contrary, or, nor, on the other hand, still, yet, rather.
   e. Time relations: afterwards, meanwhile, subsequently, then, now, soon.
2. Repetition of content (direct repetition, pronouns, or synonyms)
   Some writers repeat an idea throughout the selection. They may use three forms of repetition: restating certain content (a word, phrase, or sentence); making pronouns stand for content; and having synonyms stand for content.

3. Parallel structures

   Some writers use parallel words, phrases, clauses, or sentences to show ideas of similar importance.

4. Enumeration

   Some writers show connections by marking their ideas. They may use letters (a, b, c, . . .), or numerals (one, two, three, . . . ; first, second, third, . . .)

5. Writers' descriptions or notes

   Sometimes, in longer selections, writers tell you what ideas they present and how they arrange them.

6. Headings and subheadings

   Writers may use headings and subheadings to show relations among parts. Different orders of headings and subheadings go with different levels of complexity. The different orders of headings and subheadings are shown by the different sizes and styles of type.

How Do You Find Directly Stated Main Ideas? The writer sometimes directly states his main ideas in paragraph headings or in topic sentences. And so, look for these in the selections you read.

1. Paragraph headings

   Paragraph headings are titles telling what the paragraph is about. They may be statements or questions. Headings, of course, are easy to find. They are put in different type or print from the rest of the paragraph. They usually are in a different position from the rest of the paragraph.

2. Topic sentences

   Writers sometimes put a main idea in one or more sentences called topic sentences. Here are ways to help you find topic sentences.

   a. Look at the relations among the sentences. The topic sentence is the most general statement. The other sentences are about it more than they are about each other.

   b. Use guides to coherence. The topic sentence may be linked to the supporting sentences by phrases like "for example," "namely," "because," and so on.

   c. Use position clues. Writers may put topic sentences anywhere in the paragraph. However, in any one selection, a writer may adopt a certain style and stick to it.

—The topic sentence may be at the beginning.

People really do differ in the music they like best.
Joe tunes in to folk rock. Mary goes for country western. Joan looks for classical music. Sam will not listen to anything but hymns.

—The topic sentence may be within the paragraph.

Lightning can be dangerous. It involves big electrical discharges. *When lightning storms come, here are five safety rules to follow.* Stay indoors. Keep away from open doors and windows, stoves, TV sets, and plumbing fixtures. Do not bathe. Do not use or plug in electrical appliances. Do not use the telephone.

—The topic sentence may be at the end of the paragraph.

Overinflation, or too much air in your tires, causes faster wearing in the center groove area. Underinflation leads to faster wearing of the outside edge. Underinflation also brings on greater heat which is another cause of tire wear and failure. *The right amount of inflation is very important to the life of your tires.*

How Do You Find Implied Main Ideas? Implied ideas, of course, are not directly stated. Instead, they are suggested by the sentences in the paragraph taken together.

Ticks can be carriers for two bad illnesses, Rocky Mountain spotted fever and tularemia. Tick bites in a person's head or spine areas may lead to paralysis. This paralysis clears up soon after the tick is removed. Local infections can be caused by leaving the head when the tick is removed.

What is the main idea implied here? It is: *Tick bites can hurt people.* This idea is suggested by the troubles that tick bites cause. Finding implied main ideas takes several steps.

1. Look at the sentences in relation to one another. Go beyond the different words. Find the idea that all the sentences refer to in common. This common idea is the implied main idea.
2. Make a direct statement of your own. Directly state the implied main idea as a paragraph heading or as a topic sentence.
3. Check your statement. Test each of the writer's sentences against your statement to see if they support your statement. If yes, then you have found the implied idea. If no, then try out another direct statement. Keep trying until you get a statement that is supported by the writer's sentences.

PRACTICE

Find the main idea for each paragraph. Write it in the space given.

Set 1

THOREAU[2]

Thoreau Believed That Each of Us Is His Own Jailer. One day a week, a man should work. Six days a week, he should read, think, and tramp in the woods, observing and enjoying the beauties and wonders of nature. To Henry David Thoreau, a friend of Emerson and, like him, a resident of Concord, Massachusetts, this was the ideal life. Thoreau believed that too many people spend so much of their lives trying to amass money that they never really live. Thoreau believed further that most persons imprison themselves by living dull, meaningless, routine lives to gain possessions that are, in reality, burdens to them. To him, these were "lives of quiet desperation."

Main idea: THOREAU BELIEVED THAT EACH OF US IS HIS OWN JAILER.

Set 2

FEAR AND FRIENDLINESS[3]

The more I traveled, the more I realized that fear makes strangers of people who should be friends. Once for a period of one month I knew what it meant to be totally without fear. What I felt was harmony, honor, and complete trust of another people. They happened to be black people. They weren't civilized. They were primitive. And they themselves were the most nearly fearless human beings I have ever known. The only thing they feared was nature. Lying was beyond their comprehension. Their self-confidence was absolute and their arrogance was justified. They were the Masai tribe of East Africa.

Main idea: FEAR MAKES STRANGERS OF PEOPLE WHO COULD BE FRIENDS.

[2] Nathaniel Platt and Muriel Jean Drummond, *Our Nation From Its Creation* 2nd ed., © 1966. By permission of Prentice-Hall, Inc., Englewood Cliffs, New Jersey.

[3] Shirley MacLaine, *Don't Fall Off the Mountain* (New York: W. W. Norton & Company, Inc., 1970), p. 152. By permission of W. W. Norton & Company, Inc. Copyright © by Shirley MacLaine. Used with permission.

EMOTIONS AND YOUR DRIVING[4]

When you drive, you need to watch for danger from many sources. Many traffic accidents and a good deal of unsafe driving can be traced to emotional factors. The person who has just had a frightening experience may be too upset to do as he should behind the wheel of a car. And, many mistakes in driving judgments can be made by the person who has just had an argument, slams into his car, and drives off full of anger and resentment.

Main idea: YOUR EMOTIONS EFFECT YOUR DRIVEING

THE IMPACT OF INDUSTRIAL TECHNOLOGY[5]

The way we live and feel has been greatly affected by the widespread growth of industrial technology, the development and use of machines like the car, the telephone, and the computer. Here are three examples. First, *the urbanization of society has vastly increased* bringing the good and bad effects of city living. Second, *each person's economic independence has greatly lessened* making him much more vulnerable to economic and social forces beyond his direct control. Third, *the character of work has radically changed* leading the person to feel more powerless and separated in relation to the natural and man-made worlds.

Main idea: THE URBANIZATION OF SOCIETY HAS INCREASED, MAKING PEOPLE LESS INDEPENDENT, AND POWERLESS

[4] Center for Safety Education, New York University, *Driver Education and Traffic Safety* © 1967. By permission of Prentice-Hall, Inc., Englewood Cliffs, New Jersey.

[5] Robert L. Heilbronner, *The Making of Economic Society*, 2nd ed., © 1968, pp. 98–100. Abridged. By permission of Prentice-Hall, Inc., Englewood Cliffs, New Jersey.

Set 5

THE SCIENTIST'S TOOLS[6]

No matter what phenomena he is interested in, the scientist employs two main tools—theory and empirical research. *Theory* employs reason, language, and logic to suggest possible, or predict probable, relationships among various data gathered from the concrete world of experience. *Empirical research* is the process of gathering these data through rigorous, careful and patient observation, and of recording them in detail and with precision, so that any other scientist can check the results. Theory and empirical research are complementary. Each is empty and sterile without the other, and neither can stand alone. Theory that is not tested against fact is mere speculation; facts gathered without reference to theory are meaningless conglomerations.

Main idea: THEORY & EMPIRICAL RESERCH ARE THE TWO MAIN TOOLS USED BY SCIENTIST

Set 6

REVOLUTION AS A SYMPTOM[7]

The starting of a revolution shows that old ways of doing things no longer are right for the conditions, needs, and demands of a group of society; and that this group is large enough or strong enough to change things by force if the present leaders of society do not meet its demands. These things make revolutions happen. The purpose of the group who revolts is to change old ways of doing things in order to make them answer, more or less, to present conditions, needs, and demands. Thus, a revolution is a sad thing because it is a sign that "the times are out of joint."

Main idea: REVOLUTION SHOWS THAT CHANGE IS NECESSARY

[6] John Biesanz and Mavis Biesanz, *Modern Society. An Introduction to Social Science*, 3rd ed., © 1964. By permission of Prentice-Hall, Inc., Englewood Cliffs, New Jersey.

[7] Based on: Arnold J. Toynbee, "Revolutionary Change," in *The Great Ideas Today: 1970* (New York: Encyclopedia Britannica, 1970), pp. 4–27.

Set 7

OUR GOLDEN AGE?[8]

We have many world-wide problems in the twentieth century. For example, various historical forces have led to racial conflict, conflicts between rich and poor lands, nationalism in one-world time, and problems taking care of scientific and technological discoveries' side effects like the unbalancing of nature. On the other hand, there are many good developments in the twentieth century. Think a minute about such things as nations' taking global responsibility, the possibility of ending want, the awakening of peoples all over the world, and the good things from science and technology. In short, it must be concluded that this is an age of great problems and great opportunities, of great pride and great potential.

Main idea: THE TWENTIETH CENTURY HAS GREAT OPPORTUNITIES IN SPITE OF SIDE EFFECTS

Set 8

GETTING SPECIFIC ABOUT IDEAS[9]

The whole process of writing is like an inverted triangle ∇ . The job is to get from some broad and often vague idea down to the most specific, narrow way of explaining that idea. The idea of freedom can be used by anybody to mean almost anything. But talk about freedom is not meaningful until it is limited to a narrower, lower level of discussion. There is quite a difference between being free to complain about the mayor and being free to invade his private office, or between being free to talk about owning firearms and being free to have a closet full of them. Getting down to that level, down to the nitty gritty facts, that is

---

[8] Based on: L. S. Stavrianos, *The World Since 1500: A Global History* (Englewood Cliffs, N.J.: Prentice-Hall, Inc., 1966), pp. 655–68.

[9] Alan Casty and Donald Tighe, *Staircase to Writing and Reading: A Rhetoric and Anthology*, © 1969. By permission of Prentice-Hall, Inc., Englewood Cliffs, New Jersey.

the job of writing. It is a job that goes on all through the process of writing a paper; but it has to start with thinking about the subject, and limiting it.

Main idea: WHEN WRITING, START FROM ABROAD AREA BUT HAVE A SPECIAL POINT IN MIND.

Set 9

ABRAHAM CADY WRITES[10]

Samantha became the silent partner and privileged observer to one of the unique human experiences, the writing of a novel. She saw him detach himself from the first world of reality and submerge into a second world of his own creation and wander it alone. There was no magic. There was no inspiration that people always look for and imagine in the writer. What there was, was the relentless plodding requiring a special kind of stamina that makes the profession so limited. Of course, there came moments when things suddenly fell into a natural rhythm and, even more rare, that instant of pure flying through creative exhilaration. But what Samantha witnessed most was the uncertainty, the drain, the emotional downs, those times he did not have the strength to undress himself.

Main idea: WRITING IS A PHYSICAL AS WELL AS A MENTAL DRAIN ON THE AUTHOR AND THERE ARE NO MAGIC.

Set 10

A PLANT AND ANIMAL TAXONOMY[11]

Scientists classify particular plants or animals by using seven major ordered categories: kingdom, phylum, class, order, family, genus, and

[10] Leon Uris, *QB VII* (Garden City, N.Y.: Doubleday and Company, Inc., 1970), p. 146. Copyright © by Leon Uris. Used with permission.

[11] Neal B. Buffaloe and J. B. Throneberry, *Principles of Biology*, 2nd ed., © 1967, pp. 79–80. By permission of Prentice-Hall, Inc., Englewood Cliffs, New Jersey.

species. By way of illustration, let us consider the classification of an animal common to everyday experience, the domesticated cat. In distinguishing it as a kind (a species) of organism different from all other organisms, we can best start with the most general category of classification and proceed toward the most specific. There are two great kingdoms into which most organisms fit readily on the basis of characteristics that will be defined later on. There are the *plant* and *animal* kingdoms, and our specimen is classified in the latter group. Of the many phyla which taxonomists recognize in this kingdom, we find that the cat possesses those characteristics generally accepted for the phylum *Chordata*, a group that is made to include all animals exhibiting, among other features, a structure called a *notochord* at some time during their lives. Of such animals, one group, the vertebrates, are able to replace the notochord with a vertebral column and hence comprise the subphylum *Vertebrata*. Within this subphylum, several classes are recognized. Our animal is placed in the class *Mammalia* along with all other vertebrates whose young are nourished by means of milk and who produce hair as an external bodily covering, to mention two of their characteristics. This class is divided into several orders, one of which, the order *Carnivora* is made to include those mammals whose natural food is the flesh of other animals. The carnivores differ so much among themselves that a number of families have been established taxonomically, and the cat is placed with other carnivores to which it bears a strong resemblance in the family *Felidae* (the cat family). Within this family, two genera are recognized; one of these is the genus *Felis* which includes all "true" cats. There are several species belonging to this genus: *Felis leo* ("lion cat"), *Felis tigris* ("tiger cat"), and so on. Our cat differs from these, however, in one respect that has been selected for descriptive purposes. It can be tamed, and hence it is called *Felis domestica* ("domesticated cat"). In summary then, let us arrange the ordered classification of the house cat this way.

Kingdom: Animalia
 Phylum: Chordata
  Subphylum: Vertebrata
   Class: Mammalia
    Order: Carnivora
     Family: Felidae
      Genus: Felis
       Species: Felis domestica

Main idea: PLANTS & ANIMALS ARE SEPERATED FOR IDENTIFICATION BY SCIENTISTS

ANSWERS FOR PRACTICE SETS

Set 1

Thoreau believed that each of us is his own jailer. We imprison ourselves by our own actions.

Set 2

Fear makes strangers of people who should be friends.

Set 3

Many traffic accidents and a good deal of unsafe driving can be traced to emotional factors which operate in all of us.

Set 4

The way we live and feel has been greatly affected by the widespread growth of industrial technology.

Set 5

The scientist employs two main tools—theory and research.

Set 6

Revolution is sad because it shows that things are not in balance. People's needs are not being met by the old ways of doing things.

Set 7

This is an age of great problems and great opportunities, of great pride and great potential.

Set 8

The job in writing is narrowing broad ideas down to specifics, the actual events you can observe.

Set 9

Writing involves a lot of hard work and suffering as well as satisfaction and joy.

Set 10

Scientists classify particular plants or animals by using seven major ordered categories: kingdom, phylum, class, order, family, genus, and species.

3

Finding Supporting Ideas in Paragraphs

Ideas 1 and 3 are supporting ideas. See how they carry out the main idea about surfing and skiing. Ideas 2 and 4 are not supporting ideas. They are about related main ideas but not the one stated here.

SURFING AND SKIING[1]

Surfing and skiing have come closer together with the short surfboard; now, we can compare the two sports.

1. In both sports, you must center your body-weight over your feet.
2. The new bellyboards are less tricky than the stand-up surfboards.
3. In skiing, you keep your stance fixed. You put more weight on the downhill ski and keep it slightly behind the uphill ski. In surfing, you keep your weight on both feet until you make forward turns and cutbacks; then, you shift more weight to the back foot.
4. Running dune buggies, snowmobiles, and minicycles are other activities which are getting to be more popular.

[1] Based on Joe Cabell, "Surfing and Skiing Techniques," *Surfing*, June 1970.

DESCRIPTION

What Are Supporting Ideas? Writers use supporting ideas to carry out their main ideas. They may present these supporting ideas in several ways: giving particular cases, using a restatement, giving reasons, and making comparisons and contrasts. And, helpfully, most writers tip you off with guides to coherence.

Why Is It Valuable to Find Supporting Ideas? Finding the information the writer uses to carry out his main idea and ruling out extra ideas is important to understanding in three ways. One, it helps you grasp what the main idea means. Two, it helps you see how the writer is trying to get across his main idea. Three, it prevents your mixing up main ideas and supporting ideas—in other words, from getting confused about what the selection is about.

How Do You Find Supporting Ideas? There are four basic steps.

1. Find the main idea of the paragraph. (See Chapter 2.)
2. Find each remaining idea in the paragraph. In this process, use guides to coherence. (See Chapter 2.)
3. Decide whether these remaining ideas are supporting ideas. Check each to see whether it fits the main idea; whether the writer uses it to carry out the main idea as a particular case, a restatement, a reason, or as a comparison or contrast.
   a. Giving particular cases
      Writers may carry out the main idea by listing particulars: by giving examples, illustrations, steps, parts, members of a class, characteristics, and so on. Look for guides to coherence like "for example," "for instance," "namely."
   b. Using a restatement
      Some writers state the main idea again in different words. Guides to coherence are phrases like "that is" or "in other words."
   c. Giving reasons
      Writers often give reasons to justify the main idea or to show cause-effect relations. Watch for guides to coherence like "because," "for these reasons," "therefore," "consequently."
   d. Making comparisons and contrasts
      Writers sometimes try to get across the main idea by showing what something is like. Or they may show what it is not like. Sometimes they use both comparisons *and* contrasts—that is, both likenesses and differences.
4. Rule out duds, pads, and distractors
   Sad to say, in some paragraphs, writers put in extra ideas that do not

fit the main idea. These extra ideas are the ones that are left after you identify the supporting ideas. Ignore them. They will only confuse you.

a. A *dud* is a mistake; it happens when a writer loses control and gets off the point.

b. A *pad* is extra material the writer throws in to fill out space.

c. A *distractor* is a fooler; writers use it to lead readers astray.

PRACTICE

Pick out the supporting ideas for each main idea. Write their code numbers in the space given.

Set 1

FORM CLASSES[2]

Main idea: One category of the parts of speech consists of words that can take suffixes; that is, they can change their form (spelling) and are called form classes.

Supporting ideas: _____

1. Verbs can take inflectional suffixes like *-ing* (playing), *-s* (plays), and *-ed* (played).

2. Emphasis on any word or any group of words can come from its position in the sentence.

3. The *There is* or *There are* sentence pattern gives emphasis by delaying impact. It uses *There* to signal the reader that the subject is out of its usual position.

4. Nouns can take a number of suffixes, for example: *-s* (boys), *'s* (cat's). *-er* (player), *-ous* (joyous).

5. Adjectives inflect to indicate the comparative and superlative degrees, for instance, *-er* (taller) and *-est* (tallest).

[2] Based on: Helen C. Lodge and Gerald L. Trett, *New Ways in English* (Englewood Cliffs, N.J.: Prentice-Hall, Inc., 1968), pp. 167–231.

Set 2

THE MELTING OF SOLIDS[3]

Main idea: A special set of words has been found useful in dealing with processes such as melting and freezing.

Supporting ideas: ────────────────────────────────

1. The discovery of regularities or patterns helps the scientist more easily describe a number of separate observations.
2. Ice is the *solid phase* of water and water is the *liquid phase*.
3. After the scientist finds regularities, he asks: Why do they happen? What is the explanation?
4. The *melting point* is the temperature at which a solid turns to liquid.
5. A change that occurs when a solid melts or a liquid freezes is called a *phase change*.

Set 3

WHAT AFFECTS CLIMATE?[4]

Main idea: Several factors affect climate: the heat, the humidity, the rainfall.

Supporting ideas: ────────────────────────────────

1. Climate varies with latitude. Countries near the equator generally have a hot climate; those nearer the north and south poles, a colder climate.
2. Nearness to the water can make a difference in the climate of an area. Land nearer the water is warmer in summer and cooler in winter than land more distant from the water.
3. Temperature changes as altitude changes. The higher you go, the cooler the temperature is.
4. Weather refers to day-to-day changes in atmospheric conditions. On

[3] Based on: Robert W. Parry, Luke E. Steiner, Robert L. Tellefsen, and Phyllis M. Dietz, *Chemistry* (Englewood Cliffs, N.J.: Prentice-Hall, Inc., 1970), pp. 2–19.
[4] Based on: Sol Holt, *World Geography and You* (Princeton, N.J.: D. van Nostrand, 1964), pp. 23–30.

the other hand, climate refers to a characteristic pattern, the average of weather conditions over a long period of time.

5. A temperature over 90 degrees Fahrenheit is considered hot; under 30 degrees, cold; and between 60 and 70 degrees, comfortable.

Set 4

THE MASTER GLAND[5]

Main idea: The anterior pituitary is a very important endocrine gland.

Supporting ideas: _____

1. One of the pituitary gland's hormones is called the growth hormone. The growth hormone has a role in physical growth and control of blood sugar.

2. The anterior pituitary is often called the master gland because it secretes several hormones needed by the thyroid gland, the adrenal cortex, and the sex glands—all very important endocrine glands themselves.

3. Insulin, a hormone from the pancreas, has an important affect on the cells' use of glucose or sugar.

4. Metabolism, roughly, is the changing of foodstuffs into energy within the body.

Set 5

USE SPECIFIC, PRECISE LANGUAGE[6]

Main idea: In writing and in speaking, use explicit language rather than vague language.

Supporting ideas: _____

[5] Based on: Robert I. Macey, "Human Physiology," in William D. McElroy and Carol P. Swanson, eds., *Foundations of Biology* (Englewood Cliffs, N.J.: Prentice-Hall, Inc., 1968), pp. 561–722.

[6] Suggested by ideas in the following: B. J. Chute, "When the Writer Comes of Age," in A. S. Burack, ed., *The Writer's Handbook* (Boston: The Writer, 1970), pp. 6–14; William Strunk, Jr. and E. B. White, *The Elements of Style* (New York: Macmillan, 1959).

1. Writing and speech-making are satisfying even though they are hard work.

2. Which form shows the message better?

His gastric discomfort was immeasurably diminished subsequent to his partaking in a sumptuous repast.

His stomach ache was better after he ate a good meal.

3. Style, grammar, and content are building blocks in both writing and speaking.

4. You often have to do a good bit of rewriting to get your message into clear, specific language. What appears quite simple is often quite hard to achieve.

Set 6

ELECTRONIC MUSIC[7]

Main idea: Some composers are very interested in electronic music.

Supporting ideas: _____

1. Electronic music is music produced by electronic generators and amplified over loudspeakers. With this equipment, we can produce any gradation and range of pitch and timbre. The possibilities are much greater than the conventional semitone system and tone colors available in existing instruments.

2. Musique concrete is tape-recorder-loudspeaker music in which the basic sound material is taken from nature, not generated electronically.

3. Pure electronic music does not need any musical performers for its generation. Therefore, a composer can work directly with his medium just as a painter works directly with paint on canvas.

4. Leontyne Price, Joan Sutherland, and Marilyn Horne can produce broad ranges of pitch and timbre.

[7] Based on: David D. Boyden, *An Introduction to Music* (New York: Knopf, 1970), pp. 517–22.

ENDURING QUESTIONS OF POLITICS[8]

Main idea: In politics, there are some problems which have had men's attention continually through the ages.

Supporting ideas: _____

1. One role of art is to help man understand himself by pinpointing things as they are.

2. For the sake of humanity and enlightened self-interest, man keeps trying to solve problems related to authority, freedom, equality, constitutionalism, and government and order.

3. In most cultures, men have developed myths and other folklore around people's common joys, fears, and griefs.

4. As man has made progress with problems of constitutionalism and democracy within nations, he has made progress with problems of international society.

TWO KINDS OF SPEAKING[9]

Main idea: There are two basic kinds of speaking: original and interpretive.

Supporting ideas: _____

1. In original speaking, the speaker uses his own words to present his own ideas to an audience.

2. In opera, the talented and highly trained have a showplace for their great voices.

3. In interpretive speaking (reading aloud), the speaker presents the author's ideas in the author's words; in addition, he goes further to show their meaning.

[8] Based on: Werner Feld, Alan T. Leonhard, and Walter W. Toxey, Jr., eds., *The Enduring Questions of Politics* (Englewood Cliffs, N.J.: Prentice-Hall, Inc., 1969).

[9] Harry G. Barnes, *Speech Handbook* (2nd ed.) (Englewood Cliffs, N.J.: Prentice-Hall, Inc., 1959), p. 70.

4. In both original and interpretive speaking, the speaker must use skills to get the people's attention, to hold their interest throughout the presentation, and to make certain thoughts and feelings clear and understandable to them.

5. The recitative is a link between the literary and musical arts.

Set 9

MEASURING VOLUME[10]

Main idea: Volume is not the best measure for the quantity of solid matter.

Supporting ideas: _____

1. The density of solids affects their volume. Think about a cup of flour before and after it is sifted.

2. A balance is a measure which compares the pull of gravity on two pieces of matter. Think of a set of balance scales.

3. Solid matter can change in form without changing in quantity. Think about a piece of metal—how it grows smaller when it is cooled and larger when it is heated.

4. Characteristic properties are properties of substance that are independent of their size or shape. Think about the qualities which describe a piece of wood: as it is part of a tree, and as it is part of a chair.

Set 10

THE COMMUTATIVE PROPERTY[11]

Main idea: Addition and multiplication are commutative operations; it does not matter what order is used with the numbers. On the other hand, subtraction and division are non-commutative operations.

Supporting ideas: _____

1. These statements always are so: $7 + 9 = 9 + 7$; $3 \times 7 = 7 \times 3$.

10 Based on: IPS Group, *College Physical Science* (Englewood Cliffs, N.J.: Prentice-Hall, Inc., 1969), pp. 10–13, 33.

11 Based on: Eugene D. Nichols, *Pre-Algebra Mathematics* (Holt, Rinehart and Winston, 1965), pp. 99–109.

2. Most people use the base-ten number system more often than they use the base-seven system.

3. These statements are *not true*: $20 - 8 = 8 - 20$; $8 \div 2 = 2 \div 8$.

4. Numerals are symbols which stand for numbers.

5. $[(2 + 5) + 6 = 2 + (5 + 6)]$ is an example of the associative property of addition.

ANSWERS FOR PRACTICE SETS

Set 1
Supporting ideas are nos. 1, 4, and 5.

Set 2
Supporting ideas are nos. 2, 4, and 5.

Set 3
Supporting ideas are nos. 1, 2, and 3.

Set 4
Supporting ideas are nos. 1 and 2.

Set 5
Supporting ideas are nos. 2 and 4.

Set 6
Supporting ideas are nos. 1, 2, and 3.

Set 7
Supporting ideas are nos. 2 and 4.

Set 8
Supporting ideas are nos. 1, 3, and 4.

Set 9
Supporting ideas are nos. 1 and 3.

Set 10
Supporting ideas are nos. 1 and 3.

4

Finding Main Ideas and Supporting Ideas in Longer Selections

ILLUSTRATION

The paragraphs in this selection on car stealing are numbered. Note how the writer uses the ideas in these paragraphs. He leads out in paragraph 1 with his main idea: *Through carelessness, many people make it easy for thieves to steal their cars.* Of the four ideas listed below, ideas A and C are among the supporting ideas he uses to carry out his main idea. He gives these ideas in paragraphs 2, 3, and 6. Ideas B and D are not supporting ideas. They are related ideas but the writer does not use them in the selection.

A. Thieves find it easier to steal cars on dark streets than on lighted streets.

B. Insurance rates are higher in areas where car stealing is higher.

C. An extra ignition switch which is hidden will do a lot to protect a car from thieves.

D. After they steal them, thieves often strip and abandon cars.

HOW TO COMBAT THE CAR THIEF[1]

[1] Last year nearly 500,000 Americans helped thieves steal their cars, through plain carelessness.

[1] Robert M. Beasley, "How to Combat the Car Thief," in *Roof Lines*, (Seattle, Washington: Safeco Insurance Company, April 1970). Used with permission.

[2] How do owners help? Well, police reports reveal that more cars are stolen from dark streets than any other place, and most cars are unlocked when taken.

[3] As one thief with 30 years' experience put it: "Any car I see on a dark street, with doors unlocked or windows ajar, belongs to me if I want it. It's stupid to risk getting caught stealing a locked car on a lighted street, when I know that within a block of that one I can find another car I can take under ideal conditions."

[4] Another commented: "It's amazing how easy people make it. I've stolen lots of cars that had keys in the switch, some with titles and gas credit cards in the glove box."

[5] Teen-age joy riders, who are responsible for at least 75 percent of all stolen cars, also avoid lighted streets and generally pass up cars securely locked.

[6] The best protection is to put an extra ignition switch in a hidden spot, which opens the circuit directly at the coil or distributor. If starting is difficult, the thief will abandon the car in a hurry. A 50-cent switch concealed in the glove compartment, under the dash or under the seat will give as much protection as a $50 alarm system.

[7] In addition to dark streets, public parking lots are favorites for both professional and joy-riding thieves, because many lots make you leave the ignition key in the car. Whenever possible, find a lot where you can lock your car.

DESCRIPTION

What Are Longer Selections? Paragraphs may be grouped into longer selections: sections of articles, chapters, and books; and whole articles, chapters, and books. These longer selections also are organized around main ideas and supporting ideas. In some ways, longer selections are like paragraphs; in some ways, they are different.

1. Likenesses between paragraphs and longer selections
    a. In paragraphs, ideas are in one or more sentences. In longer selections, ideas are in one or more paragraphs.
    b. Main ideas may be directly stated in headings or titles or in topic paragraphs.
    c. The topic paragraph may be anywhere in the selection: in the beginning, in the end, or within the selection.

d. The main ideas may be implied instead of directly stated. They may be suggested by several paragraphs working together.

e. Supporting ideas may be put across in several ways; writers may use particular cases, reasons, and so on.

f. Perhaps more often than paragraphs, longer selections may have extra material: pads, duds, and distractors.

2. Differences between paragraphs and longer selections.

a. By definition, longer selections carry more information than paragraphs. They may carry more ideas. Or they may carry the same number of ideas but more details about each idea.

b. Longer selections may be more complex than paragraphs. The meaning of complex here is this. There may be a broad main idea and several broad supporting ideas. These supporting ideas, in turn, may act as main ideas which are further carried out by other, more specific, supporting ideas. This kind of complexity is hard to describe. However, it is easy to see in an outline where supporting ideas are separated from main ideas by position and by type-size and type-style.

Why Is It Valuable to Find Main Ideas and Supporting Ideas in Longer Selections? Identifying the writer's central message and the information he uses to carry it out is perhaps more important in longer selections than in paragraphs. Why? Because the length and the difficulty of a reading selection go hand in hand. As you add more material, it becomes harder to understand and remember that material. And so, it becomes even more important to see the main idea (what topic the writer is writing about) and the supporting ideas (what he is writing about that topic).

How Do You Find Main Ideas and Supporting Ideas in Longer Selections? For longer selections, you use the same steps as you do for paragraphs. (See Chapters 2 and 3.)

1. Finding directly stated main ideas

a. Headings and titles

In longer selections, writers more often use headings to show what ideas are in a section and as guides to coherence. Be careful to look for the various orders of headings to show the main ideas and supporting ideas. The table of contents and the way the print looks will help you here.

b. Topic paragraphs

Writers may state the main idea in one or more topic paragraphs. These topic paragraphs may be at the beginning or end of the selection or within the selection.

2. Finding implied main ideas

When the writer does not directly state the main idea, these steps will help you figure it out.

   a. Look at the paragraphs in relation to one another. Go beyond the differences and find the idea that all of the paragraphs refer to in common.

   b. State what you think the writer's main idea is.

   c. Check your proposed main idea. Put your proposed main idea against the writer's paragraphs to see if they support your proposed main idea. If yes, then you have the implied idea. If no, then try out other possible main ideas. Keep trying until you get a statement that is supported by the writer's paragraphs.

3. Finding supporting ideas

   a. Find the main idea of the selection.

   b. Find each remaining idea in the selection.

   c. Rule in supporting ideas. Rule out duds, pads, and distractors. Do this by checking each remaining idea against the main idea to see whether it fits—that is, whether it supports the main idea as a particular case, a restatement, a reason, or as comparison or contrast.

   d. In this process, watch for guides to coherence to help you see relations among the parts.

PRACTICE

Find and write the main idea of the selection. Find the supporting ideas which are among those the writers use. Write their code numbers in the space given.

Set 1

Main idea: _____

_____

_____

Supporting ideas: _____

1. Young was friendly with directors of the NAACP.

2. Young's goal was to get black people an equal share in America.

3. Young worked through leaders in government, labor, business, and philanthropy.

4. Young believed that one kind of monument was people helped in moments of distress, people given hope when they had reason to feel despair.

WHITNEY YOUNG: HE WAS A DOER[2]

He was Mr. Inside to the black revolution—a cool, urbane diplomat whose work began where the street marches and the picket lines left off. His single goal, in ten years as executive director of the National Urban League, was an equal break for Negro Americans; his strategy was to seek it among men who had it to give—white men of power in business and labor and government. He looked Establishment, except for his smoldering dark eyes and his equal-sign lapel button, and moved comfortably inside it, and so a good many militants wrote him off as a Tom or an Oreo cookie—black outside and white inside. It was a case of mistaken identity. Whitney M. Young Jr. died at 49 last week, while at a conference in Nigeria, and in the stock-taking that followed it was evident that few men did more with less fanfare in the whole turbulent history of the civil-rights movement of the 1960's.

That the Urban League should now be thought part of that movement was not the least of Young's victories. When he moved in as chief executive in 1961, after seven years as dean of the Atlanta University School of Social Work, the league was a sleepy place with a depleted budget, a $100,000 mortgage on its headquarters and a reputation as a job-placement service for the Negro middle class. Young set the dust flying. He opened 35 new chapters, increased the professional staff from 300 to 1,200 and the budget tenfold and insisted that the league get into the black slums where the problems were. And when the movement exploded into the streets in the early '60s, Young got into that, too, operating as a counselor and contact man between the militants and moderates and marching himself in the big parades in Washington 1963, Selma 1965 and Mississippi 1966. The league wasn't used to that sort of thing, but Young insisted. "At the crucial moments," he said, "you've got to be there and be counted."

The Art: But marching was not really his thing. His whole life pointed him toward a career in racial diplomacy—his boyhood as the son of the president of a precarious Negro boarding school in Kentucky, his Army tour as a noncom in a demoralized Jim Crow unit in Europe, his ap-

[2] "Whitney Young: He Was a Doer," *Time*, March 22, 1971, p. 29. Reprinted by permission from TIME, The Weekly Newsmagazine; © Time, Inc., 1971.

prenticeship in the Urban Leagues of St. Paul and Omaha. He had his angry moods but learned the arts of what he called "restrained anger. . . . You decide you'll only play into the other guy's hands if you get mad. The most satisfying thing is to get this man to do what you want him to—and make him think he wants to do it."

That was precisely Young's gift. Commuting to work from suburban New Rochelle every morning, he used to say, "I think to myself should I get off this morning and stand on 125th Street (in Harlem) cussing out Whitey to show I'm tough? Or should I go downtown and talk to an executive of General Motors about 2,000 jobs for unemployed Negroes?" It pained him when the hot-bloods called him "Whitey" Young and attacked him for the company he kept. White folks? "Yeah—well, they've got the jobs. *Somebody's* got to talk to the people who have something to give."

Whitney Young talked to more of them than anybody in the movement. Before his time at the league, he said once, "We used to wait six months to see an assistant to the assistant personnel director." But Young opened lines to three presidents (Lyndon Johnson became a fast friend) and dozens of board chairmen, labor barons, philanthropoids and politicians; Henry Ford II met him on a business junket—and the next Christmas sent him a $100,000 check for the league to spend any way he wanted. There was method in all of it: "I don't get so flattered by floating around on some yacht that I lose sight of my goal."

The Craft: The goal, first and foremost, was an equal share in America, and, to get it, Young was willing to cajole and badger and flatter shamelessly: he helped jolly the late Everett Dirksen into voting for one civil-rights bill by telling him he would go down in history as a "blond Moses" if he did. He appealed to consciences where he found them, hard business instinct where he did not. Long before "reparations" for blacks became a militant rallying cry, Young argued for a multibillion-dollar "domestic Marshall plan." And all of it began to pay off: he sat on seven presidential commissions, was consulted on the war on poverty and the model-cities program and helped the league land 40,000 jobs for blacks in a single year.

His relations with Richard Nixon were uneven at first—and at moments quite uncomfortable. Young for a time defended the Administration ("It isn't so bad") while much of the black establishment was attacking it—and then, in a 180-degree turn last summer, charged it with being "sort of like Jell-O . . . It's what I call white magic, you know, now you see it, now you don't." He finally did get in the door this winter, for an unprecedented audience with the president and most of his Cabinet, and came away with $28 million in federal money for league programs. When he died last week, Mr. Nixon led the mourners—"I have lost a friend—

black America has lost a gifted and commanding champion of its just cause"—and dispatched a plane to Lagos to bring Young's body home.

The End: Death came while Young was in Nigeria for the African-American Dialogue, a foundation-sponsored colloquy between U.S. and African leaders. He had been swimming with some of the Americans, among them former Attorney General Ramsey Clark, and suffered an apparent heart attack. "I looked back," Clark remembered. "I saw his arm flashing . . . Then his head went right under . . . My wife and I dragged him to shore." While someone went for a doctor, Clark and a Polaroid Corp. vice-president, Thomas H. Wyman, tried for about an hour to revive Young with mouth-to-mouth resuscitation, but he was dead.

As the news flashed back to America, the tributes poured forth from the corporate boardrooms and the chambers of government. But Whitney Young had long known the kind of epitaph he wanted. "I tell people, 'I can't guarantee you a monument in stone,'" he said once. "'Your monuments will be people helped in moments of distress, people given hope when they had every reason to feel despair.' I'm not anxious to be the loudest voice, or the most popular, but I would like to think that, at a crucial moment, I was an effective voice of the voiceless, an effective hope of the hopeless." He was.

Set 2

Main idea: _____

_____

_____

Supporting ideas: _____
1. Examples of mistakes.
2. Mistakes in testing can have a bad effect on selection for jobs, schools, and so on.
3. People who work with tests need to keep checking for mistakes.
4. Not enough tests are used in schools.

SCORE INTERPRETATION[3]

"When am I going to start failing?" a student asked me a couple of years ago. Upon being questioned, he told me this story: "My high school teacher told me

[3] Howard B. Lyman, *Test Scores and What They Mean*, © 1963, pp. 1–2, 159–60. By permission of Prentice-Hall, Inc., Englewood Cliffs, New Jersey.

that my IQ is only 88. He said that I might be able to get into college because of my football, but that I'd be certain to flunk out—with an IQ like that!" I pointed out to Don that he had been doing well in my course. I found out that he had a B+ average for the three semesters he had completed. I reminded him that the proof of a pudding lies in its eating—and that the proof of scholastic achievement lies in grades, not in a test designed to predict grades.

Last June, Don graduated with honors.

This little story, true in all essential details, illustrates many points; for example:

1. Was the test score correct? I suspect that an error was made in administering or scoring the test. Or, perhaps that score was a *percentile rank* instead of an IQ—which would make a lot of difference.

2. Regardless of the accuracy of the score, the teacher should not have told him the specific value of his IQ on the test.

3. The teacher went far beyond proper limits in telling Don that he would ". . . be certain to flunk out . . ." The teacher should have known that test scores are not perfect.

4. Furthermore, test scores do not determine future performance; demonstrated achievement is more conclusive evidence than is a score on a test intended to predict achievement. Both the teacher and Don should have known that!

If Don's case were unusual, I might have forgotten about it; however, mistakes in interpreting tests occur every day. Here are three other examples that come quickly to mind:

A college freshman, told that she had "average ability," withdrew from college. Her counselor had not added ". . . when compared with other college students." She reasoned that if she had only average ability compared with people in general, she must be very low when compared with college students; rather than face this, she dropped out of college. (There may have been other reasons, too, but this seemed to be the principal one.)

A high school student who had high measured clerical and literary interests was told that this proved that he should become either a clerk or a writer!

A personnel manager, learning that one of his best workers had scored very low on a test that eventually would be used in selecting future employees, nearly discharged the worker; ". . . the tests really opened our eyes about her. Why, she's worked here for several years, does good work, gets along well with the others. That test shows how she had us fooled!"

None of these illustrative cases is fictitious. All involve real people. And we will see a good many more examples of test interpretation throughout this book. Each one is based on a true situation, most of them drawn from my own experience in working with people who use tests.

No amount of anecdotal material, though, can show the thousands of instances every year in which the wrong persons are selected for jobs, admitted to schools and colleges, granted scholarships, and the like— merely because someone in authority is unable to interpret available test scores or, equally bad, places undue confidence in the results.

Nor will anecdotal material reveal the full scope of the misinformation being given to students and parents by teachers and others who are trying to help. Willingness to help is only the first step. There is also a lot to know about the meaning of test scores. Even the expert who works daily with tests has to keep his wits with him, for this is no game for dullards.

Common Sense

It is human to err, we are told. Most of these errors, though, could have been prevented. And we cannot blame the tests for mistakes like these.

When test results do not make sense, the test results may be wrong— or our "common sense" may be faulty. Neither is perfect.

Any testing program should call for checking at every stage where mistakes are possible. As test users, we should be prepared to check the scores that are put into our hands. If the test results do not seem reasonable, they may be wrong; on the other hand, our expectations may have been in error and the tests may be right.

Several years ago I was looking over a multiple-score test taken by a college student as part of a campus-wide testing program. I was surprised that this good student had no scores above the median. Upon checking, I discovered that one of the scoring clerks had not understood the directions for using the norms table. She had taken raw-score values from the text, entered these in the percentile-ranks column, and read out the corresponding entries in the raw-score column as percentile ranks. Since there had been no system of checking results, more than 1,000 test sheets and profiles had to be re-examined.

On the other hand:

A company was testing several people for a junior-level management position. Al Athol had been an employee of the company for several years, had a good work history, and was well-liked by fellow employees and by management. The other candidates were very recent college graduates and new to the firm. Al did as well as the other candidates except on a spatial relations test; on this, he did very poorly. The personnel director decided to select one of the other men because of this one very low score —and it is doubtful whether spatial relations skill is even involved in the management position! This personnel director should have used a little common sense, for Al was clearly superior to the other men on the various nontest factors that should have been considered.

When test results and common sense seem to be in conflict, we need to check all possibilities. There are four: (1) tests may be wrong; (2) common sense may be wrong; (3) both may be wrong; and (4) neither may be wrong.

Other Sources Too!

Tests are only one source of information. And test scores are only bits of information. In any important decision, we should make full use of all of the information available to us. As information-collectors, tests do have certain advantages—most especially their objectivity. But tests are fallible instruments, and test scores are fallible bits of information.

If tests are to be used, they should contribute something. People managed to exist and to make decisions without the aid of tests for many years—and they can today. If tests provide helpful information, we should use them—if they do not, we should not! And even if we do use tests, let us not forget to consider nontest factors as well—they, too, can be important.

Set 3

Main idea: _____

_____

_____

Supporting ideas: _____

1. Like physical discipline, mental discipline gets easier with practice.

2. Grammar is to a writer what anatomy is to a sculptor, or the scales to a musician.

3. An important part of creative writing is being able to see underlying themes in events.

4. Many writers of the past, like George Eliot, are really quite modern.

WHEN THE WRITER COMES OF AGE[4]

There is no royal road to maturity for any human being, and most certainly I know of none for the writer. Coming of age is not a chronological matter; it is a lifetime process. Fortunately, there are signposts along the way, and the signposts that guide the writer are really no different from the ones that guide everyone else.

The process of writing, like the process of growing, is one of accepting, testing and rejecting, of "holding fast that which is good." It is a process of infinite curiosity, a seesaw process of vast enthusiasms opposed by discouraging failures. For a writer, as for anyone, there are days when anything seems possible, and there are days when everything seems hopeless. Gardeners know this feeling very well. The lawn, the flower bed are full of crabgrass and a multitude of weeds, and many things done once are all to be done over again.

The first thing one learns is that this is not nearly as wasteful a pattern as it appears to be. Out of the nonsense, wildness and despair, there is always left the fine growing ground which we label experience. Experience is a dull word; another dull word is discipline. I am going to use both.

I have very strong feelings about discipline and especially about self-discipline. I have not found life at all permissive, either in the day-to-day process of living it or in the strict professional process of being a writer. This is no contradiction to my other strong feeling which is that life should be enjoyed. I am also a firm believer in day-dreaming, wasting time, staring into space or leaning against a wall watching the snails whizz by. There are certainly times when one's mind should be as open, empty and placid as a millpond. Who knows what attractive bugs will come to skitter on the surface or what wonderful white whales of the imagination will rise from its depths?

But self-discipline means doing one's work and doing it to the top of one's bent. I need hardly add that this often involves simple drudgery. There is no way to avoid it, whatever profession or calling you enter. There is drudgery in housework, in office work, in acting, painting, writing; it cannot be avoided, and the habit of self-discipline is the habit of doing what has to be done, even when dull. At any age, the ability to dodge disagreeable tasks comes naturally. I am not suggesting a permanent state of high-minded activity. I am merely urging you to avoid that intellectual curvature of the spine which results from lounging on the back of one's mental neck.

[4] B. J. Chute, "When the Writer Comes of Age," in A. S. Burack, ed., *The Writer's Handbook* (Boston: The Writer, 1970), pp. 6–14. Abridged. Based on the Mabel Williams Lecture, given at The Donnell Library Center, The New York Public Library, 1962. Used with permission.

Mental discipline is like physical discipline. It becomes easier through practice. Any athlete knows that the first aching clumsy use of untrained muscles eventually gives way to flexibility and control. The mental muscles behave in the same way, so that knowledge, sensitivity and capacity all improve through exercise.

I need hardly say that other people's exercise will not improve *your* muscles. Here, the intellect has some advantage over the physique, since other people's knowledge can enlarge yours. But only if you use it. We are the heirs of and contemporary to worlds of experience so vast as to be limitless, but these are ours only through our own effort.

Everything I have said so far applies to any kind of coming of age; but, since I am a writer, I would like to relate it to the specific problems of my own craft.

I never consciously planned to be a writer. I never pictured short stories in magazines with my name on them; I never imagined books that I would have written. I wrote because I wrote and, I suspect, also because I read omnivorously. (I will come back later to that splendid subject.) I was blessed with a grounding in grammar so solid, so stern, so basic that I have never had to think about the structure of the language at all in the purely grammatical sense. I learned it the hard way—by endless parsing, by drawing diagrams, by rote, by drill. If there is another way in which to become so firmly and surely rooted, I do not know it. I suspect there is not. Grammar is to a writer what anatomy is to a sculptor, or the scales to a musician. You may loathe it, it may bore you, but nothing will replace it, and once mastered it will support you like a rock. I have no quarrel whatever with the writer who breaks the rules of grammar intentionally, but I have a quarrel with the writer who breaks them because he has not been willing to learn them properly. The English language deserves more respect.

I learned something from learning grammar. I learned not to mind working hard for the sake of control. I learned not to trouble myself about what appeared to be wasted pages, if through the producing of them I moved closer all the time to the things I wanted to say in the way in which I thought it should be said. I am a confirmed re-writer. There is no especial moral virtue in re-writing; it merely happens to be my particular way of achieving an end, and if you can get your results on the first try, more power to your pen! What matters is not to be afraid of doing the same thing again, and again, and then again, if that is necessary. A writer will never be judged by his private vision, only by what shows of it on paper. It is no use sitting around admiring one's mental processes, however enchanting they may be. The reader is not sitting around in any such admiring state. His posture is "Show me!" and he is quite right to insist.

I can speak of drudgery casually, as a part of a writer's task, because I have learned there is no evading it. When I have finished a novel, taking it through as many drafts as needs be, to the point where I am almost satisfied, I expect to sit down at my typewriter and do the whole thing over once more from beginning to end, so that the words suit my ear, the effort to communicate has become the best effort of which I am capable, and the courtesy due to the English language has been given to it as completely as I can. This is not a sign of nobility, but it is a matter of pride. I have no wish to encounter in print words I have written that should have been written better, and there is something very immovable about that thing called movable type, once the printer has locked it up. There is no time for reconstruction after the words lie in the bound book.

Now, I want to revert to that subject I touched on earlier: reading. Reading is only another way of "listening fluently" (to borrow Langston Hughes' wonderful phrase). My first advice to any would-be writer is that he read—creatively, passionately, chronically. I am impatient with the idea of sugar-coated reading. I do not believe in padding about timidly in the tepid waters of the merely entertaining, the placidly simple. Reading is a joint creative process between writer and listener. It is a multilevel process, more than mere ability to recognize and interpret words. It is also more than mere familiarity with contemporary fiction or a dutiful sampling of the classics. The real reader needs to have a mariner's knowledge of those myriad minor writers of past centuries who compose the vast ocean of literature.

Some writers of the past are not easy to understand. They speak in idioms not always clear to us; they reflect ways of life that are now alien. They make heavy demands on the reader to respond to their strangeness. The ear complains, "But this is old-fashioned"; the mind replies, "It was modern once." Even the classics sometimes fall heavily on the senses, and after a few chapters one's attention falters and lags, and it is tempting to say, "This is not for me," and turn to the familiar.

I think part of the trouble here rises from the theory that one is a reader because one has learned to read. One would not think of himself as a tennis player because he had mastered the elements of tennis playing, or as a skier because he was able to go downhill without collapsing in a snowbank. We willingly train our muscles to the mechanical difficulty of a powerful serve, to the controlled rhythm of stem turns, but we do not as willingly train our minds to follow the involutions of an unfamiliar way of writing. This is a pity. Batting a ball earnestly back and forth, going downhill soberly and arriving upright—this is neither tennis nor skiing. They are both exciting sports, and we work hard to become adept in them so we can know their real excitements. Yet what Baudelaire called "the heavenly mechanics of the mind" is the source of an infinity of excitement, compared to which Wimbledon and the Alps seem very small indeed.

I know readers whose whole literary world seems to be related to the so-called "modern" literary world. They are experts on the Twentieth Century of prose and poetry, widely read, subtle; but, except for the great mountain peaks of Shakespeare, Homer, Dante (the names that leap to the mind), they have none of that accumulation of reading which would illuminate, broaden, deepen every modern book they read.

I think we often fail to recognize how a wide range of reading enlarges literature. Let me take two quotations from Shakespeare, a writer with whom we all have a bowing acquaintance, to show how one kind of writing, even the greatest, can be affected by all the other kinds.

The first, from *Antony and Cleopatra*, said of the great Egyptian queen herself, beautiful in death as she was in life:

. . . she looks like sleep,
As she would catch another Antony
In her strong toil of grace.

This is a marvelous bit of poetry, in and of itself. You need not be deep-rooted in literature to know that. But suppose your reading roots *do* go deep, so that the description of Cleopatra wakens within your mind a memory of other beloved women stricken by untimely frosts—Villon's "Flora, the lovely Roman," Tolstoy's achingly tragic Anna Karenina, Robert Herrick's country girls like daffodils. For the wide-ranging reader, who is not intimidated in his reading, a host of perilous and immortal women join hands. Where are the snows of yesteryear, if not imprisoned forever in the minds of the "fluent listeners"? The color from each spreads to the others, and the passage from Shakespeare, most beautiful in itself, is made more beautiful through association, through links and echoes.

The second quotation, then, from *The Winter's Tale*. A small boy is invited to tell his mother a tale "of sprites, and goblins." He is an artful storyteller, and he begins magically:

There was a man . . .
Dwelt by a churchyard: I will tell it softly,
Yond crickets shall not hear it.

This is the perfect invitation to the listener, hushed, mysterious, full of shadows. The immediate echo it wakes is the childhood one of "Once upon a time." But for the skilled reader other echoes cry like bells, calling us to come, to come and listen. I think of a modern chime in that wonderful line of Scott Fitzgerald's—"Draw your chair up close to the edge of the precipice and I'll tell you a story." I think of the legends and the ballads—"There dwelt a man in fair Westmoreland," "The king sits in Dumferling town." I remember that deceptively simple opening of Dickens' which pulls us into the world of his Curiosity Shop: "Although I am an old man, night is generally my time for walking." And I am even moved to remember the harsh, dark texture of *Beowulf*, which in high school I studied so resentfully, only to know now that its granite lies in the pit of my mind forever.

Neither writer nor reader can quite talk of coming of age until these echoes and links begin to crowd into the mind. George Eliot is too alien, too Victorian? She is one of the most modern and civilized writers on earth, with a sharp wit and a broad compassion and a capacity to translate life that you will pass by at your peril. Chaucer's Middle English makes him unreadable? But his *Troilus and Criseyde*, though written in poetic form, is one of the finest psychological novels ever written, and Criseyde is as enchanting a woman as ever a great poet loved.

Stretch, I implore you, in your reading. The words are unfamiliar to your ears? The passions are foreign to your mind? Reach up to them; do not wait until they reach down to you, because they will not. When Horatio said, "But this is wondrous strange," Hamlet replied, "And therefore as a stranger give it welcome." Leap to your place in reading. Bruise your mind, fracture your old ideas, stretch your muscles until they shriek in protest. I offer you no sympathy. I offer you, instead, the kind of delight that comes from effort, a delight you will never have unless you step out dangerously.

What I am saying then is, simply, that the mind grows in use. "Art was given for that," Robert Browning tells us. "God uses us to help each other so,/Lending our minds out."

Discipline and experience cannot be separated from the whole bright process of coming of age. Every writer, every reader, indeed every human being, knows in his heart that he has a capacity for growth that would astound a redwood tree. In one sense, none of us ever comes of age—not at twenty-one, not at fifty-one, not at ninety-one.

But, oh, the journey! And I wish you Godspeed.

Set 4

Main idea: _____

_____

_____

Supporting ideas: _____

1. Some people throw off on today's times as being the age of anxiety.
2. One source of anxiety is guilt and fear of punishment.
3. People in less modern societies are less anxious than we are; instead, they are often seriously and continually frightened.
4. Uncertainty leads not only to anxiety but also to hope.

ONE VOTE FOR THIS AGE OF ANXIETY[5]

When critics wish to repudiate the world in which we live today, one of their familiar ways of doing it is to castigate modern man because anxiety is his chief problem. This, they say, in W. H. Auden's phrase, is the age of anxiety. This is what we have arrived at with all our vaunted progress, our great technological advances, our great wealth—everyone goes about with a burden of anxiety so enormous that, in the end, our stomachs and our arteries and our skins express the tension under which we live. Americans who have lived in Europe come back to comment on our favorite farewell which, instead of the old goodbye (God be with you), is now "Take it easy," each American admonishing the other not to break down from the tension and strain of modern life.

Whenever an age is characterized by a phrase, it is presumably in contrast to other ages. If we are the age of anxiety, what were other ages? And here the critics and carpers do a very amusing thing. First, they give us lists of the opposites of anxiety: security, trust, self-confidence, self-direction. Then without much further discussion, they let us assume that other ages, other periods of history, were somehow the ages of trust or confident direction.

The savage who, on his South Sea island, simply sat and let breadfruit fall into his lap, the simple peasant, at one with the fields he ploughed and the beasts he tended, the craftsman busy with his tools and lost in the fulfillment of the instinct of workmanship—these are the counter-images conjured up by descriptions of the strain under which men live today. But no one who lived in those days has returned to testify how paradisaical they really were.

Certainly if we observe and question the savages or simple peasants in the world today, we find something quite different. The untouched savage in the middle of New Guinea isn't anxious; he is seriously and

[5] Margaret Mead, "One Vote for this Age of Anxiety," *The New York Times Magazine*, May 20, 1956, pp. 13, 56. © 1956 by the New York Times Company. Reprinted by permission.

continually frightened—of black magic, of enemies with spears who may kill him or his wives and children at any moment, while they stoop to drink from a spring, or climb a palm tree for a coconut. He goes warily, day and night, taut and fearful.

As for the peasant populations of a great part of the world, they aren't so much anxious as hungry. They aren't anxious about whether they will get a salary raise, or which of the three colleges of their choice they will be admitted to, or whether to buy a Ford or Cadillac, or whether the kind of TV set they want is too expensive. They are hungry, cold and, in many parts of the world, they dread that local warfare, bandits, political coups may endanger their homes, their meager livelihoods and their lives. But surely they are not anxious.

For anxiety, as we have come to use it to describe our characteristic state of mind, can be contrasted with the active fear of hunger, loss, violence and death. Anxiety is the appropriate emotion when the immediate personal terror—of a volcano, an arrow, the sorcerer's spell, a stab in the back and other calamities, all directed against one's self—disappears.

This is not to say that there isn't plenty to worry about in our world of today. The explosion of a bomb in the streets of a city whose name no one had ever heard before may set in motion forces which end up by ruining one's carefully planned education in law school, half a world away. But there is still not the personal, immediate, active sense of impending disaster that the savage knows. There is rather the vague anxiety, the sense that the future is unmanageable.

The kind of world that produces anxiety is actually a world of relative safety, a world in which no one feels that he himself is facing sudden death. Possibly sudden death may strike a certain number of unidentified other people—but not him. The anxiety exists as an uneasy state of mind, in which one has a feeling that something unspecified and undeterminable may go wrong. If the world seems to be going well, this produces anxiety—for good times may end. If the world is going badly—it may get worse. Anxiety tends to be without locus; the anxious person doesn't know whether to blame himself or other people. He isn't sure whether it is 1956 or the Administration or a change in climate or the atom bomb that is to blame for this undefined sense of unease.

It is clear that we have developed a society which depends on having the *right* amount of anxiety to make it work. Psychiatrists have been heard to say, "He didn't have enough anxiety to get well," indicating that, while we agree that too much anxiety is inimical to mental health, we have come to rely on anxiety to push and prod us into seeing a doctor about a symptom which may indicate cancer, into checking up on that old life insurance policy which may have out-of-date clauses in it, into having a conference with Billy's teacher even though his report card looks all right.

People who are anxious enough keep their car insurance up, have the brakes checked, don't take a second drink when they have to drive, are careful where they go and with whom they drive on holidays. People who are too anxious either refuse to go into cars at all—and so complicate the ordinary course of life—or drive so tensely and overcautiously that they help cause accidents. People who aren't anxious enough take chance after chance, which increases the terrible death toll of the roads.

On balance, our age of anxiety represents a large advance over savage and peasant cultures. Out of a productive system of technology drawing upon enormous resources, we have created a nation in which anxiety has replaced terror and despair, for all except the severely disturbed.

But in this twilight world which is neither at peace nor at war, and where there is insurance against certain immediate, downright, personal disasters, for most Americans there remains only anxiety over what may happen, might happen, could happen.

This is the world out of which grows the hope, for the first time in history, of a society where there will be freedom from want and freedom from fear. Our very anxiety is born of our knowledge of what is now possible for each and for all. The number of people who consult psychiatrists today is not, as is sometimes felt, a symptom of increasing mental ill health, but rather the precursor of a world in which the hope of genuine mental health will be open to everyone, a world in which no individual feels that he need be hopelessly brokenhearted, a failure, a menace to others or a traitor to himself.

Set 5

Main idea: _____

_____

_____

Supporting ideas: _____

1. Many people see the material benefits of science but they don't see how science affects how they think.
2. The motivations, the satisfactions, the frustrations of the scientist are not different in kind from those of other types of creative personality.
3. Leonardo Da Vinci was both a scientist and a humanist.
4. Our separation of science as a special and distinct kind of intellectual activity is relatively new—though nonetheless unfortunate.

THE TWO CULTURES: SCIENTIFIC AND HUMANISTIC[6]

It is curious how often students dislike science courses. They take them only because they are required and try to meet the requirement with a minimum of effort. Science to them seems to be an irrelevant subject, full of strange, jawbreaking words to be memorized and forgotten as soon as the final examination has been passed, of frogs and worms to be cut up, or half-forgotten algebra and esoteric formulas. The great ideas of science never come across, nor does the excitement of discovery, or a feeling for the people, great and small, who have built up this immense body of knowledge. Almost all of us like the products of science—automobiles, modern medicine, television, wide varieties of food—but few of us have much curiosity about how these things came about.

The material benefits of science are clear, but the pervasive influence of science on how we think is little understood. We now know a great deal about the earth and the sun and the moon. How could we ever assume the old common sense attitude and view the earth as obviously flat with an arched firmament above it? We no longer appease the demons that hurl thunderbolts, or exorcise those that cause disease. We may worry about gremlins and black cats and the thirteenth floor, but it is a sort of play-worry, not the real terror of the unknown and unpredictable. We have almost imperceptibly acquired a faith in the orderliness of nature and, in some cases, at least, in its predictability. We may not know the second law of the thermodynamics, but gravitation, evolution, and even relativity have become common words in our lexicon.

Intellectuals of many sorts tend to be scornful of science, and remain unconscious of the fact that the intellectual climate in which they live has been largely formed by science. Scientists themselves, as C. P. Snow has pointed out, often are not considered to be "intellectuals." The word is reserved for writers, artists, philosophers, and the like. Working scientists, on the other hand, are often scornful of other kinds of scholars, dismissing them as "fuzzy thinkers" chained by long outmoded traditions of knowledge. Snow, interviewing thousands of scientists in England during the Second World War, found them in general to be amazingly ignorant of literature and art—as he found writers and artists to be ignorant of science. The result is "two cultures" which have little contact with one another. It sometimes looks as though our intellectual world were as sharply split between scientists and humanists as the political world is between communists and advocates of democracy.

[6] Marston Bates, *Man in Nature, Foundations of Modern Biology Series,* © 1964, pp. 108–100. Abridged. By permission of Prentice-Hall, Inc., Englewood Cliffs, New Jersey.

Divided worlds, whether political or intellectual, are dangerous; and for the intellectual division there is little excuse.

Science is one of the great creative achievements of the human mind. The motivations, the satisfactions, the frustrations of the scientist are hardly different in kind from those of any other type of creative personality however different the products of the creative act may be. The products in the case of science are concepts, theories, and classifications, arrived at by experiment, observation, and analysis. These certainly are very different from poems or painting or symphonies, but they are no less great as intellectual accomplishments, no less worthy of our admiration and appreciation. Instead of contrasting sciences with humanities, perhaps we'd better look at the sciences as a part of the humanities, as one of the ways in which man has tried to understand himself and the world around him.

Our separation of science as a special and distinct kind of intellectual activity is relatively new—though nonetheless unfortunate. We can recognize many instances of scientific exploration in the ancient and medieval worlds, but the people involved generally called themselves philosophers, whatever the system they used in their inquiries. The founders of modern science in the seventeenth century still thought of themselves as philosophers and considered that they were dealing with the traditional problems of philosophy, even though they are approaching them untraditionally.

The student of science today is most often awarded the degree of "Doctor of Philosophy," but the label is about all that is left of the historic connection. There has been, in recent years, a considerable effort to develop a "philosophy of science" that would help bridge the gap, but this has not met with great encouragement from either scientists or philosophers. The trouble, one suspects, is that science *is* philosophy, today as well as yesterday—not all of philosophy, certainly, but a very live and active part that has somehow lost its family relationship, to the detriment of everyone.

ANSWERS FOR PRACTICE SETS

Set 1
Main idea: Whitney Young was a doer. He was often criticized but when you take stock, it's clear that few men did more with less fanfare during the civil-rights movement of the 1960s.
Supporting ideas: Nos. 2, 3, and 4.

Set 2

Main idea: Many mistakes are made in interpreting test scores. They can be serious and they should be prevented.

Supporting ideas: Nos. 1, 2, and 3.

Set 3

Main idea: As it is in other parts of life, so it is in writing: discipline and experience are very important to growth and coming of age.

Supporting ideas: Nos. 1, 2, and 4.

Set 4

Main idea: On balance, our age of anxiety represents a large advance over savage and peasant cultures. Out of a production system of technology drawing upon enormous resources, we have created a nation in which anxiety has replaced terror and despair for most people.

Supporting ideas: Nos. 1, 3, and 4.

Set 5

Main idea: There is little reason or excuse for the division into two cultures: scientific and humanistic.

Supporting ideas: Nos. 1, 2, and 4.

II

RAPID SEARCH SKILLS

Part Two is about the rapid search skills. These skills help you go through a lot of material and quickly get certain items you need for your particular purposes. Chapter 5, *previewing*, covers sizing up a selection to see what the writer is trying to say and how he is organized to say it, as well as any special things that may influence his work. Chapter 6 is on skimming and scanning. *Skimming* is for looking at only main ideas, and *scanning* is for finding specific bits of information like items in the dictionary.

5

Previewing

Previewing can be used to size up this selection on thinking as you read. Note how the first three questions and answers begin to give you an idea about what the selection is like before you read it. You continue the previewing by glancing at the article to find answers to questions 4 and 5.

1. What is the article about?
   Reading newspapers critically: ways to separate truth from partial truths and misinformation.

2. Who are the authors? Do they seem qualified?
   Adams and Stratton. Yes, they seem to be qualified by training and experience.

3. From what point of view do they look at the subject, *Thinking As You Read?* Are there other points of view?
   They look at the subject from the point of view of journalism—how misinformation shows up in newspapers. Yes, there are other ways to look at the subject. For example: you could look at psychological factors which explain why people fail to read critically.

4. What are some of the ideas that Adams and Stratton look at? _____
   _____
   _____
   _____

5. What are the main guides to coherence that Adams and Stratton use to show structure? _____

_____

_____

_____

THINKING AS YOU READ[1]

Can you believe what you read? Is it the truth? And if true, is it the whole truth, or just part of the truth—a part that gives you a different impression from the one you would receive if you knew the whole story?

These questions must be faced by you, as a newspaper reader. You must consider the same points when you listen to someone speak—in person, on the radio, or on the motion picture or television screens. Only through wide reading, general knowledge, and alertness can you avoid being influenced without realizing it.

A free press may publish much that would not be printed if newspapers were controlled by the government. Most American editors and writers recognize a duty to their community and readers. To the best of their ability, they report news fairly, truthfully, and completely, yet there are ways in which they can fail. They must please their readers, who are not always interested in the absolute truth. They are human beings with human feelings, and they may allow their own ideas to creep into their reporting.

The responsibility, however, is not all on the side of the newspaper. If you, as a reader, do not think as you read, you may fail to understand what a newspaper is trying to tell you. Along with the privilege of receiving uncensored news, you must accept the responsibility of reading carefully. The following steps show you what to consider as you read the news.

Step 1:   Recognize and Understand Opinion

Opinion appears in every newspaper: editorials are opinions, as are daily columns, play and movie reviews, printed quotations or speeches. In all of these, it is clear whose ideas you as a reader are receiving. Editorials state the opinion of the newspaper itself; columns and reviews have bylines and contain the authors' comments. Any news story with a

---

[1] Julian Adams and Kenneth Stratton, *Press Time* (Englewood Cliffs, N.J.: Prentice-Hall, Inc., 1969), pp. 4–10. Used with permission.

byline may include the opinion of the reporter, although the byline may be printed simply as credit for an outstanding piece of factual reporting. In addition, comments may be expressed in news stories, if they are properly placed within quotes or follow a phrase like, "Mr. Jones says that . . . ."

Most newspaper readers want and welcome opinion, when it is clearly identified, because it helps them form their own thoughts. But their problem—and yours—is to keep the difference between fact and opinion clear.

Step 2: Distinguish Between Fact and Opinion

To a reporter, anything that really happens is a fact. If someone makes a statement concerning an event, the only known fact is that he talked, but what he said must be considered his own personal opinion until it is clearly established that he was describing what actually happened. The listening reporter notes what was said, being careful to name the source. If the reporter has reason to believe that the statement is incorrect, he may qualify it in some way, perhaps with words like "assert" or "allege." He may obtain contradictory statements from other sources. But he reports them just the same!

Here, responsibility for determining the truth shifts to you, the reader. To understand what actually happened, you must analyze the statements in the story. You must make a distinction between actual facts and personal opinions. Moreover, you must watch for conclusions which someone has drawn. They are also opinions. Each time you find an opinion, consider it for what it is. Accept it or reject it; then place it in the proper corner of your mind to assist in forming your own judgment about the news event.

Step 3: Consider Each News Source

Another close distinction you as a newspaper reader must make is between facts and rumors stated as facts. Most newspapers faithfully identify news sources. They either furnish names or indicate the reporter's personal presence at a news event. But you must judge for yourself the actual authority of the person who is the source of a news story. Is he in a position to say this? Does he possess sufficient information to be capable of making such a judgment?

As a far-fetched example, suppose your mayor announces that the mayor of a large city 500 miles away is a crooked politician. Before you even consider the truth of this statement, think about what authority your mayor might have to make this statement. Where might he get his information? How reliable might this source be? Why is he saying this? What business is it of his anyway?

Perhaps even worse than the named news source who has no authority to make a statement is the unnamed source. This "individual" appears frequently in news of national or international politics. Some facts can't be announced publicly, but a reporter uncovers them and reports them as a rumor, without naming his authority. He may make no reference to a source, or he may state that his information comes from an "informed source" or a "usually reliable source."

Step 4: Watch for Slanted News

A newspaper may present news in a "biased" or "slanted" way, either accidentally or intentionally. You, as a newspaper reader, are likely to misunderstand the true facts of a slanted news story. All the facts may not be there, or may be presented so their relative importance is not clear to you.

How might a slanted news story be written? In the limited time before a deadline, the reporter may not have time to gather all the facts; he does his best, but he may miss an important part of the story. An informant who furnishes the reporter with news may not know all the facts, or he may deliberately lie about some of them, but the reporter may not find this out. Because the reporter may have a strong personal opinion about his subject, he may deliberately or unconsciously allow his opinion to creep into the story. This may be the result of what he writes, of his emphasis of certain facts, or of his omission of other facts.

Compare these leads. Which shows evidence of slant? Why?

The School Board today revealed plans for a $9,000,000 bond issue to enlarge and improve school facilities throughout the city. Of the $9,000,000, some $2,500,000 would be used to acquire land, while the remainder would rebuild two schools and provide for additions to 11 others.

The School Board revealed today that it plans to condemn private property and homes worth $2,500,000, including a square block in the downtown area, for expansion of school facilities. The condemnation would be part of a $9,000,000 school bond issue going before voters in the general municipal election.

News may also be slanted by the way stories are arranged on a newspaper page, or by the way a story is emphasized. A news item of major importance may be hidden on a back page, while sensational but unimportant stories fill the front page. Important stories may sometimes be left out entirely.

Slanted news is not always the fault of the reporter. Frequently, it is the editor or publisher who directs that a certain policy be promoted in the paper. Slanted news challenges your alertness and your ability to think clearly about what you read.

Step 5: Beware of Appeals to Your Emotions

Propaganda is the name given to any organized attempt to influence your thinking or your actions. It may be good or bad. There is no objection to much propaganda. "Join the Red Cross!" "Buy a student body card!" "Vote!" This is a kind of propaganda, expressed in slogans, news stories or editorials, that is usually constructive and worthwhile.

Nearly all advertising is propaganda. It is an attempt to persuade you to buy. Good advertising is generally honest and straightforward in its presentation of facts, although it may use some exaggeration and repetition to convince you. But the propaganda to watch for is the kind that is used to try to mislead you.

Propagandists appeal to your emotions in many ways. Half truths are common: "Doctors recommend our toothpaste." How many doctors? Who were they? For what do they recommend it? These questions are unanswered. Or another: "This cigarette proved best by extensive tests." Who conducted the tests? What kind of tests? With what other makes of cigarette was it compared?

Other propagandists want you to do something because "everybody's doing it." "Follow the crowd! Everyone's voting for this candidate!" Or a testimonial is offered: "Famous movie star, Joe Smith, chews this bubble gum." This implies that you should chew this brand because Joe is famous and wealthy, and in this way you will share something with him.

All these devices appeal to your emotions rather than to your common sense. It is easier to relax and be fooled than it is to consider carefully what you hear and read. This is why propaganda succeeds. You don't bother to think statements through, so you don't recognize propaganda when you see or hear it. Therein lies the greatest danger—as well as the greatest challenge—of today's high-speed methods of communication.

DESCRIPTION

What Is Previewing? Previewing is sizing up a selection before you read it. You look ahead to see what a selection is like. What the writer is trying to say, how he is organized to say it, and any special factors that may influence his work.

Why Is Previewing Valuable? Previewing helps you in locating, grasping, and evaluating information.

1. Locating information: Previewing helps you decide whether the selection has the material you need for your purposes.

2. Grasping information: Previewing makes material more familiar when you read it. Familiar material means more to you. In turn, meaningful material is easier to understand and remember.

3. Evaluating information: Previewing helps you see whether the writer has a special interest, what writing skills he uses, and so on.

How Do You Preview? You ask questions and then look for the answers. Most times, you don't need to write the answers. But in one situation you do need to write. When you deal with very hard material, you need to write the outline and look at it while you read.

You can ask many questions about a selection. Some sample questions are below. They are organized by three major divisions: front matter, body or text, and back matter. You don't need to use all these questions all the time. Choose the ones you like the best and which suit your purposes best. Make up some questions of your own.

Front Matter

—What does the title say? What does it mean? Can you change it into your own words? Does it show what the selection is about or is it a come-on to hook you?

—Is there a paper jacket on the book? Does it have such items as these: descriptions of the book's contents, reviewer's comments, selections from the book? Do these items show accurate information about the book or are they just bits of information to hook you?

—Who is the writer? Does he have the experience and training to write about the topic? What else has he written? Does he have a special point of view?

—What is the publication date? Is the selection up to date? Have there been new developments since it was published? If so, how do these new developments relate to information the writer presents?

—What company published the material? Do they have a good reputation in general? Are they noted for soundness in the particular field of the selection like psychology, history, English, and so on?

—Is there a preface, foreword, or introduction? Does the writer tell what he is trying to do? Does he tell what kind of material he has included and how he has organized it?

—Is there a table of contents? What does the table of contents show about the nature of the book's main ideas and supporting ideas? What does it show about their organization?

Body or Text

—What system does the writer use in the article or in the chapters in a larger book? Does he summarize his presentation at the beginning or end of the selection? Does he give study questions and exercises at the beginning or end of the selection?
—What is the writer's style? How does he treat his main ideas? Are they directly stated or implied? Where does he put his main ideas—at the beginning, the end, or within the selection? Does he use headings—how many orders and how are they shown? What kinds of guides to coherence does he use? What kinds of supporting ideas does he seem to like? How much detail does he give?
—How many orders of headings does he use and how are they indicated?
—Is there a list of references for further reading?
—What kind of graphic aids does he use: drawings, photographs, charts, tables? Do they seem accurate and up-to-date?

Back Matter

—Is there a bibliography or list of selected references? What kind of materials are these? Are they appropriate for the subject of the selection? Are they reliable? Are the publication dates suitably recent?
—Is there a glossary? What kind of material does it have? Do you understand most of the items it contains?
—Is there a subject index? An author index? Are some of the materials familiar to you? What do they show about the contents of the book?
—Is there an appendix containing additional information? What kind of information does it contain? Is that information familiar to you?

PRACTICE

Preview these selections. Use the space above the selection to write your preview questions. Then, search the selections for answers to your questions.

Set 1

Preview Questions and Answers

FRONT MATTER: BOOK²

[The material presented here was on pages i–xii of the original book. It is telescoped here to save space. Double lines are used to indicate pages.]

THE ARTS IN SOCIETY
edited by Robert N. Wilson, University of North Carolina

Prentice-Hall, Inc., Englewood Cliffs, N.J.

Prentice-Hall International, Inc., London

Prentice-Hall of Australia, Pty, Ltd., Sydney

Prentice-Hall of Canada. Ltd., Toronto

Prentice-Hall of India (Private) Ltd., New Delhi

Prentice-Hall of Japan, Inc., Tokyo

Prentice-Hall De Mexico, S.A., Mexico City

1964 by Prentice-Hall, Inc., Englewood Cliffs, N.J.

Printed in the United States of America

[p. iii and p. iv are blank]

PREFACE

This symposium was first considered during 1957 when I was a Fellow at the Center for Advanced Study in the Behavioral Sciences and an interested participant in a seminar on art and human behavior. At that time such a collection began to seem feasible; indeed, four other members of that seminar are now represented in this volume: Leo Lowenthal, Harrison and Cynthia White, and Hans Speier. In a more general sense, I have been deeply concerned about the relations between the humanities and the social sciences since my student days when I was dismayed to find that there seemed to be such a slight connection between my college studies in literature and my graduate studies in sociology and psychology.

² Robert N. Wilson, ed., *The Arts in Society*, © 1964, pp. i–xii. By permission of Prentice-Hall, Inc., Englewood Cliffs, New Jersey.

I determined to explore this connection further, the first effort being an investigation of modern poets, later published under the title, *Man Made Plain*.

The present book grows out of my conviction that is exceedingly important for the student of society to attend to the arts achieved by various social groups.

v

Behavioral scientists can learn a great deal from artists and art, primarily because writers and painters are sensitive perceivers who often see what is going on in the society or the psyche a good bit earlier than other men do. Moreover the arts are symbolic representations of *something* (no one is quite sure what) in the societies that give them birth. It is commonplace to say that people who study human behavior can gain heightened understanding through art; part of the task in this book is to enunciate more clearly what sorts of understanding may be thus derived.

Complementing the idea that literature, painting, music, and the dance have something vital to say to the social scientist is the belief that social scientists have themselves a contribution to make. One may propose, audaciously enough, that a sociologist or psychologist brings to the arts a trained intelligence and a point of view, and that he is therefore potentially equipped to enhance our comprehension of the arts themselves—for their own sakes. Further, those who believe with Edward Shils that the high culture of any age is of immense value and must be cultivated may take heart from the attempt of the social scientist to define and ultimately help to conserve the arts as a realm of social life.

The authors gathered here are concerned with both the major themes in the reciprocal pairing of art and society: what can art and artist teach us about society? What can the perspectives of the social sciences teach us about artistic careers and created works? It would be difficult to say that one theme or the other was clearly dominant, since most of the selections illuminate both ranges of questions. However, there has been throughout an emphasis on close study of the creator and the art product in the conviction that at this early stage in the development of a sociology of art we need to know much more about the precise character of the objects of our attention. That is, literature and other expressive media are not taken merely as illustrations of already-framed social psychological issues, but are seen as phenomena of intrinsic interest. It is very unlikely that any scholar can do excellent work in this field unless he has such an abiding interest and resists the temptation to use the arts as mere adjuncts to social research or convenient repositories of data.

The editorial comments attempt to place the various contributions in

vi

perspective and relate them to one another. There is, however, no intention of trying to impose a single, rigid conceptual scheme on these diverse essays; art is long and social science is short, and our correct posture should be one of humility toward the fact of art rather than an arrogant and premature disposition to sort and count. Whatever the long-run possibilities, we are surely in no position at this date to erect an accepted, conventional taxonomy or to compose textbooks on the sociology of the arts. The theoretical view which informs my discussion is catholic in nature and modest in claim. It argues only that the analysis of art cannot proceed on the sole basis of internal criticism, psychological explanation, or sociological association. The art object is complex and the artist is complex; a single-factor or unidimensional analysis is almost certain to be inadequate. To "understand" a work of art in the fullest sense requires intimate acquaintance with the created work itself, with the personality of its creator, with the social milieu which is an environing frame for artist, art, and audience. One can never know enough or see with sufficient clarity. Art is at once profoundly individual—the sacred private vision of its creator—and resolutely social—a pervasive transaction among a symbolic tradition, an artist, a medium, a company of perceivers, and a species of social organization.

I have not sought to impose form upon this volume by culling appropriate selections from extant work or suggesting topics to contributors. With few exceptions, the essays are written expressly for the symposium and printed here for the first time. From the authors I have asked only excellence, leaving them quite free to pursue any topic or point of view within the general field. This orientation is in keeping with the contention that the sociology of art is not ripe for formalization. There is no effort to "cover" all of the subjects that might be suggested by the title; for the present, a collection of lively individual voices seems more fitting than an arid comprehensiveness.

As is always the case with a book carried over several years and involving many associates, there is no accurate way to express thanks for the varieties of help received. I should nevertheless wish to mention a few of the persons whose encouragement and labor were important: Ralph Tyler, Charles Morris, Henry A. Murray, Neil Leonard, Ronald D. Scibilia, Lowell Hagan, Alys Venable, and Gay Goss. In addition, my students in

Social Relations 90 at Harvard and Sociology 70a and 26a at Yale were a constant stimulus to thought.

Chapel Hill, North Carolina   Robert N. Wilson

THE CONTRIBUTORS

Sanford M. Dornbusch is Professor of Sociology at Stanford University.

Cesar Grana is Associate Professor in the Social Sciences at the University of Chicago.

Mason Griff is Professor of Sociology, Anthropology, and Social Work at Montana State University.

Leo Lowenthal is Professor of Sociology at the University of California at Berkeley.

Dennison Nash is Associate Professor of Sociology at the University of Connecticut.

Carol Pierson Ryser is a candidate for a Ph.D. in sociology at Harvard University.

Edward A. Shils is Professor of Sociology and Social Thought, University of Chicago, and Fellow of King's College, Cambridge.

Hans Speier is a member of the Research Council of The RAND Corporation.

Cynthia White is a painter and a graduate of Radcliffe College *magna cum laude* in Fine Arts.

Harrison White is Associate Professor of Sociology at Harvard University.

Robert N. Wilson is Professor, School of Public Health, and Professor of Sociology at the University of North Carolina.

ix

CONTENTS

Set 2

Preview Questions and Answers

CAR-BRAKE PROBLEMS[3]

Although you may not be able to identify specific car-brake faults, you should be aware of the most common symptoms of brake trouble. They are:

Low pedal. If the brake pedal depresses to within two inches of the floor, you do not have enough reserve braking power to stop in emergencies.
Soft pedal. If brake pedal offers little resistance, chances are there is air in the brake hydraulic system. This could be serious, and should be checked at the first opportunity.
Locking brakes. Brakes which suddenly grab or seize cause a car to stop abruptly. When this occurs, it means there is probably foreign matter, such as grease, on the brake lining.
Brake scream. A high, piercing noise could indicate that brake lining is worn. Have the lining checked at once. A badly worn brake lining will eventually cause serious malfunctions in the brake system.

A car-brake system of the drum type works this way: Inside each car wheel is a *wheel cylinder, two brake shoes* covered with an *asbestos brake lining,* and a *metal brake drum* which revolves with the car wheel. Pressing on the brake pedal causes pressure to increase in the fluid that flows throughout the brake system. In turn, this raises pressure at each wheel cylinder, activating two metal pistons, which force the brake shoes against the brake drum, stopping the car. These parts must be in good condition if brakes are to work properly.

In a 1969 survey by *Motor,* a leading automotive journal, one out of two cars checked needed some type of brake service, ranging from a minor pedal adjustment to replacement of a brake drum. Cooperating in the survey were garage shops, service stations, and auto dealers' service departments across the country. In all, 350 cars, ranging from 1954 to 1969 models, were inspected. The majority of models were two to six years old.

By projecting these results to include all 83 million cars in the U.S., it would indicate that about 42 million cars presently need some brake work. The most common defects *Motor* found in the cars checked are:

Worn brake linings. One out of two cars checked required new lining now or within the next few thousand miles.
Leaky wheel cylinders. This problem was found in one out of every four cars.
Scored (gouged) brake drums. This problem was also found in one out of every four cars.

All of these defects are potentially serious. If a brake lining is worn out,

[3] "The Better Way: Car-Brake Problems," reprinted by permission from the May 1970 issue of *Good Housekeeping Magazine.* © 1970 by the Hearst Corporation.

the raw steel face of the brake shoes will score (gouge) the brake drum. Prolonged scoring wears down the metal drum and brake failure may occur. Similarly, if brake fluid leaks out of the wheel cylinder, pressure in the brakes will be too low to activate the brake shoes, and brake performance will become sluggish.

To keep brakes in good working order, have them inspected every other oil change. When repairs are needed, have them made at a service station, garage or dealer service department where you are known. If the car warranty is still in effect, it may cover repair costs.

Have the mechanic prepare a *repair order* before he begins. The order should itemize all repairs together with a cost estimate. A repair order is not binding. It is merely an *indication* of repair costs.

When repairs not itemized are required, ask what's needed before giving your authorization. Be wary of shops that offer cut-rate brake jobs. These jobs could mean installation of inferior brake linings, which will not give sufficient stopping power in emergencies.

Set 3

Preview Questions and Answers

KINDS OF CONSUMER CREDIT[4]

Government agencies frequently classify consumer credit into two main categories: installment and noninstallment credit. The latter is further classified as single-payment loans, charge accounts, and service credit.

1. Single-payment Loans. These are mainly short-term personal loans made by commercial banks. Such loans ordinarily account for less than 10 per cent of outstanding consumer credit. The borrower signs a promissory note. This is a written promise to pay back the amount borrowed at the end of the loan period. A comaker may or may not be required, depending on the borrower's credit rating and local banking practices.

Interest on a single-payment bank loan is usually collected in advance. This practice is called *discounting a note*. For example, if you borrow $1000 for two months at an annual rate of 6%, the interest charge of $10 ($1000 $\times$ .06 $\times$ 1/6 of a year) will be deducted at once. You will then receive $990 in cash or, more likely, that amount will be added to your checking account.

2. Charge Accounts and Service Credit. These forms of credit permit consumers to buy goods and services with the understanding that they will be paid for within 30 days or by a certain day of the next month following the purchase. Sometimes creditors will allow payment in 60 or 90 days and occasionally over a longer period. Charge accounts are used by retail stores to accommodate buyers. Service credit is often extended by physicians, plumbers, repair shops, and other service establishments.

The distinctive feature of these forms of credit is that they are interest free. The creditor expects that the additional business which he will get by extending credit will cover his extra costs. Part of the cost is bookkeeping and mailing expense. The cost of the goods or services is entered ("charged") on the creditor's books. Then once a month the consumer receives a statement of his account. Failure to pay within the allowed time may mean loss of further credit. The creditor must also expect some cost in the form of bad debts.

Charge-account customers ordinarily are provided with a means of identification, often a *charge plate*. This permits the customer to get possession of the goods without waiting for credit references to be checked.

A popular form of charge account which can be used at a variety of business establishments is the *credit card*. Some credit cards are issued

[4] Kennard E. Goodman and C. Lowell Harriss, *Economics* (Boston: Ginn, 1966), pp. 202–3. Used with permission.

for particular goods and services, such as air transportation or gasoline service-station products. Others are issued by business concerns for use in a wide variety of restaurants, hotels, theaters, and specialty shops. The cost to businesses honoring these general-purpose credit cards is about 7 per cent of the customer's bill. For this the credit-card distributors handle the billing and collecting.

3. *Revolving Credit Plan.* This combines certain features of charge accounts and installment credit. The customer decides how much he can afford to pay each month, and the total amount which he may charge is based on this figure. For example, if a customer believes he can pay the store $15 a month, he may be allowed to charge his purchases up to a limit of $150. Thus a buyer who charged goods worth $50 would still have $100 in credit available. After a monthly payment of $15, his available credit would rise to $115. Ordinarily stores make a service charge for such credit. Some banks also offer revolving credit accounts.

4. *Installment Credit.* About 80 per cent of consumer credit is installment credit. The plan by which the customer pays only part of the cost of merchandise when he obtains possession (the down payment) and spreads payments for the balance over a period of time is called *installment buying*. It is used chiefly in the purchase of durable goods, such as an automobile or household appliances and furnishings.

Installment payments may extend from six months to three years, depending on the size of the debt and ability of the customer to pay. Often the seller cannot afford to be without payment for such a long time, so he arranges with commercial banks or sales finance companies to "carry" the unpaid balance. The interest on an installment loan is frequently called a *carrying charge*.

Installment credit also includes installment loans. Banks, consumer finance companies and credit unions make personal loans with provision for repayment in installments. Sometimes consumers borrow money so that they can pay cash for merchandise, or they may need money to pay old bills. An installment loan differs from an installment purchase chiefly in that no down payment is required.

The cost of installment credit may range from 10 per cent to 30 per cent or more a year. If a bank, for example, charges 6 per cent on a one-year installment loan, the true interest rate is about 12 per cent, since the borrower does not have the use of the entire loan over the entire interest period. Credit unions ordinarily charge 1 per cent a month on the unpaid balance. The yearly interest rate in that case is also 12 per cent. In some states finance charges are as high as 3 per cent a month on unpaid balances, or 36 per cent a year, on small loans of $500 or less. A person receiving $500 to be repaid over two years at $25 a month will pay an average interest rate of 18 per cent.

Set 4

Preview Questions and Answers

INVENTION: WHAT TO SAY[5]

The techniques for finding material vary with the paper you are writing. At one extreme there is the brief paper or theme whose material comes completely out of your own head. Invention here is subjective. The assignment only asks that you think about a subject and then express your ideas, observations, opinions, or recollections in an essay. That withered old chestnut "What I Did on My Summer Vacation" is the classic example of the essay requiring this kind of invention. As long as you can remember what you did that summer, or can invent, you have your material. Although we may remark snidely on this tedious topic, some very sophisticated types of writing—from autobiography to pure creative thought in philosophy or economics—require very similar invention, largely from the writer's head. At the other extreme is the paper drawn from material quite external to the writer. Here invention is heavily objective. It depends wholly on research (whether in books or in the laboratory) and aims only at an unadulterated, undeviating report of that research. Examples of this kind of paper are the book report or report on the literature of a subject without any comment or interpretation from the writer and the straight report on an experiment in the sciences or social sciences without any effort from the writer to interpret and comment.

Obviously most undergraduate papers stand somewhere in the rather considerable range between these extremes. An ordinary history or sociology essay assignment, for instance, usually demands that you combine research in the relevant books with your own ideas and comments. Here invention is both objective and subjective. The degree to which it is effectively one or the other varies with the assignment, of course, but it is hard to exclude the writer from most predictable assignments. In the most heavily researched paper he will make himself known by his introduction, his arrangement of externally derived material, and his verbal tone. As he cites various authorities, arranges them against each other, then discriminates between them, sides with some, or synthesizes, he manifests his own way of seeing the subject. The invention of such a paper thus involves as sources both the writer's head and his research.

In spite of the variety of writing assignments, two stages are necessary for the invention of almost all kinds of papers. They are the collection of raw material and the imposition on that raw material of a thesis or focus.

[5] Thomas H. Cain, *Common Sense About Writing,* © 1967, pp. 30–43. Abridged. By permission of Prentice-Hall, Inc., Englewood Cliffs, New Jersey.

Finding raw material

Searching the Topics. If you are inventing an essay by getting material largely out of your head, your main difficulty may lie in simply getting started. How do you get ideas to offer themselves? A *classical rhetorical technique for breaking into invention is to begin by asking yourself questions about the subject.* The old rhetoricians called such a process "searching the topics." This phrase denoted the use of handy general headings or categories ("topics") that the writer put to himself as questions about the subject.

One form of this is the seven "circumstances" taken from Cicero's treatise *On Invention* and memorized by schoolboys for centuries as a means of cracking open a resistant subject. Thomas Wilson, a sixteenth-century English rhetorician, put these circumstances into a rhyme of the "thirty days hath September" kind so that students could memorize them more readily:

Who, what, and where, by what help and by whose,
Why, how, and when do many things disclose.

Whereas all these questions may be appropriate only to a narrow range of subjects, such as description of a human act or of a narrative or historical event, they suggest that searching the topics may offer a basically useful and adaptable technique for finding material. Implicit in the process of searching the topics is an assumption most of us have accidentally found to be true: that we know more about many subjects than we can recall on short notice. (Examinations have a way of bringing this to mind.)

Cicero's so-called circumstances furnish only a limited list of topics to use in searching for matter. Another list of topics adaptable to a greater range of subjects might include these: *comparison, contrast, definition, division, example, contradiction, objection, qualification, implication.* Not all of these are likely to be relevant to any one subject, of course, but a few of them will often prove helpful in getting the collection of material under way. Comparison and contrast are especially useful, for you begin to see what the essence of your subject is when you see what it is like and unlike. Suppose, for instance, that you are writing about the American Revolution. What is unique about it? This question becomes less difficult if you begin to answer by searching the topic of comparison. Compare it to another revolution of which you know something, perhaps the French or the Russian Revolution. It begins to look not much like either of them. Conflict between social classes is not so prominent an element in the American Revolution, for instance. It does not decline into a bloodbath and purges as does the French, nor does power shift hands when the smoke clears as with the Russian. Whether you actually mention the French and Russian Revolutions in your essay on the American Revolution is not so relevant as the fact that comparing them with it gives you an insight into its uniqueness. It helps isolate the special characteristics of the subject.

In the same way you can turn other topics into questions and apply them to a subject to "search" it for material. Here are further examples of the procedure:

1. *Definition.* Do the terms need to be defined? (E.g., what does "revolution" mean? Is the American Revolution a "revolution" in a strict sense? Or is it a "War of Independence"? or a "Revolutionary War"? Is it perhaps a civil war?)

2. *Division.* Does the subject divide readily into parts? (What are the main military phases of the American Revolution? What steps led up to the firing at Lexington of the "shot heard round the world"? What were the major factions?)

3. *Example.* What illustrates the subject most clearly? (Is there a battle or other event that most typifies the Revolution or some important stage of it? What men represent it best?)

4. *Contradiction.* Is there a contradiction inherent in the subject? (Is the Revolution a war to gain political independence or an internal economic and class struggle for power? Or are both true? Is it both a challenge to and an affirmation of traditional Anglo-Saxon rights?)

5. *Objection.* Can I foresee any objection to this idea? How can I meet it? (How can I show that the Revolution is more than a war to gain political independence? What can I say to the argument that it is nothing more?)

6. *Qualification.* Would this idea work better or be more accurate or convincing if it were qualified? (Would it be more precise to say that the Revolution is primarily an internal economic and class struggle that rapidly acquires international overtones?)

7. *Implication.* What does the subject imply? Where does it lead? (What does it suggest about the nature of imperialism? About the problems of ruling colonial territories? Why do so many spokesmen for contemporary wars of "national liberation" claim the American Revolution as their historical justification? Is this often true, or is it usually propaganda?)

There could be many more. The point is not that you burden your mind with a list of specific topics or the questions they give rise to. Rather, remember that when you must find information, begin by asking yourself questions about the subject. Even when they simply point out only what you don't know, they serve to indicate where your thinking and research should begin.

Common Sense About Time. No matter where your material originates, it is essential that you allow yourself adequate time for its invention. If you employ efficiently your knowledge of the separate operations of writing, you will find that invention properly carried out takes far more time than either disposition (which takes least) or expression. This is not to say that "just writing it up" can be a casual act. But when you have searched out adequate material for an essay, the other steps suggest themselves. Also, your time for finding material is always limited (papers tend to be due on a fixed day), and you cannot always foresee or control the amount of thinking or reading or both that it will take to find enough material. So you must begin as early as possible to provide for whatever effort a respectable amount of material may require. Though I realize that this runs counter to the near-suicidal procrastination of many undergraduates, it is true all the same. There is simply no point in knowing about the various writing operations if you don't allow yourself time to exploit the distinctions between them.

Flexibility. Searching the topics and giving your unconscious time to work are useful elements of invention, which in very short papers written out of your head may supply most or all the material you need. For longer papers or papers involving reading and research, however, you will also need a method of recording the relevant information as you come upon it. Such a method will be practical only insofar as it is flexible. Until you have all the material you will need and have arranged it in a disposition, you cannot be completely sure where and how and under what heading you may wish to use any one piece of it. So your system of notetaking must let you switch and manipulate your pieces of information with the greatest freedom and the least effort.

The notes designed for maximum flexibility will always contain the following:

1. a heading indicating the relevance of the note to your subject;
2. accurate reference to source (author, work, page) so that when you use this information you can document it precisely in a footnote;
3. the information itself, in quotation marks if you are quoting but carefully paraphrased *in words of your own* if you are not.
4. (One more element may appear: a comment or question from you, perhaps to remind you how this information fits into your conception of the subject. Always put such a comment in brackets or initial it to distinguish it from your notes.)

Common Sense About Research. This point is so obvious that I would not state it here were it not for my experience of undergraduates' research habits as well as my own. Common sense suggests that your research should generally progress from more elementary to more advanced studies, and that in subjects where some of the material is difficult for you to master, you should prepare yourself by consulting less advanced sources first. But common sense is spectacularly uncommon.

You should be aware of three clues to the intelligent control of the progress of any research, although their relevance depends on the nature of the source material:

1. Proceed from the most detailed basic treatment that you can understand to more advanced treatment.
2. When an advanced study goes beyond your depth, find one of intermediate difficulty and use it to prepare yourself for the advanced.
3. But don't spend too much time on very elementary material and unnecessary background, or you may never get the paper written at all. Writers who begin reading very far away from their subject and hope to build up a complete background for it usually are not being practical about time. Often they simply capitulate or else at the last frantic moment do only minimal research and write papers thin in content.

Finding an Argument or Focus

As the last stage of invention, you must assume an attitude toward your subject that will coordinate it and give it a single direction. This attitude may take the form of either an argument or a focus. By *argument* I mean simply a defensible position regarding the subject (i.e., the form taken by most debating resolutions). "Dutch elm disease" is a subject, but "Dutch elm disease can be controlled" is an argument, implying automatically that its opposite is untrue. By *focus* I mean any non-argumentative way of seeing unity in the subject. Focus usually reflects a discernible principle inherent in your raw material. "How Dutch Elm Disease Spreads," "The Effect on Rural Landscapes of Dutch Elm Disease," "Urban Spraying Programs for Controlling Dutch Elm Disease" —these hypothetical titles bring three unifying focuses to bear on the subject. They are not argumentative but are instead simply approaches to the subject "Dutch elm disease" that allow you to begin ordering your collected raw material.

This stage of invention will be irrelevant if the topic set for the paper has forced you to collect your material with the intention of taking a predetermined position. Essay assignments that begin "Show that," "Argue," "Defend," "Prove," "Criticize," or "Reply to" obviously have argument built into them. Topics like "The Social Effects of Heroin" or "The Administration of the Federal Reserve Bank" obviously have a controlling focus inherent in them: the variety of the effects or the shape of the administration will automatically structure your collection of material. In such topics, argument or focus has been externally imposed, and consequently this second stage of invention is not relevant.

But in topics where only a subject without imposed argument or focus has been assigned, it will be necessary for you to find one.

Finding when necessary an argument or focus is legitimately an aspect of invention because, until you have done it, you really don't know the limits of your material, what is relevant in it, and whether you need to look for more. When found, it provides the principle for selecting and sorting your material and shows you what to look for if you need more. You can usefully make your argument or focus take the form of a single sentence; for example, "By foreshadowing the rest of *Hamlet* the first scene becomes indispensable"; or "Three varieties of illusion characterize the first scene of *Hamlet*." Such a sentence epitomizes the structure of the whole paper. It need not necessarily appear in your finished essay, but having it in front of you is an invaluable technique in arranging your material: by summing up your attitude toward your material it furnishes the clue to disposition.

Points to Remember

1. Search the topics. Ask yourself questions about the subject.
2. Allow adequate time for invention.
3. In impromptu essays, allow one-quarter of your time for invention.
4. Give your unconscious time to work.
5. Record material in the most flexible form.
6. Proceed in your research from basic to more advanced material.
7. Look for the principle inherent in your raw material—whether argument or focus—and use it to help limit and select your final material.

ANSWERS FOR PRACTICE SETS

There is no one set of answers. Many preview questions could have been asked. And different people probably asked different questions. Look back at the questions listed in the description section. They are examples of questions you could have asked about the selections in the practice sets.

6

Skimming and Scanning

Skimming and scanning were used to quickly find answers to questions about the blind men and the elephant. See how fast you can search through the material and find the answers given.

A. Find the pairs of words the writer used for each blind man: the first word showing the part of the elephant he touched; the second, his idea about the nature of the elephant.

First blind man:	side—wall
Second blind man:	tusk—spear
Third blind man:	trunk—snake
Fourth blind man:	knee—tree
Fifth blind man:	ear—fan
Sixth blind man:	tail—rope

B. What did the writer state about the blind men's rightness and wrongness?

"...each was partly in the right/and all were in the wrong."

THE BLIND MEN AND THE ELEPHANT:
A HINDU FABLE[1]

It was six men of Indostan
To learning much inclined,
Who went to see the Elephant
(Though all of them were blind),
That each by observation
Might satisfy his mind.

The First approached the Elephant,
And happening to fall
Against his broad and sturdy side,
At once began to bawl:
"God bless me! but the Elephant
Is very like a wall!"

The Second, feeling of the tusk,
Cried, "Ho! what have we here
So very round and smooth and sharp?
To me 'tis mighty clear
This wonder of an Elephant
Is very like a spear!"

The Third approached the animal,
And happening to take
The squirming trunk within his hands,
Thus boldly up and spake:
"I see," quoth he, "The Elephant
Is very like a snake!"

The Fourth reached out an eager hand,
And felt about the knee.
"What most this wondrous beast is like
Is mighty plain," quoth he;
" 'Tis clear enough the Elephant
Is very like a tree!"

The Fifth who chanced to touch the ear,
Said: "E'en the blindest man
Can tell what this resembles most;
Deny the fact who can,
This marvel of an Elephant
Is very like a fan!"

[1] John Godfrey Saxe, *The Poetical Works of John Godfrey Saxe* (Boston: Houghton Mifflin, 1889).

The Sixth no sooner had begun
About the beast to grope,
Than, seizing on the swinging tail
That fell within his scope
"I see," quoth he, "the Elephant
Is very like a rope!"

And so these men of Indostan
Disputed loud and long
Each in his own opinion
Exceeding stiff and strong
Though each was partly in the right
And all were in the wrong!

DESCRIPTION

What Are Skimming and Scanning? Skimming is a rapid search technique for finding main ideas in a selection. Scanning is a rapid search technique for finding details.

Why Are Skimming and Scanning Valuable? You can use skimming and scanning to find certain information you need without reading other material you do not need. Thus, they save you work and time. And they help you stay on the point and keep from getting distracted.

How Do You Do Skimming and Scanning? Here are some main steps.

1. Before you start, be very clear about your purpose. Know exactly what information you are looking for in your rapid search.

2. Preview thoroughly. (See Chapter 5.) Pay particular attention to organizational features like headings and subheadings to see what ideas the writer includes and how he arranges them. Note the writing patterns he uses. Such previewing helps you search and find your answers rapidly. For example, look back at the illustration, *The Blind Men and the Elephant.* See how the writer puts the supporting ideas first and the main idea last. Look at his writing pattern. In each case, he uses numeral, part of the elephant's body, and descriptive noun: first, side, wall; second, tusk, spear; and so on. You can answer the questions quite quickly once you see the organization and writing style in the selection.

3. Use keys to organization and location like headings, numbers, guide words, and so on.

4. Stay very active and alert. Look only at the information you are searching for. Do not let yourself get distracted by other information.
5. Make yourself move fast. Go over the pages very quickly.

PRACTICE

Each set starts with questions about certain information in the selection. Quickly search the selection for answers and write them in the space given.

Set 1

1. Relevance is a complex idea. We can't discuss it sensibly until we ask what kind of questions?

   REVELANCE TO WHAT, WHOM, AND WHEN

2. State what follows from this sentence: "Relevance, then, has a time dimension."

   WHAT STRIKES YOU AS IRREVELONT Now MAY HAVE TREMENDOUS IMPORTANCE A YEAR FROM NOW. (A EXPLANATION OF WHEN)

3. What is a do-it-yourself relevance program?

   STUDENTS CAN ORGANIZE PROGRAMS TO MAKE SUBJECTS MORE REVELANT TO WHATS HAPPENING TODAY

HOW RELEVANT ARE YOUR COURSES[2]

Students across the country are clamoring for changes in the traditional academic curricula. *The Catcher in the Rye,* many feel, is more pertinent

[2] David Klein, "How Relevant Are Your Courses?" Copyright © 1970 by Tri-

than *Silas Marner* and Black Studies more relevant than Latin or Greek. In both high school and college, relevance has become a crucial issue, even for the passive students, who suffer quietly through courses they "can't see the use of" or who simply drop out of school. Such attitudes may reflect your own feelings. You may feel that your studies just aren't relevant to your life, your needs or the real problems of the world today.

Relevance is a complex idea. We can't discuss it sensibly until we ask: "Relevant to what?" "Relevant to whom?" and "Relevant when?" The physical therapy student who labels her freshman humanities course irrelevant has a different complaint from the psychology major who finds her required statistics course dull or the sociology student who argues that her courses ought to deal with real social problems instead of theory. Each of these girls complains of irrelevance. But each has a different perspective and requires a separate answer.

If the physical therapy student is interested only in learning the techniques of physical therapy, humanities is irrelevant. But techniques alone won't make her a good physical therapist and they will do little to make her an interesting, sensitive person. Today's work week absorbs about one-third of our waking hours and in ten years this fraction may well drop to one-fourth or less. Courses in art, literature and political science are likely to make the therapist's leisure time happy and creative instead of a restless period between work shifts.

The psychology major's complaint about her statistics course may stem from a basic misunderstanding. A person attracted to the field because she "loves people and wants to learn what makes them tick" is likely to find statistics dry and boring because she hasn't yet grasped that psychology really is the scientific study of behavior. Whether the psychologist is investigating how laboratory rats make decisions or why some children do better at school than others, she can understand very little and communicate even less until she has learned the techniques of interpreting statistical findings of other investigators and of presenting her own. Whether the statistics course is fun or not may depend on the teacher, but a course may be highly relevant without being fun—and vice versa.

Bright, motivated students who are sensitive to current problems sometimes feel that their courses don't offer enough in the way of solutions. Why, they ask, does the economics course deal with supply and demand curves and not with cures for poverty? Why does the instructor in sociology spend so much time on abstract discussion of "group membership" and so little on the elimination of racial discrimination? Why do

angle Publications, Inc. Appeared originally in *Seventeen* ®. Reprinted by permission of McIntosh and Otis, Inc.

courses in international relations concentrate on such dull subjects as the balance of payments instead of on the prevention of war?

There are two answers to these questions and though neither is completely satisfactory, both deserve attention. To begin with, many students have far more faith in the power of science than do the scientists. Many students believe, for example, that sociologists know how to eliminate poverty; sociologists agree that they have learned a good deal about why poor people remain poor, but they are a long way from being able to offer practical cures. Professors do, of course, hold opinions about the solutions to social problems, but many of them feel that handing these to students is dangerously close to brainwashing them and that they serve the students better by offering "just the facts."

Sometimes students who are impatient for "instant" solutions are not aware that most social problems persist because their solution is extremely complex and often depends on apparently unrelated factors. One can't thoroughly understand the causes of war without knowing something about the balance of trade. Racial problems cannot be solved without some understanding of such abstractions as group membership and community structure. Viewed in this way, what may seem irrelevant becomes not only relevant but essential.

Relevance, then, has a time dimension. What strikes you as irrelevant right now may develop tremendous importance for you in just a year or two. What seems most pertinent today may turn out all too soon to have been a waste of time. The Black Studies programs now being offered on dozens of campuses are a striking example of this. In a general sense, Black Studies programs are relevant for both white students and black because typical courses do tend to neglect the contributions made by black people. For black students from the ghetto, such courses offer an almost irresistible, immediate attraction in inculcating a feeling of pride and dignity. Yet for such students what is crucially important (though far less appealing) is courses that are designed to correct the educational deficiencies developed in ghetto schools. Again, it's a matter of timing. Black Studies may have relevance when you're a B-average junior, but not when you're an untried freshman.

The same point applies to the independent study programs offered by an increasing number of high schools. A research project on disarmament may seem much more challenging than the standard courses you would otherwise take. But as a senior in high school, are you really equipped to do research—or will your "research paper" make you blush when you read it a year from now? Might you not do better to take an advanced or college-level course? This may save you time at college and thus permit you to do independent study when you are really capable of doing it well.

What we have said this far is, of course, a defense of the establishment —or at least a plea that you give it the benefit of the doubt. But irrelevance does occur—when a professor lectures from ten-year-old notes because revising them seems just too much trouble, or when he assigns a five-year-old textbook because changing it would mean changing his five-year-old exams—or even when he resists updating his own mental set, which may require still more effort. It occurs also when a professor is so involved in his research that he fails to point out the broader implications of his subject to his students.

Students have found a number of ways of successfully coping with obvious irrelevance. With the cheerful cooperation of the administration, students on many campuses have set up "free universities"—loosely organized groups of not-for-credit tuition-free courses offered on such subjects as the mass media and student unrest. These courses tend to be lively, free-wheeling sessions that bridge the relevance gap between the traditional academic subjects and "what's happening." All that is required is a dozen interested students, an empty classroom and a couple of instructors.

Some students have made subjects more relevant by organizing informal discussions on pressing social problems, then inviting professors to form panels to demonstrate what each of their disciplines can contribute toward solutions. Such sessions can be organized for high schools as easily as for colleges.

If you're convinced that the irrelevance of a course is real and irreversible, a committee of like-minded students can visit the department chairman to discuss the problem.

In addition, you can begin a do-it-yourself relevance program. Today so much worthwhile, thought-provoking material is available in magazines, books, journals, television documentaries and other sources that you can build your own study program on any subject that interests you. Such a program may not only provide you with the meaningfulness you seek in your studies, but surprisingly, may give your school work a relevance you never suspected it had.

Set 2

1. Briefly, what are the contents of the book, *The Sound of the City, The Rise of Rock and Roll?*

IT EXAMINES ORIGINS OF R&B, REGIONAL CONTRIBUTIONS TO ROCK & ROLL, AND BRINGS THIS HISTORY UP TO THE PRESENT DAY

2. Look at the information on the book, *The Rise of the Colored Races.*

Who is the author? *KEITH IRVING*

Who is the publisher? *W. W. NORTON*

What is the cost? *$10.00*

BRIEF BOOK REVIEWS[3]

FROM NOWHERE TO SOMEWHERE, by *Joseph Harold Wiley, Kenneth Jeffries* and *Charles T. Brooker.* The three black men who wrote this book were born in poverty. One grew up in a rural area of the South, another on city streets and the third in a small town. None of them had special talents or abilities. They were not writers, artists, athletes or singers. They were average, and millions of black youth can relate to them. They escaped their background, rose to a middle-income level, established homes and families and now enjoy a degree of peace, security and genuine happiness. Chilton Book Co. $4.95.

BLACK HUMOR, by *Charles R. Johnson.* This is a collection of cartoons by a Southern Illinois University student who is currently featured in "Charlie's Pad," a "how-to" television series on cartooning for fun and profit, to be syndicated nationally this year. The cartoons in this book satirize various aspects of the race problem. Johnson Publishing Co., Inc. $3.95.

THE THIRD LIFE OF GRANGE COPELAND, by *Alice Walker.* The black hero's life in this novel is analyzed in terms of how he copes with white oppression. He experiences the hopelessness of life in the South, finds it is not much better in the North and reaches old age a wiser, more responsible man. He concludes that the oppression he suffers is no rationalization for the mistreatment of others. Harcourt Brace Jovanovich, Inc. $5.95.

THE SOUND OF THE CITY, THE RISE OF ROCK AND ROLL, by *Charlie Gillett.* The book traces the sources of rock and roll in "the urban pioneer" of rhythm and blues, examines regional contributions to rock 'n roll (with sections on Northern studio teen beat, Southern rock 'n roll, the Detroit sound, etc.); and brings the history of rock 'n roll up to the

[3] Ebony Book Shelf, *Ebony,* October 1970, 28. Reprinted by permission of EBONY Magazine, copyright 1970 by Johnson Publishing Company, Inc.

present day, including a section on its trans-Atlantic echoes. Outerbridge & Dienstfrey. $6.95.

INTRODUCTION TO AFRICAN CIVILIZATIONS, *by John G. Jackson*. "The picture we get today of Africa in past ages from the history taught in our schools is that Africans were savages and that, although Europeans invaded their lands and made slaves of them, they were in a way conferring a great favor on them, since they brought to them the blessings of Christian civilization," writes the author. His book challenges all of the standard approaches to African history. University Books, Inc. $10.00.

FIRE AND BLACKSTONE, *by John R. Fry*. The author, a white Presbyterian minister who came to national attention in 1968 when he was attacked before a Senate committee investigating the use of OEO funds to "pay off" street gang leaders, charges that his efforts to bring peace and progress to Chicago's black ghetto have been shafted by official stupidity, public apathy and the spiritual poverty that pervades the church today. J. B. Lippincott Co. $5.95.

THE BLACK SITUATION, *by Addison Gayle, Jr*. This collection of essays ranges over the contemporary black experience. Chapter headings include: "White Experts–Black Subjects," "Black Power and Existential Politics" and "Cultural Nationalism: The Black Novelist in America." Horizon Press, $5.95.

PREJUDICE AND RACE RELATIONS, *edited by Raymond W. Mack*. From the pages of the New York Times the editor has drawn some of the analyses of prejudice and race relations that have appeared in the past decade. In his introduction, he discusses the swift and drastic changes that have occurred in some patterns of race relations in American Society, and how other patterns have resisted change and thereby outraged many Americans, black and white. Quadrangle Books, Inc. $2.45.

THE SOUTH AND THE NATION, *by Pat Watters*. The author sees the Southern experience as one which the rest of the country will soon follow. He uses a variety of methods—reportorial, analytical, anecdotal —to present what he calls "the South in the kind of rambling complexity that is its reality. . . ." Pantheon Books, $7.95.

THE RISE OF THE COLORED RACES, *by Keith Irvine*. The author traces the story of interracial relations from the epoch of the Flood to the time of Patrice Lumumba, illuminating facets of intercontinental history hitherto hidden by colonial myth or by white—and black—fear of being cast in a villainous role. His survey moves from antiquity—when, since some men were thought to have two heads and others eyes in their stomachs, the question of skin color or curliness of hair seemed practically irrelevant—down to the era when Europeans subjugated other continents. W. W. Norton & Co. $10.00.

Set 3

What type of plastics are used to make these objects?

Object	Type of Plastic
Ex.: photographic film	celluloid
1. airplane propellers	*BAKELITE*
2. costume jewelry	*LUCITE - PLEXIGLAS*
3. electrical insulators	*STYRENE*
4. food wrappers	*VINYL*

SOME COMMON PLASTICS[4]

Cellulose nitrate is made by treating cellulose with a mixture of concentrated nitric and sulfuric acids. The nitrated cotton is dissolved in a mixture of alcohol and ether. After the solvent has evaporated, a soft jelly-like mass remains. This is molded into any desired shape and heated until it becomes solid. *Celluloid,* the oldest commercial plastic, is made by dissolving cellulose nitrate in camphor. It is very inflammable and burns with a flash when set on fire. It is used for making combs and brushes, photographic film, toys, fountain pens, and many other articles. *Collodion* is a solution of cellulose nitrate in alcohol and ether.

Cellulose acetate is produced by treating cotton cellulose with acetic acid anhydride. It burns more slowly than does cellulose nitrate. Although it is more expensive to manufacture, it finds extensive use as "safety film," artificial leather, screwdriver handles, etc., and as the interlayer in safety glass.

Bakelite is prepared from phenol and formaldehyde. It was discovered by Dr. Leo Baekeland. It is a thermosetting plastic which is used in making automobile parts, electric appliances, and lampshades, as a binder in plywood, and in making laminated materials. Laminated means built up in layers. Sheets of paper or cotton cloth are dipped in Bakelite and are laid on top of other sheets treated in the same way, until the desired thickness is attained. The pile is then placed under a hot hydraulic press.

[4] L. E. Young and W. M. Petty, *Chemistry for Progress* (Englewood Cliffs, N.J.: Prentice-Hall, Inc., 1957), pp. 546–47. Abridged. Used with permission.

A hard, tough sheet results. Laminated plastics are used for making airplane propellers and gears, and to replace many metallic parts in airplanes.

Plastics from milk are made by treating casein, the protein found in milk, with formaldehyde. These casein-formaldehyde resins color easily and are used for making beads, buckles, and buttons.

Lucite and *Plexiglas* are made by polymerizing methyl-acrylic acid (an organic acid) with light, heat, or peroxides. These plastics are crystal clear and are often used for making lenses, costume jewelry, and toilet articles. Bomber noses are made from this plastic material.

When urea, $CO(NH_2)_2$ is heated with formaldehyde in the presence of a suitable catalyst, a plastic of great strength is formed. Unbreakable water tumblers and dishes, buttons, and many other common articles are made from this plastic.

Styrene resins are made by polymerizing styrene. They are crystal clear, are resistant to shock, are not reacted upon by common chemicals, and do not absorb water. They are used in making electrical insulators.

Vinyl resins are made by polymerizing vinyl chloride and vinyl acetate, two organic compounds. They do not burn and do not react with ordinary chemicals. They are extensively used as interlayers for safety glass, as food wrappings, in transparent suspenders and belts, and in many lacquers and adhesives.

A new type of plastic is being made from fluorine derivatives of hydrocarbons. *Teflon* is an example. These plastics are very resistant to the action of acids and alkalis even at high temperatures.

Set 4

1. What may internal conflicts result from?

   PERSONAL FACTORS AND PHYSICAL LIMITATIONS

2. What is an approach-approach conflict?

   IS WHEN A PERSON MUST RESOLVE A CONFLICT BETWEEN TWO DESIREABLE GOALS

FRUSTRATION[5]

When we cannot satisfy a need or solve a problem because an obstacle is blocking our efforts, we experience feelings of frustration that disturb us, distract us from our other responsibilities, and interfere with our capacity to remain rational. If our inability to overcome the obstacle continues, further problems and conflicts arise. Handling frustration is an important aspect of personal adjustment. Sources of frustration are discussed below.

SOURCES OF FRUSTRATION

The frustrating obstacles that prevent us from satisfying our needs or solving our problems may be either (1) external or *environmental* conditions, or (2) internal or *personal* factors, or a combination of both. Let us briefly consider these two types of factors.

Environmental Conditions

These include any obstacles we may encounter in our physical environment. If we need to prepare an early breakfast, and we discover that we are out of eggs and bread, and the stores are still closed, we are caught in a frustrating situation. If we have an important appointment and find that the car will not start or that the road has been washed out, we are again frustrated. The man in prison finds the bars frustrating; so may the child in his playpen. Both are blocked by physical restraints.

In attempting to achieve our goals we may also find ourselves in conflict with environmental obstacles raised by sociocultural mores. We Americans, for example, place great stress on getting ahead, on beating the other fellow. But we also stress cooperation and consideration for our fellow man. Thus there emerges a frustrating conflict between competition and cooperation.

Personal Factors

Internal conflicts may arise as a result of personal factors that make it necessary for us to choose between conflicting needs and goals, or conflicting approaches to a goal.

We may, for example, need to study and yet, at the same time—because we are lonely and have few friends—need to become better ac-

[5] George F. J. Lehner and Ella Kube, *The Dynamics of Personal Adjustment*, 2nd ed. (Englewood Cliffs, N.J.: Prentice-Hall, Inc., 1964), pp. 95–100. Abridged. Used with permission.

quainted with the fellow-student who drops by. In such a situation we are frustrated by incompatible personal needs.

We may have a goal to bolster our finances by taking a summer job and at the same time have a goal to make a bicycle tour of the country with a group of friends. In such a situation we are frustrated by incompatible personal goals.

We may wish to achieve financial security as soon as possible. We can spend four years at a university learning a profession that would help us get a good job or we can accept a friend's offer to get in on the ground floor of a "deal" that promises rich financial rewards immediately. In such a situation we are frustrated by having to choose between incompatible approaches toward a goal.

The essence of these frustrating conflicts is that no one can go in two different directions at once. Each conflict must be resolved before any action can be taken.

Personal factors can serve as frustrating barriers even when they exist only in our imagination. Such barriers may prevent us from attempting to acquire new skills because we imagine we would be clumsy and inept. We may, for example, forego tennis or skating or dancing for this reason, while at the same time envying those who are able to enjoy these activities.

Physical limitations may also serve as sources of frustration. An athlete may suffer a frustrating injury that forces him to the sidelines. A girl may be frustrated because she thinks she is too short to look chic.

Certain personality or behavior characteristics may frustrate our efforts to make friends. If I am hypercritical of others, for example, or ill-tempered, I may receive few social invitations. My desire to be accepted by others will then be frustrated, and I may not even realize why. My reaction to this frustration may be anxiety, loneliness, or anger. Or I may eventually take a good look at myself and realize that if I change my behavior my social relationships will improve.

Internal conflict situations are generally classified into three types according to the contradictory nature of the goals or alternatives. These are:

1. The *approach-approach* conflict, in which a person must resolve a conflict between two equally desirable goals—between two excellent job opportunities, for example.

2. The *avoidance-avoidance* conflict, in which a person must make a choice between two equally undesirable goals—must decide, for example, whether to sell his car or move to a cheaper room in order to avoid going further into debt.

3. The *approach-avoidance* conflict, in which a person is both attracted

and repelled by the same goal—as might be the case when a young man wishes to marry a girl who is extremely beautiful (encouraging the approach reaction) but who is also aggressive and demanding (encouraging the avoidance reaction). These mixed feelings of positive and negative factors, of approach to and avoidance of the same object, we also speak of as *ambivalent* feelings.

The need to make a choice in any of these three types of conflict can block our progress toward our goal and thus create a frustrating situation. We cannot proceed until we make one choice or the other or until we devise a satisfactory compromise.

This frustrating internal turmoil and conflict that often attends the making of choices is described in an interesting way by William James (1842–1910), the famous American psychologist.

"I am often confronted by the necessity of standing by one of my empirical selves and relinquishing the rest. Not that I would not, if I could, be both handsome and fat and well-dressed, and a great athlete, and make a million a year, be a wit, a bon-vivant, a lady-killer as well as a philosopher, a philanthropist, statesman, warrior, and African explorer, as well as a 'tone-poet' and saint. But the thing is simply impossible. The millionaire's work would run counter to the saint's; the bon-vivant and the philanthropist would trip each other up; the philosopher and the lady-killer could not well keep house in the same tenement of clay. Such different characters may conceivably at the outset of life be alike possible *to a man*. But to make any one of them actual, the rest must more or less be suppressed. So the seeker of his truest, strongest, deepest self must review the list carefully, and pick out the one on which to stake his salvation. All other selves thereupon become unreal, but the fortunes of this self are real. Its failures are real failures, its triumphs real triumphs, carrying shame and gladness with them. This is as strong an example as there is of that selective industry of the mind on which I insisted some pages back. Our thought, incessantly deciding, among many things of a kind, which ones for it shall be realities, here chooses one of many possible selves or characters, and forthwith reckons it no shame to fail in any of those not adopted expressly as its own."

Set 5

1. What two kinds of things can you do to keep down mistakes in testing?

LEARN TO TAKE TESTS & DEAL ACTIVELY WITH THEM.

2. At what three stages do you use reading skills as tools in taking a test?

PRE PAREING, WARMING UP, AND TAKING THE TEST

READING AND TAKING TESTS

Definition of Tests

Tests are sets of activities called test items. They are used to sample your behavior. Your responses to the test items are samples of your behavior. These behavior samples are used to make judgments about two things: what you can do now and what you probably will be able to do in the future.

Test items are questions or statements which you respond to. Several types are used: multiple choice, completion, true-false, matching, enumeration or listing, and essay.

Kinds and Uses of Tests

Two main kinds of tests are achievement tests and intelligence or aptitude tests. Achievement tests sample what you know about a given area. Aptitude tests sample how well you can probably achieve in an area.

Achievement tests are used in your courses to measure your progress. You probably call them examinations. Sets of achievement tests and aptitude tests are used in placement to help judge whether you can succeed. Examples of placement situations are admission to college and hiring for jobs like civil service jobs.

Mistakes in Testing

Much can be said for tests. Much can be said against them. However, as things now stand, you need to be very, very careful about tests because your test performance can have a big influence on your life. For example, your test performance can influence your grades in courses. It can influence whether you get admitted to certain training programs and whether you get certain jobs. The sad thing is that tests may not show what you know or what you can do. Why? It's hard to explain briefly. But here are some main points. Remember, tests are used to get samples of your behavior to use in making judgments.

—A sample of your behavior means that only a part of your behavior in an area is looked at, not all of your behavior. When you sample a basket of peaches, you look at only several peaches, not every peach in the basket.

—Judgments are predictions about what probably is so. They are not sure things or certainties.

—Many mistakes can be made in sampling your behavior and making judgments. These mistakes can be made by anyone who takes part in the testing.

—You can make mistakes in taking the tests. For example, you might not read the questions right.

—People who build the tests may make mistakes. For example, they may make up poor items.

—People who give the tests may make mistakes. For example, they may get mixed up on timing.

—People who score the test may make mistakes. For example, they may use the wrong answer key.

—People who interpret the tests may make mistakes. For example, they may make statements which go beyond the test results and their agreed-on meaning.

Keeping Down Mistakes in Testing

You don't have to be at the mercy of tests. If you are, it's your fault. You can do two kinds of things to keep down mistakes: learn to take tests, and deal actively with test results.

Learn to Take Tests. Taking tests is like many things; learning how is part of the problem; actually doing is the other part. You can learn to be a better test-taker by learning skills that will help you get higher test scores.

Deal Actively with Test Results. Think for yourself when you get test results. Don't just accept test results passively if they don't make sense—that is, if they don't seem to show what you think you can do. Do something. Ask questions about the results. Ask for a check for mistakes. If no mistakes can be found, ask for another test.

Role of Reading in Testing

Reading is involved two ways in tests: as the behavior tested and as a tool in taking the test.

As the Behavior Tested. Some tests have items for measuring your reading skills. They check how well you know the reading skills and can use them.

As a Tool. In some tests, you use reading as a tool to get the message about what you are to do. You have to read directions, read questions, and, on some tests, read the possible answers to select from. In addition, you may use reading in getting ready for tests.

Reading Skills as the Behavior Tested

Most reading tests sample how well you can deal with vocabulary and connected material.

Vocabulary. In vocabulary items, you deal with sets of single words. Items test how much you know about word meanings and how well you can use (manipulate) words in relation to other words. Four kinds of often-used items are synonyms, antonyms, verbal analogies, and sentence completion.

1. Synonyms are the simplest kind of vocabulary questions. You have to mark words or phrases which mean the same as the key word.

Euphoria means _____.
(A) sense of well-being
(B) act of friendliness
(C) ability to speak well
(D) eagerness to agree

The main vocabulary skill used here is dealing with synonyms. However, if you have to figure out the word meaning, then use phonetic analysis and structural analysis skills. Of course, dictionary skills are ruled out, and there is no way to use context clues.

2. Antonyms or opposites are used more often than synonyms. They

are harder and more searching in testing your ability to use vocabulary. Why? They test not only your knowledge of definitions but also your skill in shifting mentally to find the opposite of denotative meanings.

> Cognizant is the opposite of _____.
> (A) afraid
> (B) ignorant
> (C) aware
> (D) optimistic

Use skills for dealing with synonyms and antonyms.

3. Verbal analogies are almost always used in tests because they are the most searching sample of your vocabulary. Why? They test three things: one, your knowledge of word meanings; two, your knowledge of, or ability to see relations among word meanings; three, your ability to apply these relations to other sets of words—that is, to find these relationships in other sets of words.

> Cool : cold : _____
> (A) meat : lunch
> (B) winter : spring
> (C) money : dollar
> (D) pink : red

Use the skills for dealing with verbal analogies.

4. Sentence completion items test your ability to deal with vocabulary in the context of a sentence. Sentences may have one or two words missing.

> A _____ may give you wrong advice and cause you trouble.
> (A) taciturn
> (B) valence
> (C) charlatan
> (D) pleased

> The beautiful _____ was the center of all _____.
> (A) picture—attention
> (B) remarks—informative
> (C) mundane—tractable
> (D) chains—connects

The main skill needed here is using context analysis.

Longer Connected Material. Here, you have to deal with paragraphs or longer selections. Most often, the test items sample whether you can get information presented in a selection. Less often, they sample your ability to evaluate the material.

Use three sets of skills for such test items which cover longer connected material:

1. Use mainly the comprehension skills: following guides to coherence; finding main ideas in paragraphs, finding supporting ideas in paragraphs, and finding main ideas and supporting ideas in longer selections. You especially need to be able to find implied ideas.

2. Use the rapid search skills also: previewing to see what questions you need to answer before you read the selection; and skimming and scanning to find particular information asked for in the questions.

3. When questions call for evaluation, of course, use the evaluation skills: separating fact and opinion, finding writing tricks, finding faulty reasoning.

Reading Skills as Tools in Test-Taking

You use reading skills as tools at three stages: in preparing for the test, in warming up, and in taking the test.

Preparing for the Test. The task in preparing for a test is to learn and remember the material you will need in taking the test items. Here, you need reading skills used in studying.

Warming up for the Test. Warm-up activities are just as important in test-taking as they are in other activities like pitching a baseball or playing the piano. Warming up for test-taking means practice with the content to be tested and with the types of test items to be used. The task is to get yourself reacting in the way you will need to react on the test. Warming up keeps you from wasting time in figuring out what you are supposed to do, and with it, you will be less likely to miss important clues.

1. Use collections of practice materials. These have been prepared for aptitude tests and the aptitude–achievement tests used in placement. Examples are *The Handbook of College Entrance Examinations, Civil Service Examinations, Tests for Dental Assistants,* and so on. There are a great many books like these. You can find them in public libraries and school libraries. Also, you can buy them in book stores.

2. For achievement tests in your courses, review the materials in the

course. Ask your teacher for sample items. Or try to figure out the types of items you will have, make up your own items, and then answer them. In this process, use skimming and scanning in rapid searches for specific information.

Taking the Test. Here, you need a variety of skills:

1. *Previewing.* Preview the entire test. Locate the items you are sure you can answer and the items you are not sure of. Also, preview the answers before you do the stem of each multiple-choice question. That is, alert yourself ahead of time to clues you need to look for as you read the selection.
2. Reading skills for test requirements. Read the test directions and the test items carefully.

—Be sure you understand what you are to do. Sadly, many people miss questions for which they know the answers. The problem is that they do not grasp what the questions are asking. Use several skills: the comprehension skills and certain vocabulary skills—using phonetic and structural analysis, dealing with homonyms, synonyms, and antonyms, and using context analysis.

—For essay items, construct your answers carefully. Use the processing skills. You use these skills on material you have read in relation to the problem posed by the essay test question. Important skills here are checking relevance, analyzing and outlining, summarizing, and synthesizing.

—Watch out for the effects of simple words. In true-false tests, pinpoint the words which nearly always make an overgeneralization and are thus false—for example: all, always, never, none, no, only. Also, in true-false tests, pinpoint words which limit generalizations and thus make it possible for broad statements to be true—for example: some, sometimes, usually, more, most. In essay tests, note the key verb in the question and do exactly what it says—for example: compare—show the similarities between two subjects; contrast—show differences between two subjects; define—give the meaning of the subject; describe—give the characteristics of the subject; discuss—give the pros and cons related to the subject; list, name, or enumerate—give a number of points on the subject called for, *i.e.*, characteristics, causes, and so on; evaluate—give an opinion backed up by reasons; and explain—give reasons for an occurrence or characteristics of an event.

ANSWERS FOR PRACTICE SETS

Set 1

1. Questions like: Relevant to what? Relevant to whom? Relevant when?

2. Relevance has a time dimension because what strikes you as irrelevant right now may become very important for you in a year or two. What seems pertinent today may turn out soon to have been a waste of time.

3. A do-it-yourself relevance program: you can build your own study program on any subject that interests you. Also, you can start your own action programs and other group programs to apply your knowledge.

Set 2

1. Sources of rock and roll, regional contributions to rock and roll, history of rock and roll to the present including a section on rock and roll in other countries.

2. Author: Keith Irvine. Publisher: W. W. Norton and Company. Cost: $10.00.

Set 3

1. bakelite

2. lucite and plexiglas

3. styrene resins

4. vinyl resins

Set 4

Motivation is a stimulating condition, either external or internal or both, by which a process of behavior is initiated and continued until a state of equilibrium is restored.

Set 5

1. Learn to take tests. Learn the skills that will help you get higher test scores. Deal actively with test results; don't accept them if they don't seem to show what you think you can do. Ask questions about results. Ask for a check for mistakes, or even for another test.

2. In preparing for a test; in warming up for a test; in taking the test.

III

EVALUATION SKILLS

Part Three looks at the evaluation skills. These skills involve ways of judging the accuracy of written material. Chapter 7, on *separating fact and opinion*, concerns learning to tell the difference between an actual event and a person's notions about an event. Chapter 8, *finding writing tricks*, is about catching wrong ideas the writer can give you when he seems to say one thing and actually says another. Chapter 9, *finding faulty reasoning*, deals with spotting the ways you can avoid inaccurate reading of material.

These chapters go into ways for judging the truth value of the written material itself—the way ideas are presented. They don't cover the critical evaluation of *content*, of ideas. Criticizing content is a special study in the various fields. Each field has its own types of evidence, rules of evidence, and methods for getting and analyzing evidence. These things are beyond reading, as such. For an example of how to do critical evaluation in one field, literature, see "The Theme of Evaluation" by Roberts.[1]

[1] In Edgar V. Roberts, *Writing Themes About Literature* (Englewood Cliffs, N.J.: Prentice-Hall, Inc., 1969).

7

Separating Fact
and Opinion

Statements 3, 5, and 6 are facts. They are about actual events. Statements 1, 2, and 4 are opinions. They refer to people's feelings and judgments.

1. The movies being made today are more interesting and meaningful than movies used to be.
2. That part of the country is really beautiful.
3. In that pet shop, the kittens cost less than the puppies do.
4. Walnut furniture is just too expensive.
5. Dogwood trees bloom in the Spring.
6. Canada is north of the U.S.; Mexico is south.

DESCRIPTION

What Are Facts and Opinions? A fact is an actual event. The truth is in the event. It can be checked out by evidence you get through the five senses—hearing, seeing, smelling, tasting, and touching. People cannot disagree. On the other hand, an opinion is a judgment or feeling about an event. It is based on a person's interests, experiences, and so forth. The truth is in the people who judge and feel. An opinion cannot be checked out by evidence obtained through the five senses. And since people differ, their opinions may honestly disagree.

Why Is Separating Fact and Opinion Valuable? Facts and opinions are both useful but you need to keep them separate so that you can react differently to them. Why? Because of the way they affect your actions. If you don't separate them, you may waste time, money, and effort, or you may hurt yourself or someone else. A simple example: Fact: Water is not fuel for your car. Action: Plan on gas money. Opinion: It's better to use high-test gas rather than regular gas. Action: Spend or don't spend the extra money for high-test gas depending on whether you agree with that opinion.

How Do You Tell the Difference Between Fact and Opinion? It's pretty hard sometimes. Here are three steps:

1. Read the material very carefully. Be sure you get the writer's message. Especially look for clues to opinion statements in such expressions as "I think," "I believe," "In my opinion," "Everyone agrees that . . . ," and so on. (See the Comprehension Skills in Part One.)

2. Size up what people say and think for yourself. "Chicken tastes better when it's fried than when it's baked." That's an opinion. Think about it. Some people like it better fried; some, baked.

3. Get evidence. You have a fact if the evidence is information obtained through one of the five senses, and if you get the same information every time you check. You have an opinion if the evidence is information about what people like, feel, or think, or if different people give different information about what they like, feel, or think about the same thing.

PRACTICE

Set 1

The sentences below are statements of facts and statements of opinion. Mark each statement as either a fact (F) or opinion (O).

_O_ 1. More people watch football games than tennis games.

_F_ 2. Subtraction takes less steps than long division.

_O_ 3. Fear and anxiety are more upsetting than anger.

O 4. The middle ages were the least interesting time in the recorded history of mankind.

O 5. Geology is the most important study in the physical sciences.

F 6. Oregon has more mountains than Kansas.

F 7. Babies begin learning language during their first year.

O 8. Baseball is a great deal of fun to play and to watch.

O 9. It is more fun to be in Los Angeles than in San Francisco.

F 10. Columbus first sighted the American continent in 1492.

Set 2

O 1. Winter is not a nice time of the year.

O 2. Situation comedies on TV are fun to watch.

F 3. The Statue of Liberty is in New York Harbor.

O 4. *True* is a magazine designed mostly for men.

F 5. J. F. Kennedy was president after D. D. Eisenhower.

O 6. Galsworthy's *Forsyth Chronicles* is very interesting.

F 7. Shakespeare wrote *Hamlet* and *Macbeth*.

O 8. Everybody needs a car and a TV.

F 9. The Beatles influenced popular music.

O 10. College freshmen are not mature enough to study psychology.

Set 3

F 1. H_2O is the chemical formula for water.

F 2. Adjectives and adverbs serve as modifiers for nouns and verbs.

O 3. Proteins are more important to your health and well-being than carbohydrates.

O 4. Teachers give students too much work to do.

F 5. Australia is located in the southern part of the Pacific Ocean.

O 6. Mathematics is the most important study for a student.

F 7. Scientific knowledge has increased a great deal in the twentieth century.

O 8. Joe Namath is a better player than Red Grange was.

O 9. The world is moving so fast that no one can keep up.

F 10. The English language has been affected by the languages of the Romans and the Greeks.

ANSWERS FOR PRACTICE SETS

Set 1
Facts: nos. 1, 2, 6, 7, 10.   Opinions: nos. 3, 4, 5, 8, 9.

Set 2
Facts: nos. 3, 4, 5, 7, 9.   Opinions: nos. 1, 2, 6, 8, 10.

Set 3
Facts: nos. 1, 2, 5, 7, 10.   Opinions: nos. 3, 4, 6, 8, 9.

8

Finding Writing Tricks

These statements have writing tricks. Look at how they seem to say one thing when they really say something else.

1. "This is the season when many people get bad colds. For bad colds, doctors say stay warm and dry, rest in bed, drink plenty of fluids, and take aspirin. Brand X aspirin is excellent. People have used it for years. So take Brand X and do the other things the doctors say and you'll be well soon."
   This statement suggests that doctors say take Brand X along with the other things. However, it really does not say that.

2. "I have to keep clean clothes for ten children and for a husband who is an automobile mechanic. Brand X soap gets our clothes cleaner."
   This statement suggests that Brand X soap does a perfect job and works better than other brands. However, it doesn't say that. It doesn't say Brand X gets clothes clean enough and it doesn't say which other brands get clothes less clean than Brand X.

3. "Come to see us when you need money. We want to loan you the money you want."
   This statement suggests that a person will be loaned all the money he wants. However, it doesn't say that. It only says that the lender *wants* to lend what a person wants; not that the lender *will* lend that much.

DESCRIPTION

What Are Writing Tricks? Writing tricks are ways some writers use for trying to fool you without actually giving you false information. Some writers may try to do various things, for example: make you think they are saying something when they really aren't, make you feel certain things to get your mind off the point, or make you get mixed up. They may have various purposes. Sometimes novelists use writing tricks to keep you from getting the plot or the solution of a story too quickly. And, sadly, some writers may try to take advantage of you and other people.

Why Is Finding Writing Tricks Valuable? The main value is to help you deal with writers who try to take advantage of the public. Being able to find writing tricks can keep you from being fooled by statements that give false suggestions even though they don't give false information—this can keep you from hurting someone else or yourself, from wasting work and time, from losing money, and so on.

How Do You Find Writing Tricks? Use these three steps.

1. Pay very close attention to what you read. Be sure you get the message. Size up the material. Make judgments about its correctness and freedom from special interests. (See *Comprehension Skills* in Part One and *Previewing* in Chapter 5.)

2. When you make important decisions, check several sources of information on the same topic. Be particularly careful if they disagree.

3. Get to know some common writing tricks. Watch for them. Some often-used writing tricks are unfinished comparisons, misleading statements, slanted words and stereotypes, slogans, wrong or meaningless phrases, misleading writing style, left-out information, appeals based on misleading authority, and appeals to inappropriate emotions.

Unfinished comparisons

Some comparisons are not finished. In a true comparison, one thing must be put against one or more other things. Otherwise, the statements don't mean much.

—"Brand X is 10 hours fresher." Fresher than what other brands? The writer doesn't say and the statement means nothing.

—"Brand X does the best job of cleaning your clothes." Better than what other brands?

—"Buy our cars. We have better ideas." Better ideas than whom? Better ideas about what?

Misleading statements

Some statements seem to say one thing when they really say another. What they *suggest* would be good if it were true; what they *really say* is less desirable, though true.

—"Brand X is *recognized* by the American Dental Society." This statement suggests that "Brand X is *recommended* by the ADS." This suggestion is not true. The statement really says that the ADS knows about the brand. So do many people.

—"No brand is better than Brand X for solving your problems." This statement suggests that Brand X is better than other brands. However, it really doesn't say that. The statement could mean that Brand X is better or that Brand X is the same as the other brands.

—"This TV is 100% more reliable than our reliable TV of four years ago." How reliable was the former model? The current model could still have more bugs than comparable brands.

—"Be thinner. Drink our milk. It's 98% fat-free." "Lose weight. Our peanuts are not cooked with oils which add fat." Milk and peanuts both still have plenty of calories and are not the best foods for weight reduction.

—"These bedroom suites are on sale for $189.95. Compare at $400." This statement suggests that bedroom suites costing $400 have been marked down. But it really says that you can look at suites that cost more. If the bedroom suites were marked down, the seller would certainly say so in clear, direct words.

Slanted words and stereotypes

Over time, we learn to have good or bad feelings when we hear or see certain phrases. In most cases, the things these phrases describe are neither *all* good nor *all* bad. Look at how these phrases can show different feelings about the same person.

—free young people . . . undisciplined youth
—selfless dreamer of the impossible dream . . . wild-eyed idealist
—determined . . . stubborn
—advanced thinker . . . absent-minded professor
—the now generation . . . wild and crazy young people
—the command generation . . . the then generation

Slogans

Some phrases become slogans. They are used to stand for an idea which is an over-simple and not complete description of the real thing. Further

and sadly, such statements are often so tied up with truly desirable things they are hard to question or argue with. Look at these statements. What do they mean? How can they be carried out?
—Stand by Old Glory.
—If it's not my bag, I won't do it.
—Tell it like it is.

Wrong or meaningless phrases

Some phrases may sound good but they are either wrong or unlikely.
—"Sally instinctively liked John." Instincts are born in people. They are not learned. Tastes for friends are learned.
—"His heart was broken when he lost her." Sadness may affect health and many things may happen to the heart. However, the heart doesn't actually break.

Misleading writing style

Some writers try to mix up readers or try to get readers' minds off the point. They use such things as double negatives, irrelevant material, very complex sentences and paragraphs, very hard words, "gobbledygook," unrounded numbers, and so on.
—"I'm not unsanguine about the team's prospects this season." This statement means: "I think the team will do well this season."
—"If they would use critical reading, *viz.*, assess what they read and not be intimidated by the printed word, most readers, but not all, could save themselves and others untold confusions and difficulties." This statement means: "Most readers would stay out of trouble if they evaluated what they read."
—"We are letting these new model cars go at $1995.50." Somehow, $1995.50 doesn't sound as costly as $2000. But when you're spending that much money, what difference does $4.50 make?

Left-out Information

Some writers may try to put across their ideas by leaving out information that fits but doesn't agree with their ideas. They include only information which supports their case.
—"This car costs less to buy and run. It has no frills. It gets 37 miles to the gallon. It is light and compact with no wasted space." Here are some things that are not told about the car: How easily it skids and turns over; how uncomfortable it is to ride in; how hard it is to carry things in; how quickly the body caves in in an accident; how little pick-up and quick-turning it has when the driver gets in a bad spot.

Appeals based on misleading authority

Some writers call on authority so that you will accept an idea. Broadly, an authority is someone who is supposed to know a great deal about something. Or authority can be a source such as research, statistics, common law, the constitution. In itself, quoting an authority is not wrong; in fact, it is common practice in legal and other types of scholarly writing. The misleading part comes in at least two ways: when the writer does not tell exactly who or what the authority is and how the evidence was gotten; when the authority cited is not qualified to comment on the particular idea.

—"Research says that children like baseball better than swimming." What research? What evidence? How was it gotten?

—"Leading physicians recommend this product for headache." Which physicians? What are their special qualifications?

—"My days as a basketball star are past. But I still eat Brand X to keep me feeling young and frisky." How does being a basketball star qualify a person to recommend food?

Appeal to inappropriate emotions

A writer may try to get you to accept an idea by appealing to your emotions. In itself, there is nothing wrong in using emotional tone or other devices to arouse emotion. The problem comes when the emotions are false, misplaced, shallow, or exaggerated; or when the emotions distract from any false evidence or lack of evidence that the writer may have.

—"Give to our new charity and save a poor, sick, starving child from going to bed hungry tonight."

—"Think about the honor of our school. Have you no pride? No loyalty? We can't let the other team win the title."

PRACTICE

Some of these statements have writing tricks. Some do not. Mark (X) each statement that has a writing trick and describe what's wrong with it.

Set 1

————1. He works long and hard on his studies. ———————————

X—2. Free public education is available to children between six and

eighteen years old. *EDUCATION IS NOT FREE IT IS PAID FOR IN TAXES*

X—3. Take these special pills for your headache. One part of them is

the pain reliever that doctors recommend most for headaches. *WHAT DOCTORS, WHAT PAIN RELIVER*

X—4. We signed a contract. Now let's fulfill it. *EMOTIONAL OBLIGATION*

X—5. We have spent many years developing this medicine. It's good

for overcoming tiredness. *HOW MANY.*

X—6. With our gasoline, you get more miles to the gallon and less

pollution. *HOW MANY MORE MILES HOW MUCH LESS POLUTION*

X—7. You are an adult, U.S. citizen. You have the right and re-

sponsibility to vote in public elections. *YOU HAVE THE RIGHT) BUT YOU ARE NOT RESPONSIBLE*

X—8. I can't go today. My head hurts too much—it's really splitting.

THE HEAD IS NOT REALY SPLITTING

X—9. Our records were checked by Mr. Smith, a certified public
accountant. He testified that we are in sound financial condition.

A CPA WOULD NOT KNOW ABOUT OVER-ALL FINANCIAL CONDITIONS

Set 2

X—1. Vote for our candidate. He will clean up city hall sooner.

CLEAN UP WHAT, SOONER THAN WHOM?

_X_—2. This car costs less to operate than any other car on the market

today. _HOW MUCH LESS, WHAT MARKET._

—————3. In comparison to a hand saw, a power saw saves time and work.

However, it is more dangerous and expensive to operate. ——————

——————

_X_—4. Their interest in the Beautiful People is really un-American.

WHAT IS AMERICAN— UN AMERICA N

—————5. The physician tapped the child's knee. His purpose was to

check the child's patellar reflex. ——————

_X_—6. Are we men or mice? Are we going to stand by and let those

outsiders come in here and tell us how to run our business? _APPEALING_

TO EMOTION - WHAT ARE THEY BEING

TOLD TO DO

_X_—7. This cleanser has bleach in it. _HOW MUCH ? WHAT_

KIND

_X_—8. Inexorably, those male individuals in our society who have not
attained their chronological majority and commitments to wives and
children are subject, with only a few exemptions, to potential selection as
participants in this country's armed services in the defense establishment

throughout the world. _AN ATTEMPT TO CONFUSE_

BY THE USE OF COMPLICATED WORDS

_X_—9. The results reported by Jones (1964) and McDonald (1967)
demonstrate that this method is accurate more than 90% of the time.

WHO ARE JONES & McDONALD - 90% OF

WHAT?

—✗—1. If you want the good students, you ought to choose our group. Check the grade point averages and you'll see that we've never been beaten by another group. GOOD FOR WHAT?

—✗—2. Since this elementary-school pupil resorts to physical means of winning his point or attracting attention, a school-home program of action needs to be arranged without delay to plan amelioration before he finds himself in conflict with his entire peer group. MISLEADING WRITING STYLE, CHILD FIGHTS A LOT.

———3. Traveling by bus is cheaper than traveling by plane. ———

—✗—4. I have been an actress for ten years and I sincerely recommend this special drink. It's good for you. BEING AN ACTRESS DOES NOT QUILIFY HER ON FOOD

———5. The candidate has a good record. He was honorably discharged from the Army. He had a B average in college and an A average in law school. ———

—✗—6. He planted the electrode in a special place in the dog's brain— the kill center. WHAT IS A KILL CENTER?

———7. He is careful and fair. We should get him as a judge in the contest. ———

—✗—8. We must protect our American Way of Life. FROM WHAT—WHAT IS THE AMERICAN—

———9. You have five years of advanced training. Are you ready to start working on your own? ———

Set 4

X—1. How can you possibly allow scientists to use defenseless little

puppies and kittens in their research? *WHO SAYS PUPPIES*
AND KITTENS ARE DEFENSE LESS

———2. The college library has more of the materials we need than the

city library does. _____

———

X—3. The teacher must meet the felt needs of the child. *WHOS*
FELT NEEDS

———4. The school was closed when 67% of the students got the flu.

———

X—5. Our furniture is sturdier and more long-lasting. *STURDIER*
AND MORE LONG LASTING THAN WHAT

———6. She is very conscientious about fulfilling her responsibilities.

———

X—7. In 1953, the candidate was a member of the New Movement
Society. This society expressed some of the same sentiments as did

governments hostile to our country. *WHAT SENTIMENTS*
WHAT GOVERNMENTS

———8. It is false economy to buy cheap material if it is a very poor

quality. _____

———

———9. Write the directions clearly and simply so that we won't make

a mistake. _____

———1. The airline passenger companies observe many safety proce-

dures. _____

———2. He is a plodding drudge, a real grind, when it comes to school

work. *A MIS STATEMENT HE DOES NOT*

REAL BAD DRUDGE OR GRIND

———3. One role of imaginative literature is to show the nature of man.

_____

———4. Leading lawyers assure us that our proposal is legally correct

and foolproof. So invest in our company today. *INCOMPLETE*

INFORMATION

———5. Our party wins elections more often than your party does.

_____

———6. When will you understand? A woman's place is in the home.

MISGUIDED OPINION

———7. The National Boating Association recommends this book on

water safety. _____

———8. You cannot take time for a tryout. If you think the material
is good, you can't keep it away from the thirsting minds of the eager

little children. *CHILDRENS MINDS DO NOT*

THIRST

———9. The play aroused deep unconscious fears of magic laid down

through the history of mankind. _____

_____

Set 6

X—1. We all accomplish our appointed tasks if our interest and initiative are frequently stimulated. *MISLEADING WRITING STYLE*

———2. On a long trip, I would rather fly than drive. Flying costs more but it is quicker and less tiring. ————————————

———X—3. Join our Aid Society and work with people in this new and underdeveloped country. The salary is high. The rewards are many. *AN APPEAL TO EMOTION: THE COUNTRY IS NOT NEW.*

———X—4. She has been a secretary for seven years. She says that your company's typewriter has a very light touch and is easy to use. *RESORTING TO AUTHORITY, INCOMPLETE INFORMATION WHAT ARE THE BAD POINTS*

———5. By law, people can be punished for reckless driving. ————

———X—6. One is a leftist and the other is a rightist. The best people won't vote for them. *BIASED OPINION LEFT OF WHAT, RIGHT, OF WHAT, WHO ARE THE BEST.*

———7. In the long run, people do what they want to do when they have the choice. ————————————

———X—8. The American Psychological Association recognizes this new book on ways to reach mental health. *MISLEADING STATEMENT*

X——9. Statistics prove that three out of four people prefer this brand

of furniture. *APPEALS TO AUTHORITY INCOM-*

PLETE INFORMATION

ANSWERS TO PRACTICE SETS

The writing tricks in the practice sets are pinpointed and explained below.

Set 1

3. Misleading statement. The pain reliever is aspirin. You don't need a special pill to get aspirin.

5. Omitted information. For example: What does the medicine cost? Are there side effects?

6. Unfinished comparison. More miles and less pollution than what other fuel?

8. Meaningless phrase. Headaches do not split heads.

Set 2

1. Unfinished comparison. Sooner than who else?

4. Emotionally toned words and stereotypes: Beautiful People, un-American.

6. Appeal to emotion. Question raised about courage in dealing with outsiders.

8. Misleading writing style. It says: Young men without exemptions can be drafted.

Set 3

1. Misleading statement. It sounds like our group is better but it says that other groups are the same as, or worse than, we are. All of us could be bad.

2. Misleading writing style. It says: Since this child fights a lot, his parents and teachers need to straighten him out.

4. Appeal to authority. Being an actress does not qualify her to recommend food.

6. Meaningless phrase. There's no such thing as a "kill center" in the brain.

8. Slogan. American Way of Life.

Set 4

1. Appeal to emotion. Picking on puppies and kittens who can't help themselves.

3. Slogan. Meet the felt needs of the child.

5. Unfinished comparison. Sturdier and more long-lasting than what?

7. Omitted information. For example: Was an unlawful link to another government proved? Did the candidate stay in or resign?

Set 5

2. Emotionally toned words and stereotypes. He probably considers that he works carefully and hard.

4. Appeals to authority. What leading lawyers? What evidence do they give?

6. Slogan. A woman's place is in the home.

8. Appeals to emotion. Depriving little children.

9. Wrong or meaningless phrases. Specific fears are learned, not inherited.

Set 6

1. Misleading writing style. It says: We do our work if we are led or pushed.

3. Omitted information. For example: What are the dangers? Do the people want help? How long does one sign up for?

6. Emotionally toned words and stereotypes. Leftist. Rightist. Best people.

8. Misleading statement. The statement suggests that the APA "recommends"; it actually says that the APA "knows about."

9. Appeals to authority. Statistics prove. What statistics? How were they collected? What are they based on?

9

Finding Faulty Reasoning

These statements have faulty reasoning. Think about how they are false and what is wrong with the reasoning used.

1. The winters in Southern Florida and Southern California are always mild and sunny.
   This statement is an overgeneralization. Part of the time both Southern California and Southern Florida have mild, sunny weather. Other times, sadly, the weather is cool, rainy, and foggy.

2. Have you washed the car yet? I think we need to take the car in for an oil change and lubrication job.
   This statement has avoided the question. The answer should be yes or no. The answer given pertains to another question, for example: What work does the car need?

3. I know those ladies really like football because they go to the game every week.
   This statement has an inference unsupported by evidence. The ladies may indeed like football. However, they may go for other reasons—for example to keep their husbands company, for the social contacts, for the fresh air, for the crowd excitement, and so on. Without more information, we can't tell whether the ladies like football or not.

DESCRIPTION

What Is Faulty Reasoning? Faulty reasoning is a mistake in reasoning. Reasoning is the process we use when we try to explain things; that is, when we try to figure out why something happens, how it happens, and what it will lead to.

Why Is Finding Faulty Reasoning Valuable? We should not use information based on faulty reasoning. Therefore, finding faulty reasoning can help save us from making mistakes through acting on inaccurate information we read; that way we can keep from hurting others or ourselves and not waste time, work, and money.

How Do You Find Faulty Reasoning? Use the same steps you use in finding writing tricks (Chapter 8).

1. Pay close attention to what you read. Be sure you get the message. Size up the material for correctness and freedom from special interests. (See *Comprehension Skills* in Part One and *Previewing* in Chapter 5.)

2. When you make important decisions, check several sources of information on the same topic. Be particularly careful if they don't agree.

3. Learn to recognize the types of faulty reasoning. Some kinds of mistakes in reasoning which people make very often are over-generalization, making inferences not supported by the information given, assumption of proof by failure to find an opposite case, special pleading, avoiding the question, begging the question, the false dilemma, the false sequence.

Overgeneralization

A generalization is a statement that is true for all cases. An overgeneralization is applied to all cases, but it is not true for all cases even though it may sound true.
—"All men were once boys." This statement is a generalization because all cases are true.
—"All men like to eat." This statement is an overgeneralization because some men do not *like* to eat even though they must eat to live.
Pay very close attention to the truth of statements which begin with all-covering words like the following: all, always, never, every, completely, absolutely. Also, look carefully at statements which have such words implied but not stated. For example, "All men like to eat" could be written "Men like to eat."

Making inferences not supported by the information given

Inferences are ideas supported by specific information that is given. Sometimes, people go beyond the information given to make inferences that are not supported and that cannot be supported without further information which is not given.

—Was Little Miss Muffet a child? That's how she's shown in pictures. But look at the words: "Little Miss Muffet/ sat on a tuffet/ eating her curds and whey./ Along came a spider/ and sat down beside her/ and frightened Miss Muffet away."

The words do not show Miss Muffet's age, only her size. She could be any age.

Assumption of proof by failure to find an opposite case

To prove something, you must have positive evidence, evidence that it is true. You can't prove something by saying that there is no evidence against it. Why? Because you never know what further evidence will be found, especially when new tools or methods of study become available.

—"We know that men don't live on Mars because we have never seen a man from Mars."

The first part of this statement is faulty. Whatever we expect, we can't know about life on Mars until we get there and see what's there.

Special pleading

A person uses special pleading when he uses one set of standards to judge his side of the argument and another set, often harder, to judge the other side.

—Look at these judgments of people who keep on trying in spite of one failure after another. Our side: "They are brave and determined." Other side: "They are stubborn and unwilling to face reality."

Avoiding the question

Information that doesn't fit is often used to avoid the question or issue. A person may answer with information not related to the question. The unrelated information may be the answer to another question (*non sequitur*) or it may be an attack on the person asking the question (*argumentum ad hominem*).

—Mr. Smith asked the company president: "Why does your company sell that product for 25 times more than it costs to make it?"

Answer 1: "Our product helps many people lead better lives." This answer may or may not be true; but it does not go with the question that Mr. Smith asked. It goes with a question Mr. Smith did not ask: "What is your product good for?"

Answer 2: "Mr. Smith is a troublemaker. When he was a boy, he made his teachers mad. Now, his wife can't stand him." This is a personal attack. It may or may not be true. However, it has nothing to do with the question Mr. Smith asked.

Begging the question

Begging the question involves circular reasoning. A person supports a statement with information which is the same as the statement.

—"You need a sense of humor to be happy because happiness depends on being able to see the funny side of things."

The false dilemma

The false dilemma involves two things: the dilemma—equally unwanted choices, and falseness—choices that are not the only ones possible.

—"Does my dress look better than you expected it to look or does it look worse?"

—"Would you rather be a do-gooder or a selfish person?"

The false sequence

The false sequence is sometimes described as *post hoc, ergo propter hoc.* The false idea is that if one event follows another, then the second event must be caused by the first event.

—"More accidents happen within fifty miles of people's homes. Therefore, it is safer to drive on long trips than it is to drive around town." Of course more accidents happen near people's homes because more people spend more time driving near home. There is no basis here for believing that it is safer to drive far from home.

PRACTICE

Some of the statements have faulty reasoning. Some do not. Mark (X) the statements or answers with faulty reasoning and tell what is wrong.

✗ 1. Marcia always gets eight hours' sleep before exams and she has an A average. Get plenty of sleep and you have nothing to worry about.

MAKING INFERANCES NOT SUPPORTED BY INFORMATION GIVEN.

✗ 2. Advertising is designed to fool the buyer. *NOT ENOUGH INFORMATION GIVEN TO SUPPORT OPINION*

———3. Six-day-old babies do not fix their eyes on objects. ———————

———4. If you want to be happy, keep active. Why? Because activity keeps you from being sad. *FALSE SEQUENCE*

———5. Joe has a good job, money in the bank, and a record of always

paying his bills on time. He deserves an excellent credit rating. ———

———6. That boy and girl are really interested in their school work.

They go to the library every evening. *NOT ENOUGH Supportive INFORMATION*

———7. He is a popular singer. He has had twenty-two gold records.

———8. Have you bought your new suit yet? No. I spent my money to

get my car fixed. ————————————

———9. Did the American settlers take land from the Indians? The settlers brought European culture and civilization to this continent; for example, organized schools, medical knowledge, technology, government,

and so on. _AVOIDING THE QUESTION_

————1. The temperature outside has dropped fifteen degrees in two

hours. The cold front is moving in fast. ——————

————2. As a group, men are physically stronger than women. ———

——✗—3. Why should I be charged extra for the twenty-four-hour rush
service? Students with long hair like yours are just trouble-makers.

AVOIDING THE QUESTION

—✗—4. She walks to work every day. Her friends decided that she can't

afford a car. _INFERANCES ON INCOMPLETE_
INFORMATION   AUSUMPTION OF PROOF

——✗—5. I brought two records with me today. Which one would you

rather hear first? _FALSE DILEMA_

——✗——6. Students started dressing casually and then we started having
trouble. If you want to clear up student unrest, get students to change

their personal appearance. _FALSE SEQUENCE_

——✗—7. Why do you say that the mayor has done a poor job? Because

he just hasn't done his job well. _BEGGING THE QUSTION_

X̶—8. There is no cure for the common cold and we won't find one.

ASSUMPTION FROM LACK OF EVIDENCE

———9. Should he be elected representative again? Yes. He did his job very well during his last term. ——————

Set 3

X̶—1. Mental retardation is always caused by heredity. *OVER GENERLIZATION*

———2. The self-reliant boy questioned widely and tried to figure out his own answers. ——————

X̶—3. What's on TV tonight? This TV season is really a good one. Really, I've never seen a season with so many good shows. *AUSSUMPTION FROM LACK EVIDENCE*

———4. He was a good leader. He helped the people get closer to reaching their goals. ——————

X̶—5. There are two things you can depend on. Where there is marriage without love, there is love without marriage. Where guns are outlawed, only outlaws have guns. *FALSE DELEMA*

X̶—6. A three-minute mile is the fastest running speed possible. *ASSUMPTION FROM LACK OF CONTARY EVIDENCE*

———7. Children usually go through a stage in which they engage in parallel play. ——————

X —8. The students reached the room at 8:55 A.M. They were not

late for the 9:00 o'clock class. *INCOMPLETE INFORMATION*

X —9. He kept revising his term paper without complaining. He

was willing to work hard on it. *PLEADING THE QUESTION*

Set 4

X —1. During football season, we should not expect football players

to do as much homework as the other students in the same classes. ___

——2. The car has plenty of gas but it won't start. It may need fixing.

X —3. We used that toothpaste and the children didn't have cavities

this year. Brand X prevents cavities. *OVER GENERALITIES*

——4. Some used cars are poor buys. Why? Because not all used cars

are good buys. *BEGGING THE QUESTION*

X —5. Twentieth-century novelists are only concerned about the place

of the individual in a complex society. *OVER GENERALITIES*

——6. Adults can usually stand more frustration than children can.

———7. Why won't the owner allow smoking near the gas tanks? He

doesn't want an explosion. _____

_____

——✗—8. I think he is one of our most talented painters. I don't agree

with you. For years, he hasn't paid his bills on time. *AVOIDING THE*

ISSUE. PAYING BILLS HAS NOTHING TO DO WITH ART

———9. When they are ill, students should be able to postpone their

exams without penalty. _____

_____

Set 5

———1. Are you going to work this summer? No. I'm going to stay at

the beach and rest. _____

_____

———2. It is a very good book. It has the latest accurate information

on the subject. _____

_____

——✗—3. Do you have your term paper done? I've really had a bad cold
in the last two weeks. Also, my friend has needed a lot of help with his

math. *AVOIDING THE QUESTION*

_____

——✗—4. He will not be here for an hour. Shall we wait here or go

somewhere else? *FALSE DILEMA*

_____

———5. The phonograph is getting electricity but it won't work. It

may be broken. _____

_____

_X_ 6. Deaf children can never be taught to talk normally. _____

OPINION FROM LACK OF INFORMATION

_X_ 7. If you are not for this idea, you are against it. _FALSE_

DILEMA

_____8. Extremely anxious people have more trouble learning facts

than less anxious people do. _____

_____9. The newspapers must print information important to the
public welfare. They should not be subject to libel laws as private citizens

are. _SPECIAL PLEADING_

Set 6

_____1. After a period of eating all they wanted of a balanced diet, the
children gained weight and showed more alertness. An ample, balanced

diet is helpful to good health. _____

_X_ 2. That girl who fell down must be in great pain. See. She is
crying. _INFERENCE - WITH OUT SUPPORTING_
INFORMATION

_____3. That car is a good buy. The price and credit charges are low

and the car is in good condition. _____

_____4. Stop talking about changing the nation. Love it or leave it.

_____5. Should we elect him senator? He was born rich; he may have

worked all his adult life but he hasn't had to. _____

———6. When they saw the monsters in the movie, the children turned pale and started screaming and crying. The movie scared them quite a bit.

_____

———7. The students worked very hard all week. On the weekend, they

were ready to play. _____

———8. Week after week, the TV show had a very small audience.

Consequently the program director cancelled it. _____

———9. That stubborn, stiff-necked little nation is objecting to our

building an air base on its soil. _____

ANSWERS FOR PRACTICE SETS

In the sets below, the instances of faulty reasoning in the practice sets are pinpointed and explained.

Set 1

1. False sequence. Rest is important but getting good grades depends on more than rest alone.
2. Overgeneralization. Some advertising is on the level.
4. Begging the question. The first and second statements say the same thing.
6. Inference not supported by the information given. Students could be in the library for many reasons; for example, they may have nowhere else to meet.
9. Avoiding the question with a *non sequitur*. The information in the answer is accurate but it does not go with the question.

Set 2

3. Avoiding the question with a personal attack. The student's personal appearance is not pertinent to the question.
4. Inference not supported by the information given. She could be walking for many reasons; for example, she may want the exercise.

6. False sequence. Student unrest has sources other than clothing and personal appearance. More specifically, student unrest and changes in students' personal habits possibly both happen for the same reason.

7. Begging the question. The two statements carry the same information.

8. Proof by failure to find an opposite case. When we have more advanced information, we may be able to find the cure.

Set 3

1. Overgeneralization. Mental retardation has several causes.

3. Avoiding the question with a *non sequitur.* The information given does not pertain to the question.

5. False dilemma. In both instances, other actions are possible.

6. Proof by failure to find opposite case. Faster speeds may be possible when we know more, have improved nutrition, and so on.

Set 4

1. Special pleading. Requirements should be the same for all students.

3. False sequence. Several things cause cavities.

4. Begging the question. The information in the first and second statements means the same thing.

5. Overgeneralization. Twentieth-century novelists have more than one concern.

8. Avoiding the question with a personal attack. Financial responsibility is important but it has nothing to do with judging talent in painting.

Set 5

3. Avoiding the question with a *non sequitur.* The information given does not pertain to the question.

6. Proof by failure to find an opposite case. With new discoveries, we may be more successful in teaching.

7. False dilemma. You can accept an idea with reservations.

9. Special pleading. Libel laws should apply equally to all.

Set 6

2. Inference not supported by information given. The girl could be crying for many reasons; for example, she may have torn her dress.

4. False dilemma. It is possible to suggest improvements in things and people one loves.

5. Avoiding the question. Personal attack on the man about things that do not pertain to how qualified he is to be senator.

9. Special pleading. People in the small nation probably consider themselves to be determined and full of self-respect.

IV

PROCESSING SKILLS

Part Four is about the processing skills. These skills help you take the material you read and change it to a form that suits your particular needs at the time. Chapter 10, *checking relevance*, concerns deciding whether information you read fits a particular topic. Chapter 11, *analyzing and outlining*, looks at breaking down and blueprinting a selection to show its parts and the relations among those parts. Chapter 12, *summarizing and note-taking*, goes into ways of stating the writer's message in a shorter form and to record that summary. Chapter 13, *synthesizing*, deals with putting together separate bits of information about a main idea and showing the relations among them.

10

Checking Relevance

Look at the problem and the main idea used in carrying it out. Ideas 1, 3, and 4 fit the main idea about fear and anxiety; they can be used in the speech. Ideas 2 and 5 fit another main idea, one about anger. They should not be used in the speech.

FEAR AND ANXIETY[1]

Problem: To prepare a speech on the relation between fear and anxiety.
Main idea: Fear and anxiety have both similarities and differences.
Relevant ideas: nos. 1, 3, and 4.

1. Some people speak of fear and anxiety as if they mean the same thing. Others do not. But, people agree about three things: both fear and anxiety represent unpleasant states of mind, both are a response to a danger or threat (real or imagined), both involve physiological reactions.

[1] Arthur T. Jersild, *Child Psychology*, 6th ed., © 1968, pp. 348–49, 366–67. Abridged and paraphrased. By permission of Prentice-Hall, Inc., Englewood Cliffs, New Jersey.

2. Through anger, a person asserts himself, gives a sharp edge to his demands and retaliates against those who block or hurt him. Anger is a way of dealing with a threatening environment. The person takes action against the threat.

3. Both fear and anxiety, especially when severe, involve the sympathetic division of the automonic nervous system. As a result, fearful or anxious people may show such signs as: a faster heart rate, slower action of the digestive system, muscular tension, and sweating.

4. Mainly fear and anxiety are separated on the basis of degree of objectivity-subjectivity. Fear is a response to a real and observable danger or threat of danger: for example, fear at the approach of a growling dog. On the other hand, anxiety is a vague feeling of dread even though no real, observable danger is present; it cannot be explained in terms of the actual situation. For example: a very well-prepared student's anxiety about a routine examination.

5. A person's anger is essential to his well-being. But, to get along comfortably with others, he must learn a wise degree of control of it. One of the hardest tasks people face is to maintain the ability to become angry and at the same time manage that anger so that it does not cause more trouble than it relieves.

DESCRIPTION

What Is Checking Relevance? Checking relevance means checking whether information fits a particular problem—whether it serves as a supporting idea for a particular main idea. You use the skill when you are reading to find information to support a main idea you are developing; you check to see that each idea you read fits your main idea.

Why Is Checking Relevance Valuable? Checking relevance helps you rule in material that fits your main idea and rule out material that does not. It is surprisingly hard to do and it takes work and time, but it is very necessary. It helps you pinpoint and focus on a writer's notions on your particular problems, and it helps you cut down confusion and mistakes.

How Do You Check Relevance? There are four main steps in checking relevance:

1. State your main idea or topic. Be sure you are clear about what your main idea is. Your main idea serves as your target. You can't decide whether other information fits your main idea if you don't know exactly what your main idea is.

2. Survey new material. Be sure you understand the new information. Check it for accuracy and freedom from special interests. (See the *Comprehension Skills* in Part One and *Previewing* in Chapter 5.)

3. Check new ideas against your main idea, making sure they fit as a particular case, a reason, a restatement, or as a suitable comparison or contrast.

4. Take action. If the new information fits your main idea, work with it. If it does not fit, rule it out.

PRACTICE

Check the selections for relevance to the problem and the question which start each set. Write the code numbers of the relevant selections in the space given.

Set 1. Motor Bikes

Problem: To buy a motor bike.
Question: Which motor bike has the features you want and the lowest cost?
Relevant Selections: _1, 3, & 4,_____

(1) SUZUKI[2]

What price acceleration? $4,100 too much, we think.

Because Suzuki's T–500 III Titan will cover a quarter mile quicker than most of Detroit's supercars. 13.2 seconds, 120 mph speed range.

What hauls you that quick is the world's first production two-stroke 500cc engine, 47 horses, 7,000 rpm. Twin cylinders, twin VM 32 carbs, twin pipes.

All of it going through a 5-speed gearbox, turning special 18″ red line tires.

[2] U.S. Suzuki Motor Corporation, Advertisement, *Hot Rod*, July 1970, p. 109. Used with permission.

Plus: dual leading shoe brakes (8″ drum in front; 7″ in rear), Posi-Force Lube, oil-dampened suspension all around, and one of the sleekest-looking designs anywhere.

About the only extra you'll get with the supercar is 3800 lbs. more machinery.

But think of it this way: The pounds you don't get you don't pay for.

In dollars or E.T.U.S. Suzuld Motor Corp., Dept. 408, 1767 Freeway Dr., Santa Fe Springs, California 90670.

(2) MINI DUNE-BUGGY[3]

Desert Fox, a fiberglas-bodied mini dune buggy with a 12–bhp air-cooled engine, has just been released by Gerim Manufacturing Co., Dept. DB, Hudson, Iowa 50643.

The buggy features bucket seats, padded steering wheel, safety belts, rack-and-pinion steering, 12 V. battery, electric starter, and automatic torque converter drive.

The Desert Fox is 45-in. wide, 30-in. high, and 87-in. long . . . small enough to fit inside a station wagon. Optional equipment includes a golf bag carrier on the back, a convertible top, and a gun toting rack. Adding flotation tires and skis to the front wheels in winter converts it to a snowmobile.

(3) RUPP TC–1 CYCLES[4]

NEW! RUPP TC–1* Cycles

Looks and rides like big bikes. Compact fun cycles with wire wheels. Groovy around town. Gutsy in the bonnies. New TC–1 Torque Converter takes you anywhere without a hitch. Five fun models. On street legal. A new breed . . . from Rupp. See your Rupp dealer or send 25¢ for catalog. Rupp Manufacturing, Inc., Dept. HR77, P. O. Box 1095, Mansfield, Ohio, 44903.

[3] "Mini Dune Buggy," *Dune Buggies and Hot* VW's, August 1970, p. 16. Used with permission.

[4] Rupp Manufacturing Company, Advertisement, *Hot Rod*, July 1970, p. 144. Used with permission.

(4) HONDA[5]

Honda motorsports literally glide over the rough country.

Take the new SL–175, for example. Take it anywhere. The famous Honda four-stroke twin-cylinder engine delivers the power to keep you flying—19 horses at 9,500 rpm.

Large knobby tires, extra heavy-duty suspension and the soft pleated seat level the roughest terrain. And the constant-mesh five-speed trans shifts quickly and smoothly . . . heading into back country or climbing steep grades.

When it comes to styling, there's no stopping the Motorsport 175, either. The radical new "Dynamic V" frame is strong, yet very light. And its upswept design makes other dirt bikes look like they're stuck in the mud.

See for yourself. Take a test flight at your local dealer. From mighty to mini, Honda has it all in motorbikes.

(5) BASIC AUTO REPAIR MANUAL[6]

If you've ever thought about doing your own car repairs to save expensive labor costs but perhaps lacked the nerve to try it, there's a book that can give you the courage—and more important—the know-how to tackle the job.

Peterson's new "Basic Auto Repair Manual No. 2" not only shows you how to repair and/or replace components for all the important systems on your car, but helps you diagnose the difficulty. This revised second edition has specially compiled extensive troubleshooting guides that offer you the invaluable analytical wisdom of master mechanics.

There are 384 pages of recommendations on how to pick the right tools, interpret specifications, get the best buy in parts, tips on lubrication and maintenance, engine tuneup, even VW servicing basics. From changing spark plugs to doing a major engine overhaul, this book brings you the information you need.

Whether you're a backyard grease monkey, or just a cost-conscious car owner, the newly revised edition of Petersen's "Basic Auto Repair

[5] American Honda Motor Company, Advertisement, *Car Life*, August 1970, Back cover. Used with permission.

[6] Peterson Publishing Company, Advertisement, *Hot Rod*, July 1970, p. 144. Used with permission.

Manual" can be as important to you as your driver's license or your gasoline credit cards. So drive—don't walk—to your newsstand for your copy. The $3.95 price tag is not a cost but an investment in car repair savings.

If your car isn't running, just send $4.20 (includes 25¢ for postage and handling) to Petersen Publishing Co., 5900 Hollywood Blvd., Los Angeles, California 90028. We'll send you a "Basic Auto Repair Manual" that'll help you fix it.

(6) TRANSVAIR II SEDAN KIT[7]

Whether it be a VW Sedan, full body Buggy or Sand Railer, a Transvair equipped machine offers you speed, reliability, low cost and easier installation. The ENTIRE Corvair drive train, not just the engine, bolts to both Sedans and Buggies. Almost any buggy body will fit with no alterations. All moving parts are standard GM parts. No transaxle "Beefing" necessary. Compatible stock gear spacing. 4 transmission and 3 rear-end ratios as near as your Chevy dealer. Auto, 3- or 4-speed trans bolts right in. Linkage hookups included. The Transvair II Sedan Kit surrounds Transvair equipped VW sedans with style and classic design plus plenty of room from competition. Transvair II includes precision quality fiberglas fenders, twin scooped deck lid bumperettes and all necessary fasteners.

Set 2. Studying

Problem: To prepare a speech on methods for studying.
Question: What are some methods which help people learn more easily.
Relevant Selections: ___2, 3 & 6_____

(1) SPEAKING[8]

By the time we become adults we are seldom conscious of how we sound to others. We have grown up in a community in which certain

[7] Hadly Chassis Engineering, Advertisement, *Dunebuggies and Hot VW's*, August 1970, p. 15. Used with permission.

[8] Johnnye Akin, *And So We Speak* (Englewood Cliffs, N.J.: Prentice-Hall, Inc., 1958), p. 4. Used with permission.

phonetic responses are used and understood. We take our speech for granted just as we do our manner of walking or our allergy. It has become a definite and inseparable part of our personality. More and more our social integration is dependent upon our adequacy of fluency in expressing ourselves. We live in a social order which demands this fluency.

(2) READING

Specialists have suggested several methods for using reading in studying. The methods are alike in having the same three steps: getting ready, reading, and reacting. People often describe the methods with sets of letters that they call formulas. Six formulas are outlined below under the three steps—getting ready, reading, and reacting.

Formula	*Getting Ready*	*Reading*	*Reacting*
PQRT	Preview, Question	Read	Test
PQRST	Preview, Question	Read	Summarize, Test
SQ4R	Survey, Question	(1) Read (4) Reread	(2) Recite (3) Review
S-Q/S-R/S-T	Survey-Question	Study-Read	Summarize-Test
OK4R	Overview, Key Ideas	(1) Read (4) Review	(2) Recall (3) Reflect
Triple S	Scan	Search	Summarize

(3) CODING

One type of coding is to identify key letters in words and then make up a sentence using words starting with those letters. For example: In biology or psychology, you may be studying the names and numbers of the twelve cranial nerves. A code here is the sentence: On Old Olympus Towering Top, A Finn And German Viewed Sipping Hops. This code can help you learn the cranial nerves when you study.

Word	Key Letter	Name of Nerve	Number of Nerve
On	O	Olfactory	1st
Old	O	Optic	2nd
Olympus	O	Oculomotor	3rd
Towering	T	Trochlear	4th
Top	T	Trigeminal	5th
A	A	Abducent	6th
Finn	F	Facial	7th
And	A	Acoustic	8th
German	G	Glossopharyngeal	9th
Viewed	V	Vagus	10th
Sipping	S	Spinal Accessory	11th
Hops	H	Hypoglossal	12th

(4) IDENTITY[9]

Occasionally the confusions and frustrations around a sensitive person become so strong that he feels his own existence is without meaning. It is as if he had lost his plan in the story of his life he had been telling himself.

Some cynical or sophisticated people joke about the person who asks "Who am I"? The question seems easy yet unanswerable. Perhaps the laughers laugh because they think they know who they are. They may say they are lawyers, doctors, mechanics, teachers—persons who are identified by the jobs they do and the acts they perform. They may have forgotten how important it is to be someone known for himself and not his role. Their joking may imply that they attach little importance to the development of a person's sense of individuality, his concept of who he is apart from what job he does, how he dresses, or what his "thing" is.

(5) HOW TO SEE[10]

The first problem in breaking out of old ways of looking at things is to know *how* to see, how to investigate and to experience something, rather than to rush in, to judge it, and label it.

[9] Wallace Kaufman and William Powers, *The Writer's Mind* (Englewood Cliffs, N.J. Prentice-Hall, Inc., 1970), p. 1. Used with permission.
[10] Kaufman and Powers, *The Writer's Mind*, p. 146. Used with permission.

Many people live like the housewife who empties the ash tray each time someone stubs out a cigarette and who keeps all the bookshelves filled and the magazines neatly in the rack. A little disorder wouldn't give her guests malaria, but she is afraid the disorder will quickly multiply. So in other areas of life, people are quick to put things in order by categorizing, labeling, or pigeonholing them. That keeps things arranged in ways which for a while may prove secure, at least if no one relates that secure *status quo* to any of the troubles in the "changing world."

(6) VERBAL MEDIATORS

Verbal mediators are words, phrases, and sentences that help you deal with connections between items. You identify these mediators and use them when you try to remember items. For example, look at the words "abstruse" and "stationary" and "stationery."

Word	*Meaning*	
abstruse	difficult to understand	Abstruse reminds me of abstract. Abstract is a synonym of abstruse and also means difficult to understand.
stationary	fixed in one place	The word meaning fixed in one place has the letter *a* as in st*a*nd.
stationery	paper for writing letters	The word meaning writing paper has the letter *e* as in l*e*tter.

Set 3. Spelling

Problem: To prepare a paper on spelling.
Questions: Why is spelling important? How can one learn to be a better speller?
Relevant Selections: _____

(1) THE REASONS WHY[11]

Correct spelling is important for at least two reasons.
1. Accurate spelling is expected of all educated people. Incorrect

[11] Thomas Clark Pollack and William D. Baker, *The University Spelling Book,* © 1955. By permission of Prentice-Hall, Inc., Englewood Cliffs, New Jersey.

spelling is penalized heavily in our society. Indeed, misspelling is the most commonly accepted sign of illiteracy.

Careful thought and clear expression are, in the last analysis, more important than correct spelling; but misspelled words stand out like sore thumbs and give the reader the impression, before he has a chance to decide for himself whether or not the writer's thought is clear, that the person responsible for the misspelling is ignorant. First impressions are hard to erase. Consider, for example, the impressions left by the following letter, in which the misspelled words are italicized.

Root #2
South Bend, Indiana
Febuary 20, 1955

Personal Manager
Acme Tool Company
3723 Marigold Street
Chicargo, Illinoise
Dear Sir:

I have recently been *seperated* from the Army and wish to apply for a position in your company. Before entering the Army, I took metal work *coarses* in high school and worked six months for *Johnsons Survice Stateion* as a garage *mecanic*. While I was in the *survice*, I supervised the tool *dispensery* for my *survice* company in Germany.

If Acme has any *opennings* for *mecanics*, I should like the *oppertunity* to *submitt* myself for an interview.

Yours *truely*,

2. The ability to spell correctly gives a person confidence with language; he knows he can use easily in writing the vocabulary he commands in speech. He is free from the hesitations and frustrations which undermine the self-confidence of a person who is uncertain about the spelling of the words he wants to use. Writing becomes fun.

Happily, it is not difficult to learn to spell correctly if you are willing to persevere. Two things are required. First, you must give your full attention to each word you are learning to spell. Look at it carefully, pronounce it, divide it into syllables. Second, you must develop the habit of writing the word correctly. Noticing the correct spelling is an important first step; but practicing writing the word correctly is what fixes the habit in your mind—or rather, in your fingers. You no longer have to think how to spell a word which you have really learned to spell, your fingers just write it correctly whenever you want to use it.

(2) METHODS[12]

There are many methods for learning to spell. Some work well; others do not. Enough scientific research has now been done on spelling to indicate that one method is successful above all others. It is effective and efficient, and if it is followed to the letter, the results are likely to be permanent. This system was devised to use the shortest path to learning; it supplants the old method of writing a word one hundred times.

This scientific five-step method of learning to spell a word correctly calls for attention and conscious effort. Follow it step by step for any words you misspell.

The Five-Step Method

Note: This method assumes that you have looked up the word in a dictionary or elsewhere and are sure of its meaning.

Step 1: Look carefully at the letters in the word and pronounce each syllable.

Step 2: Close your eyes and recall the way the word looks.

Step 3: Look at the word again to check your memory.

Step 4: Write the word from memory and then check your spelling.

Step 5: Repeat the writing and the checking twice. If at any point you misspell the word, go back to step one and begin again.

(3) VALUES[13]

Questions and doubts about values are a real problem for poets and for other people as well. Which values are real? Which are false? Today we have a very extreme empiricism. An insistence that to be of value a thing must be capable of being observed by one of the five senses and capable of being used. Some poets may feel that this empiricism is like an acid eating away at any non-utilitarian concept of life's values. This is so whether the concept stems from patriotism, morals, religion, or love.

[12] Pollock and Baker, *The University Spelling Book*, p. 2. Used with permission.
[13] Maynard Mack, Leonard Dean, and William Frost, eds. *Modern Poetry* Vol. VII, 2nd ed. (English Masterpieces Series) (Englewood Cliffs, N.J.: Prentice-Hall, Inc., 1961), pp. 8–9. Used with permission.

(4) PRODUCING SPEECH[14]

The highly specialized system that is used for producing speech is used for life-health purposes also. The production of speech requires a high degree of coordination of the speech system from the moment of drawing in breath until the sound has been produced, resonated, and finally shaped into meaningful auditory symbols that are received by the ear and interpreted. Other features such as intonation, rate, pitch, and rhythm are important to the production of speech.

(5) RULES[15]

Using spelling rules is an important help in learning to spell accurately. Spelling rules are generalizations about the groupings of letters which form words. The words, not the rules, were invented first. The rules are simply an attempt to explain how to spell some of the words. After carefully observing a number of words with similar characteristics, the observer is usually able to make certain generalizations about these words. And then there are usually exceptions!

The three rules listed here are those which experience has shown to be basic. They are the most useful to learn in a select list of practical spelling rules. All other rules, and there are approximately thirty-five more, are either learned in early elementary grades (e.g., the plural of most nouns is formed by adding s or es), or they cover specialized words (like musical terms or compounds), capitalization, possessives, or contractions. A few other rules give generalizations about prefixes and suffixes. But the three basic rules you should learn are these: the *I-E Rule*, the *Final E Rule*, and the *Doubling Rule*. Before you study these rules, however, it is wise to consider a few cautions.

Caution Number 1

It should be clearly understood that the rules are to be applied only if you have some difficulty with a particular word. For example, if you wish to write hope with an *-ing* ending, and if the letter formation, *hoping*, naturally comes to mind, you do not need to bother applying the

---

[14] Akin, *And So We Speak*, pp. 6–7. Used with permission.
[15] Pollock and Baker, *The University Spelling Book*, pp. 26–27. Used with permission.

Final E Rule. If your fingers and pen seem to write the word without much conscious prompting from your mind, it probably is not necessary to pause to apply the rule. Most good spellers have excellent arm and pen "motor memories," and poor spellers usually have imperfect ones.

Caution Number 2

The *application* of the rules, not mere memorization, should be your goal. Practical application exercises are presented after each rule in this book so that you may get the "feel" of applying the rules. Use the rules whenever you proofread, to correct or check a word that looks wrong. Use the rules, also, to check the spelling of a word as you are writing it.

Caution Number 3

Since there are exceptions to the rules, and since the human memory is not infallible, *use the dictionary* whenever you have serious doubt about a word. Although it would be impractical to look up every word you write, it is better to check too many than too few. Certainly you should do this until you feel that you have acquired a sufficient degree of "spelling confidence." Sometimes a rule may apply to only one part of a word; if you have doubt about another part of it, go to the dictionary. *When in doubt, use a dictionary.*

Caution Number 4

The *reverse* of each spelling rule is as important as the rule itself. For example, the I-E Rule states that when the sound is like *ee*, then *i* comes before *e*, except after *c*; the *reverse* states that when the sound is not like *ee*, then *e* comes before *i* when there is no *c*. When the rules are presented in this book, the reverse of each will be presented immediately after the rule. Do not pass over it as an exercise in abstract logic. Once you have learned the rule, it is a simple matter to learn its reverse. Think of the reverse as an integral part of the rule, and keep in mind that each part of the rule is important.

(6) MEANING[16]

In some modern poems, there is evidence that the poet has experienced a loss of meaning in nature. This experience of loss of meaning

[16] Mack, Dean, and Frost, *Modern Poetry*, p. 11. Used with permission.

in nature, in a parallel way, is shown in poets' loss of meaning in history. Is history an empty chain of exciting but random catastrophes? In the nineteenth century, the phrase "survival of the fittest" seemed to imply a comforting answer to this question. Today, many people are less sure. How, after all, did Darwin know which species *were* the "fittest?" Simply by checking on which ones, in fact, survived. Why not use the more exact phrase: "The survival of the survivors?" There is a doctrine of inevitable progress through history. Even though this doctrine persists today as an unexamined assumption in the popular mind, for poetry it is no longer a source of strength.

ANSWERS FOR PRACTICE SETS

Set 1
Relevant: nos. 1, 3, and 4.

Set 2
Relevant: nos. 2, 3, and 6.

Set 3
Relevant: nos. 1, 2, and 5.

11

Analyzing and Outlining

This topic outline came from analyzing the selection on fuels. Look at the selection and the outline together. See how the outline shows the parts of the selection and the relations among those parts.

1. Introduction
   a. Definition
   b. Guides for choosing fuels
2. Solid Fuels
   a. Wood
   b. Anthracite coal
   c. Bituminous coal
   d. Coke
   e. Lignite
   f. Peat
3. Liquid Fuels
   a. Crude oil
   b. Gasoline
   c. Kerosene
   d. Alcohol
4. Gaseous fuels
   a. Natural gas
   b. Coal gas

c. Water gas
d. Producer gas
e. Acetylene
f. Propane and butane

5. Summary

FUELS[1]

A fuel is something that burns and supplies heat to the surroundings. In choosing a fuel for our homes, we should look for the following advantages: it should furnish a large amount of heat at low cost; it should leave little ash and not produce too much smoke or soot or unpleasant odor; it should be easy to handle and store; and it should permit the temperature of the building to be controlled.

Solid Fuels. *Wood* is a solid fuel which is relatively cheap and gives out a large amount of heat. It was probably the first fuel to be used by man. However, the most extensively used solid fuel is *coal*. *Anthracite coal*, which is about 90 per cent carbon, burns with much heat but very little flame and almost no smoke. It is suitable for furnaces. *Bituminous coal* contains more volatile matter than does hard coal; therefore it burns with a brighter flame and more smoke. It can be used in stoves and fireplaces. *Coke*, which is a solid that remains after all volatile matter has been driven out of coal by destructive distillation, liberates a large amount of heat and burns with an almost smokeless flame, leaving very little ash. *Lignite* is a softer coal than bituminous. It burns with a smoky flame and gives out less heat. *Peat* is partly decayed vegetable matter which is often cut into blocks and dried for use as fuel. It burns with a very smoky flame and gives out little heat.

Liquid Fuels. Liquid fuels have replaced solid fuels for heating purposes to a great extent. They require less storage space, they liberate a large amount of heat, and they are delivered to the burner through pipes. Many household heaters and furnaces burn fuel oil and crude oil. Some oil burners are controlled by a device called a thermostat, which regulates the flow of oil into the burner, and in this way maintains a constant temperature. Other common liquid fuels are gasoline, kerosene, and alcohol.

Gaseous Fuels. Gaseous fuels are replacing solid and even liquid fuels for use in our homes and factories. Gases are led through pipes

[1] L. E. Young and W. M. Petty, *Chemistry for Progress* (Englewood Cliffs, N.J.: Prentice-Hall, Inc., 1957), pp. 538–41. Abridged. Used with permission.

directly to the burner, and the flame is easily regulated. If plenty of air is mixed with the gas while it is burning, an almost colorless, smokeless flame is produced and there is no ash to be removed from the burner. Most of the fuel gasses in use today yield a large amount of heat per volume of gas. At present, the principal gaseous fuels are natural gas, coal gas, producer gas, water gas, acetylene, and butane and propane.

Natural gas is composed of 80 to 85 per cent methane, 15 to 20 per cent hydrogen, and small amounts of ethane. It is obtained by drilling into deposits under the surface of the earth. It produces more heat per cubic foot than any other gaseous fuel. Some natural gas, especially that found in Kansas, Oklahoma, and Texas, contains small amounts of helium. Most of our supply of helium comes from this source.

Coal gas, the first gaseous fuel to be produced, is prepared by the destructive distillation of soft coal. The purified gas consists of methane and hydrogen. During the refining process, coal tar, ammonia, and hydrogen sulfide are removed.

Water gas is a mixture of carbon monoxide and hydrogen. It is made by passing steam through a bed of red-hot coke.

$$C + H_2O \rightarrow CO + H_2$$

Water gas is "carburetted" by passing it through hot brickwork that is saturated with petroleum oil. The large petroleum molecules are "cracked" into smaller ones by the heated bricks. These hydrocarbon molecules mix with the carbon monoxide and hydrogen, giving the gas a strong odor and increasing the heat content.

Producer gas is a mixture of carbon monoxide and nitrogen. It is made by forcing a blast of air through a tall column of coal or coke. The heating value of the gas is low.

Acetylene, C_2H_2 has been used extensively for heating and for illumination in isolated farm houses. It is usually generated as it is required by allowing drops of water to fall on calcium carbide.

$$CaC_2 + 2H_2O \rightarrow C_2H_2 + Ca(OH)_2$$

When an abundance of air or oxygen is supplied in a special type of burner, acetylene burns with a clear, white light. When it is burned with oxygen in the oxy-acetylene blowpipe, a temperature of 2500° C is produced.

Propane and butane are obtained from petroleum. They can be compressed in large steel cylinders and make an excellent fuel for homes, hotels, and motels that cannot be supplied with ordinary piped gas.

Summary. A fuel is a combustible substance that is used to produce heat. A good fuel should furnish a large amount of heat at low cost, should leave little ash and not produce undesirable waste products, should be easy to handle and store, and should allow the temperature of the building to be controlled.

Important solid fuels are wood, anthracite coal, bituminous coal, coke, lignite, and peat.

Important liquid fuels include crude petroleum, its products such as gasoline, kerosene, and fuel oil, and alcohol. Liquid fuels are more convenient to store, produce large amounts of heat, and are more easily regulated by automatic devices than solid fuels.

Important gaseous fuels are natural gas, coal gas, water gas, producer gas, acetylene, propane, and butane. Gaseous fuels are convenient to use because they flow through pipes, can be regulated easily, and leave no solid ashes.

DESCRIPTION

What Are Analyzing and Outlining? Analyzing and outlining are ways of finding and showing the organization of a selection.
—Organization means the structure of a selection: what the parts are and how the parts are related or put together.
—Analyzing is breaking down a whole selection into its parts and relations: finding main ideas, supporting ideas, and guides to coherence.
—Outlining is making a blueprint: doing a written description of the organization you find by analysis. There are two types of outlines: sentence outlines, in which ideas are in complete statements; and topic outlines, in which ideas are in words, phrases, or clauses.

Why Are Analyzing and Outlining Valuable? Analyzing and outlining are very important to understanding and remembering what you read. Seeing structure helps keep you from mixing up main ideas and supporting ideas. It helps you see the importance of each idea in relation to other ideas.

How Do You Analyze Organization? Here the task is to find the parts and the relations among them. Use these steps:

1. Find the ideas in the selection. Find the ideas that are implied and the ideas that are directly stated in headings and in topic sentences and topic paragraphs. (See Chapters 2, 3, and 4.)
2. Find the relations among the ideas. Decide on the levels of com-

plexity. Find the broadest main idea. Find the ideas that support this main idea. Check, in turn, to see whether these supporting ideas become main ideas supported by more narrow ideas. Continue until you find the most narrow or specific ideas. In this process, use the guides to coherence.

How Do You Outline? Here the task is to write a description of the selection's organization. Use these major steps:

1. Decide on type of outline. If the writer used headings to show his organization, then copy these headings as they stand: topics or sentences. If the writer did not use headings, then decide which type you like best.
2. Use parallel form. Throughout your outline, use the same form for a given order of headings. Sentences should parallel sentences, nouns should parallel nouns, and so on.
3. Use orders of headings to show levels of complexity, the relations among parts.
   —First-order headings: the broadest main ideas
   —Second-order headings: the ideas that support the first-order main ideas
   —Third-order headings: the ideas that support the second-order ideas
   —Fourth-order headings: the ideas that support the third-order ideas
   —Fifth-order headings: the ideas that support fourth-order ideas
   With most selections, you don't need to go beyond second- or third-order headings. However, with some longer materials, you have to go to fifth-order headings.
4. Use appropriate spacing to show the various orders of headings.
   —Place the title or most general main idea at the top.
   —Start each first-order heading at the left-hand margin.
   —Indent, or move over two or more spaces, for each new order: that is, indent once for second-order headings, indent again for third-order headings, and so on.
   —Keep each order of heading (equally important ideas) at the same level of indentation.
5. If you wish, you can also show the several orders of headings with numerals and letters. There is no one particular way to use numerals and letters. Figure out which form you like best and use it. One often-used form is this: For the first two orders of headings, use Roman numerals and capital letters followed by periods. For further orders of headings, use Arabic numerals and lower-case letters followed by periods and parentheses. Here is an example.

I. (First order)

    A. (Second order)

        1. (Third order)

        2. (Third order)

            a. (Fourth order)

            b. (Fourth order)

                1) (Fifth order)

                2) (Fifth order)

    B. (Second order)

II. (First order)

    A. (Second order)

Another form is to mark first-order headings with capital letters and then to mark the rest of headings with Arabic numerals and lower-case letters with periods and parentheses.

A. (First order)

    1. (Second order)

    2. (Second order)

        a. (Third order)

        b. (Third order)

            1) (Fourth order)

            2) (Fourth order)

                a) (Fifth order)

                b) (Fifth order)

B. (First order)

Another form is to use only Arabic numerals. Then, orders of headings are shown with decimals.

1.0 (First order)

    1.1 (Second order)

    1.2 (Second order)

        1.21 (Third order)

     1.22 (Third order)
          1.221 (Fourth order)
          1.222 (Fourth order)
             1.2221 (Fifth order)
  2.0 (First order)
     1.1 (Second order)

PRACTICE

Analyze each selection. Write the outline. Put your answers on separate sheets of paper.

Set 1

FATIGUE[2]

    Everyone is tired or fatigued at some time. The major cycle in your life is work, fatigue, and rest, in that order. Fatigue is characteristic of your body. It does not occur in a man-made machine, which operates as long as its parts are intact and it has fuel. But your body, a living machine, has a definite limitation; if its work continues, it gradually loses its responsiveness, becomes less irritable, turns out less work, and finally may not respond at all.

    The feeling of fatigue usually expresses itself in three ways. First, there is a feeling of tiredness and a marked desire for rest. Second, efficiency is greatly reduced. Third, there may be definite physiological changes in your body, low blood pressure, loss of muscle tone, tremors, and poor muscular coordination, and in other ways.

    Fatigue, however, may express itself in many ways, for there are many different forms of it. The fatigue of a student, for example, who has worked all evening on a difficult lesson, is different from that of a laborer who has worked all day at a back-breaking task, or that of a business executive who worries with the stress and strain of organization.

[2] Cleveland P. Hickman, *Health for College Students*, 3rd ed. (Englewood Cliffs, N.J.: Prentice-Hall, Inc., 1968), pp. 78–80. Used with permission.

Causes of Fatigue

Several factors cause fatigue, but in general, they come down to two main causes: lack of fuel or food, and the excessive accumulation of by-products of activity. Muscle activity uses up stores of glycogen or sugar. It also must have oxygen, for a muscle deprived of it will soon cease to contract. Lactic acid and carbon dioxide are the chief by-products of muscle activity, but there are also toxins from other sources which may help produce fatigue. Some of these toxins may come from bodily infections and some may be absorbed from breathing or from the digestive process. But in addition to these factors, there are certain causes of fatigue which are more or less obscure. Some of these are less physiological than psychological, such as lack of interest in what you are doing. When you do something that bores you, you tire easily; if you are interested in your work, you forget the amount of energy you put into it. You also tire more quickly when standing than when you are walking, for in walking each leg rests half of the time.

Another cause not related directly to the amount of work you put out is an upsetting of homeostasis, or constancy of the internal environment. If there is an imbalance in the constituents of body fluids, such as loss of salt in sweating, fatigue appears sooner than usual. Nerve cells may be involved in fatigue, for they are sensitive to toxic products. Nerve endings are especially sensitive to fatigue products. Stagnation of lymph or blood, which often occurs when you are inactive, brings about premature fatigue. Adolescents use much more of their energy for growth, so they have less for work and tire quickly.

Three Common Types of Fatigue

The three common types of fatigue will be described as clear-cut and definite. There are intermediate types also, having the characteristics of more than one major type.

Normal Physical Fatigue. Ordinary muscular fatigue is a normal physiological result of activity. It is initially experienced as an uncomfortable feeling, which mounts in intensity the longer the activity is prolonged, and eventually it develops into pain. This protects the body and warns that the muscles are becoming exhausted. Physiological symptoms of this type of fatigue include erratic and uncoordinated movements. This fatigue is quickly corrected by rest, which gives time for fatigue products to be removed.

Psychological Fatigue. Chronic fatigue has little relation to your amount of activity. It has its basis in your mental and emotional life, and is greatly promoted by anxieties and tensions. Such fatigue leaves you unrefreshed by a night's sleep. During the course of the day, as you get into the heat of your work, your tiredness wears off, and you actually feel better in the evening than in the morning.

Certain types of personalities are plagued with this fatigue more than are other types. Businessmen and executives are prone to it because of the conflicts and tensions of their work. Correcting psychological fatigue involves reconditioning the patient to his work, helping him to gain a balanced philosophy of life, and a program of regular exercise and relaxation to direct his interests into channels other than routine work.

A variant of psychological or nervous fatigue is the combat fatigue of soldiers. Combat fatigue has characteristics of both physical and mental fatigue. It is hard to say which is the most responsible, but the fact that certain soldiers suffered more than others is perhaps evidence that psychological factors played a prominent role. It was often found under conditions when men were very active, had no time for rest, and had insufficient nutrition. Added to these were fear, despair, the death of friends, and a general hopelessness in their situation. World War II and probably all those before had thousands of such cases. Recovery in most instances was usually very quick when the men received proper rest and other care. Psychiatric cases, however, did not respond as well.

Fatigue was also responsible for many fractures among soldiers while hiking. In these cases, soldiers became so tired that they allowed their body weight to be borne by the ligaments and bones of their ankles and feet instead of by muscles. This caused irregular and abnormal movements which resulted in fractures of ankle and other bones. More than 300 cases of fatigue fracture were reported at Camp Wheeler alone during 1943.

Disease Fatigue. Most diseases will produce fatigue. Many forms of chronic fatigue are due to diseases which remain hidden for long periods of time. Diseases especially inclined to cause fatigue are tuberculosis, diabetes, heart trouble, and underactivity of the thyroid gland. The person who feels tired most of the time without any apparent cause should consult his doctor. The symptoms of disease fatigue, like those of other types, may include low blood pressure, exaggerated reflexes, a general lack of energy, and poor muscular coordination. General nervous disorders may be common such as nervousness, irritability, and insomnia.

Fatigue: A Major Problem Among College Students

Surveys taken of college students reveal that fatigue is one of their most common health problems. Worry, anxiety, and tension are among the chief causes. Most college fatigue is due, therefore, to psychological factors, although definite physiological changes may also be a direct cause.

Many college students have low blood pressure and blood sugar. Emotional problems due to tensions built up in class may upset normal routine work.

It is not always easy to determine the underlying causes of college fatigue. Not all students adjust well to college life. Some are puzzled by their academic work. Many do not know how to study. Personal interviews for improving methods of learning and for relieving tensions are valuable in solving problems. In a study made at the University of California, it was found that interviews which involved a study of student tensions and attitudes towards praise and affection were decidedly helpful in the majority of cases.

Another aspect of fatigue is its relation to disease. Fatigue commonly lowers resistance to disease, which may explain the relative frequency of glandular fever (mononucleosis) among college students.

Set 2

THE CIVIL RIGHTS OF CITIZENS[3]

We Americans have always been concerned about what we call "rights." A right is the freedom to do or not to do something, as recognized by law or custom of the country. We have two principal kinds of rights: civil and political.

Civil rights are those freedoms we have against interference by our government. We have the right to choose our own religion without approval or disapproval by the government. We have the right to speak and write freely, even about the government itself, without being punished for what we write or say. We have the right not to be imprisoned without regular court processes and to be secure in our own homes from unlawful search and seizure by government officials. Many more of our civil rights are included in the provision that no one is to be deprived of his life, liberty, or property without due process of law.

Our Bill of Rights

The Declaration of Independence states the philosophy of American government. That is, it explains what the signers thought the United

[3] Harris G. Warren, Harry D. Leinenweber, and Ruth O. M. Andersen, *Our Democracy at Work*, 2nd ed., © 1967, pp. 29–42. Abridged. By permission of Prentice-Hall, Inc., Englewood Cliffs, New Jersey.

States government should be and what it should do in general. They felt that the most important rights are the right to "life, liberty, and the pursuit of happiness," the right to set up our own government, the right to alter or to abolish a government that does not adequately protect us, and the right to establish a new government. These general points serve as the basic ideas for bills of rights in today's fifty state constitutions and in the United States Constitution.

Our civil rights may be classified in several ways. For convenience, we shall group them under three principal headings. The first group is primarily concerned with protection: protection of life, liberty, and property. The second group is concerned with freedom of expression: freedom of speech, freedom of press, freedom of assembly, and freedom of religion. The third group is concerned with fair treatment before the law.

The Right to Protection

Protection of Life. Every citizen has the right to be safe from all bodily harm caused by the careless or deliberate acts of other people. To maintain his life, everyone has the right of self-defense. This right also includes defense of his family, home, and property.

Every citizen has the right to have local police protection against assault, robbery, and other violence. If his life and the lives of his family are threatened by mob violence or rioting, he can expect the state militia to guard him and his family. When tornadoes, hurricanes, earthquakes, and other natural disasters devastate an area, the National Guard moves in at once to help the people and to protect their property from looters. if we are threatened by foreign invasion or by missile attack, the national government will use the armed forces to protect us.

Protection of Liberty. We think of personal liberty as the right to govern our own actions without unreasonable interference by a government. Often one hears the question, which is in fact a statement: "This is a free country, isn't it?" It is, indeed; and we enjoy a great amount of freedom, or liberty.

A few centuries ago persons often were thrown into prison and held without being told the reason for their imprisonment. Such unfair imprisonment finally led to passage of the Habeas Corpus Act in 1679 in England. This law was enacted to prevent holding persons in prison indefinitely without trial. The protection of this law was extended to the English colonies in America and has come down to us.

Slavery also came down to us from the time we were English colonies.

After the war was over, Congress passed the Thirteenth Amendment to abolish slavery, and the states ratified it in 1865. This amendment forbids slavery or any other form of involuntary servitude except as a punishment for crime. The amendment freed Negro slaves, but it applies to everyone in the United States.

The Fourth Amendment provides more safeguards of our liberty. This very important amendment states: "The right of the people to be secure in their persons, houses, papers, and effects, against unreasonable searches and seizures, shall not be violated, and no Warrants shall issue, but upon probable cause, supported by Oath or affirmation, and particularly describing the place to be searched, and the persons or things to be seized."

An *oath* is a religious act calling upon God to witness and to punish if the truth is not spoken. An *affirmation* is a solemn pledge that the speaker is telling the truth. The word "God" does not appear in an affirmation. (Some religions forbid a person to say "I swear" but permit "I affirm.")

This amendment has been interpreted many times by our courts to protect individual liberties. A federal officer of the law cannot, therefore, search any house unless he has a search warrant. A search warrant, to be legal, must describe the property to be searched and state what shall be seized, and it must be signed by an officer of the court. Until recently our courts held that the Fourth Amendment applied only to the federal government, but in 1949 the Supreme Court decided that it also applies to state governments. Every state constitution, however, provides protection against unreasonable searches and seizures by state officers.

Since we live in groups, we cannot do everything we may want to do. Other people have exactly the same rights that we have, and our liberty does not permit us to interfere with the liberty of others. Laws and regulations are necessary to make it possible for people to live together in groups. Think of the danger and confusion that would exist if there were no traffic regulations! How many needless deaths would occur if anyone who decided to be a doctor could practice medicine without meeting rigid standards! Think of the state of the nation's health if those who can and package our food did not have to obey the pure food laws! It is our duty to submit to reasonable restrictions and regulations in order to safeguard ourselves and others from injury.

Protection of Property. Every person has the right to own property and to be protected in his ownership. He has the right to buy and sell as he pleases, subject to whatever restrictions may be imposed by law. For example, persons under twenty-one years of age may not buy or sell certain forms of property without the approval of a parent or guardian. This restriction helps to prevent unscrupulous persons from cheating minors.

A person who owns a lot in a city may discover that he cannot build anything he wants to on that lot. Laws called zoning ordinances, passed by village and city governments, regulate building. Such laws cover the kind of building that may be erected, its height, how far it must be set back from the sidewalk, what it may be used for, and other matters.

Private property may be taken from a person only in accordance with the law. Property may be taken by order of a court to pay taxes, or to satisfy the claims of creditors, or if it is needed for a public project. At the present time our country is being improved by the building of many superhighways. To obtain the land necessary for these highways, state governments have the power to force landowners to sell whatever is needed. This power of a government to take property for public use is called the power of *eminent domain*. The state, however, must pay a reasonable price for the land that it takes, and it must prove that public welfare demands that the land be used for public purposes.

Freedom of Expression

Freedom of Speech. One of the most important of all civil rights is that of free speech. Freedom of speech is the right to express one's opinion without fear of punishment. This right is most important in democracies because free discussion of all subjects is necessary to enable the people to act intelligently on public questions. Citizens of a democracy should be able to discuss and criticize officers of their government and their acts without fear of being punished. Only with such freedom of criticism can we be sure our officers will respect our wishes and our rights.

As with all of our liberties, we have freedom of speech as long as it does not injure other persons. We do not have the right to lie about other people, or to start untrue and harmful rumors about anyone or anything. Nor should we be so lacking in respect for others as to use language offensive to our hearers. Furthermore, we may not say things that would be likely to cause riots which might injure people or property.

Freedom of the Press. This freedom is closely related to freedom of speech. Freedom of the press means the right to print or to publish without unreasonable restrictions by government. It is essential in a democracy that newspapers, magazines, pamphlets, and books be printed to enlighten the public. What the citizen knows about his government he learns from what he reads as well as from what he hears and sees. Therefore, if the citizen is to be kept informed about his government, he must have honest sources of information available.

There are limitations on freedom of the press. Just as one cannot say everything he may want to say, neither can one print just anything. One may not publish material that is intended merely to defame (injure the reputation of) other persons, or that is harmful to the general welfare. Employees of our defense agencies, members of the armed forces, and officers of companies that manufacture highly secret military equipment are forbidden to reveal military secrets. They cannot write articles or books about what they know of these things.

Freedom of Assembly. Freedom of assembly means that people may meet peaceably at any time to hear speeches or to discuss subjects in which they are interested. The only restriction on this right is that the assembly must be peaceable. It must not be a public disturbance.

Freedom of Religion. Only after long and bitter struggle both in Europe and in America did our ancestors win the right to worship as they pleased. Government and religion were closely connected for many centuries in European countries. People who refused to follow the official religion were called heretics, and many were tortured, imprisoned, or killed because they refused to give up their beliefs.

Now our national and state bills of rights include provisions that no religion shall be made the official religion of the government and no one may be forced to attend religious meetings or be required to contribute to the support of any church. We are free to attend and support the church of our choice; or, if we prefer, we need not attend or support any church at all.

Although religious freedom means the right to pursue our religious beliefs without governmental interference, it does not give us the right to violate the law. Acts or practices which are illegal or which are generally considered immoral are not permitted under the claim of religious freedom.

Fair Treatment Before the Law

Protection Against Unjust Imprisonment. We have already noted that the English Parliament in 1679 passed the Habeas Corpus Act. Not only does this law protect personal liberty, but also it helps to guarantee that everyone will be treated fairly before the law. Our federal Constitution states in Article I that "The privilege of the writ of *habeas corpus* shall not be suspended, unless when in cases of rebellion or invasion the public safety may require it." Notice that this is not in the Bill of Rights but in the Constitution as originally adopted.

A writ is a court order; the term *habeas corpus* means literally "(that) you have the body." When a person is imprisoned he has the right to be represented by a lawyer. The lawyer may go to a judge and ask that the judge issue a writ of *habeas corpus*, that is, an order to the jailer either to release the prisoner or to show legal cause why he is being detained. Even if his client is accused of a crime, the lawyer can, in most cases, arrange for a prisoner's release until the trial is held.

Due Process of Law. Two articles in the amendments to our national Constitution provide that no citizen may be deprived "of life, liberty, or property without due process of law." The exact meaning of this phrase is difficult to explain, since each case involving "due process" has to be examined carefully to determine exactly what has occurred. In general, it means that a person's life, liberty, and property may be taken only in accordance with the law, or by regular court action. A judge, for example, cannot legally order a person punished for a crime unless the usual steps in a criminal case have been taken. Furthermore, no person may be punished for an act which was not a crime when he committed it. This is what is meant by the provision in the Constitution which states that "no *ex post facto* law shall be passed." The "due process" clause is very important in preventing judicial tyranny and in protecting innocent people from being convicted of crimes they did not commit.

The Right to a Fair Trial. Every person accused of crime in the United States is entitled to a fair and impartial trial. The accused must be formally indicted, or charged, with violation of a law; he is entitled to a speedy and public trial where the crime was committed. He must be informed of the charge against him and be allowed to be present at his trial. He must be permitted to employ lawyers to defend him, and, if he is unable to hire lawyers, the court is required to appoint a public defender to represent him. He must be allowed to hear all evidence against him, and he is entitled to have the aid of the court in compelling witnesses to appear and to testify in his behalf.

Safeguards Against Injustice. There are, in addition to these guarantees of a fair trial, other safeguards against injustice. No person may be compelled to confess or to testify against himself. It is assumed that he is innocent until his guilt has been proved beyond reasonable doubt, and it is the duty of the prosecution to prove guilt. An accused person may, by establishing a strong defense, prove his innocence; but we must remember that in our system of justice the prosecutor must prove guilt, and the accused does not have to prove his innocence.

No person may be placed in *double jeopardy* of life or limb. This means that a person who has been tried for a crime and acquitted cannot be tried again for the same crime. If a trial results in a "hung" jury in which no verdict can be reached, another trial may be held. The use of the word "hung" in this case is an Americanism, that is, something that Americans have added to the language. To be "hung up" means to be unable to move or proceed. Hence the expression "hung jury."

Amendment VIII contains three other important safeguards against injustice. First, excessive bail shall not be required. This means that a person accused of crime may be permitted to stay out of jail until his trial, provided he deposits a reasonable amount of money to guarantee his appearance when called by the court. If he doesn't appear, the bail is forfeited. Often in minor law violations, such as some traffic violations, the court just takes the bail money in place of a fine and cancels the case. In more serious law violations, the bail is forfeited, and the court orders officers to bring in the accused.

Second, excessive fines shall not be imposed. This is a restriction on both courts and legislatures. The legislatures determine fines and terms of imprisonment for the violation of most laws. A law may read in part: "punishable by a fine not to exceed $1,000, or by imprisonment for a term not to exceed one year, or both." Such a provision allows the judge to set both the amount of the fine and the length of imprisonment, if any, within limits set by the law.

Third, cruel and unusual punishments shall not be inflicted. This refers primarily to physical punishment. Persons convicted of crimes may, by law, be deprived of life, liberty, or property as punishment; but they cannot be made to suffer physical torture.

Civil Rights in a Democracy

To protect life, liberty, and property, to permit freedom of expression, and to insure fair treatment before the law are outstanding aims of a democratic nation. It is not sufficient that we have the right to take part in government; we must also be protected from government officials who might otherwise try to deprive us of our rights. In other words, we cannot have a democracy unless civil rights are guaranteed to us.

Set 3

POETRY[4]

An Introduction

GENERAL METHODS

Poetry is the most highly organized and compressed form of expression. Because every word in a poem must contribute a greater weight of meaning than in prose, a poet must always assume that what does not positively add to his effect detracts from it. Therefore, every word in a poem must justify its existence or be eliminated.

Because a poem must be so compact, it is very dependent upon conventions. The following poem, a highly organized experience, illustrates how poetic conventions help to satisfy the reader's need for order.

[4] Gene Montague and Marjorie Henshaw, *The Experience of Literature: Anthology and Analysis,* © 1966, pp. 123–218. Abridged. By permission of Prentice-Hall, Inc., Englewood Cliffs, New Jersey.

JOHN KEATS

On First Looking into Chapman's Homer

Much have I travelled in the realms of gold,	a
And many goodly states and kingdoms seen,	b
Round many western islands have I been	b
Which bards in fealty to Apollo hold.	a
Oft of one wide expanse had I been told	a
That deep-browed Homer ruled as his demesne	b
Yet did I never breathe its pure serene	b
Till I heard Chapman speak out loud and bold.	a
Then felt I like some watcher of the skies	c
When a new planet swims into his ken;	d
Or like stout Cortez when with eagle eyes	c
He stared at the Pacific—and all his men	d
Looked at each other with a wild surmise—	c
Silent, upon a peak in Darien.	d

This poem, written by John Keats when he was 21, expresses his surprise and delight at first reading George Chapman's translation of Homer's *Iliad*. Keats could not read Greek; other translations of Homer had not inspired him. Chapman's translation illuminated for him the greatness and the beauty of Homer. There is the real experience, which sounds flat, badly stated, as do all summaries or paraphrases of works of art. It is Keats's problem to communicate that experience so that it seems urgent and important. He does this by organizing it. To organize, the writer must arrange the subject in a certain order, compare it with something else, or use both methods. (Notice how the methods of the scientist and the artist are identical in this respect.) Keats does both.

First, he employs several conventions. He chooses a highly organized and very familiar form for his poem—the Italian sonnet, a poem composed of fourteen lines which divide into two units of eight (the octave) and six (the sestet). The first eight rhyme always the same way, abba, abba, whereas the sestet may rhyme any of several ways so long as it includes no more than three (c, d, e) new rhymes. Because of its two-part division, the Italian form, as opposed to the four-part English or Shakespearean form, is ideally adapted to dealing with an experience that involves describing an experience and commenting on it, asking a question and answering it, or posing a problem and solving it. Many readers will be familiar with this pattern. Thus, Keats establishes an expectation in the reader by deciding to use this form and then satisfies that expectation by using the form conventionally.

Next, he uses a metaphor, a figure of comparison, to describe his experience, since it is almost impossible to state emotion and emotional experience directly and flatly. He portrays himself as a traveler and explorer: the *Iliad* and the *Odyssey* deal often with the experience of Odysseus—one of the great travelers and explorers in literature. This figure of speech is maintained throughout the poem; all the references are to actions of some kind of traveler or explorer. Again Keats has satisfied the desire for order and symmetry.

Then Keats organizes the experience chronologically and spatially. Notice that the octave, while maintaining the explorer image, becomes increasingly specific with each line. The first two lines tell us that the poet has traveled much "in the realms of gold"—that is, he has read widely in literature—and has found many great books there—"goodly states and kingdoms." Then he narrows his compass. Apollo was the god of, among other things, poetry; therefore, in lines three and four Keats says that he has read a large amount of poetry. Becoming more specific, in lines five and six he says that he had been told of "one wide expanse" that Homer ruled. The reference here is to epic poetry. Finally, narrowing even farther, he tells us that he never really read Homer until he read Chapman's translation of Homer. This account has been expertly organized.

lines 1 and 2—literature as a whole

lines 3 and 4—poetry, one branch of literature

line 5—epic poetry, one branch of poetry

line 6—Homer, the greatest epic poet

lines 7 and 8—Chapman's translation of Homer

The octave is built like a pyramid standing on its apex. But the experience is incomplete. Thus far Keats has told us what he did but not how he felt about it. He does this in the sestet. Keeping the same figure, Keats says he felt like an astronomer who discovers a new planet (the only kind of space explorer possible in Keats's pre-astronaut days) or like Cortez when, first seeing the Pacific, he and his men were awed by the realization that here at last was the greatest body of water in the world. (Many readers will be bothered by the fact that Balboa, not Cortez, discovered the Pacific, but the lines, after all, do not say that Cortez discovered the Pacific, just as Keats was not the first discoverer of Chapman.) At that moment, Keats, like Cortez, stood alone on a peak of experience, seeing what few other men had seen.

Our account is still flat and stale because it is still paraphrase. No summary of a work of art ever approximates the experience of art. The paraphrase has not described the reader's pleasure of discovery as he recreates the experience line by line. Nor has it even mentioned the melody and the rhythm in the lines. It is not necessary to do those things here to illustrate how an experience is organized. A satisfactory account of the poem as a whole would certainly include these matters. Yet even such an account would not explain the experience fully because it would describe how all these elements appear separately when what is important —but impossible to communicate—is how all the elements work together simultaneously. This is one reason why poetry must be read, rather than discussed, to be appreciated.

Because poetry is compressed rather than diffuse, the poet must choose words that have the largest number of meanings. In practice, this means that he wants the word with the greatest number of relevant overtones to it. As a result, although a poet can achieve great precision of statement, he also often achieves ambiguity, that is, multiple meanings. A discussion of the causes of ambiguity follows.

Metaphor. Metaphor, in poetry, generally refers to any figure of comparison. It may be a metaphor proper. ("There is a garden in her face"), a simile ("Her cheeks were like roses"), or even an analogy ("Her face was a storm cloud; and when the angry rain began to fall, lightning flashed from her eyes.")

Symbols. A symbol is an emblem; it represents something else without ever announcing that an identification or a comparison is being made, as the metaphor does.

As in dealing with metaphor, the reader must exercise discretion in recognizing and accepting symbolic meaning. Again, the total poem must be the basis for accepting or rejecting symbolic meaning. One of the best known poetic symbols occurs in the concluding lines of Browning's "My Last Duchess." Because of what the reader knows of the Duke by the time he reaches these lines, he sees that, whatever the conscious reason for the Duke's mention of the statue of Neptune taming a sea horse, the statue symbolizes his cast of mind. The Duke is a man whose pride of ownership leads him to regard everything in his area of influence, including people, as property to be handled as he pleases. If these possessions do not conform to his desires, they must be "tamed."

Paradox. A paradox is an apparent contradiction, a true statement that is made up of seemingly incompatible elements. Richard Lovelace's "I could not love thee dear so much/Loved I not honour more" is a paradox. Paradoxes are always emphatic because they demand inspection. Thus, John Donne concludes a sonnet with the striking paradox, "Death, thou shalt die," and Shakespeare with

To give away yourself, keeps your self still,
And you must live drawn by your own sweet skill.

CONVENTIONS OF DICTION

Since every poem in a sense establishes its own vocabulary and since fashions in poetic diction have changed so often in literary history, conventions of diction are fluid. The history of British poetry, for example, has been a series of reactions against the "poetic diction" of a preceding age, and each new school of poetry has claimed that it was restoring "natural" language to poetry. In fact, none of them did that; they simply replaced one set of conventions with another. The early nineteenth-century Romantics said they were returning to nature and natural language in opposition to the highly artificial diction of the eighteenth-century Neo-Classical school. The Neo-Classicists had argued that they were restoring natural language to poetry as a reaction against the rough, over-specialized language of the seventeenth-century Metaphysical school. In turn, the Metaphysicals were reacting against the artificial diction of the sixteenth-century sonneteers.

The responsibility of the reader, then, is to acclimate himself to the vocabulary the poet is using. A good poem is one that is compatible with its own logic. If the diction of the poem harmonizes with the subject matter and theme, it is probably appropriate. A very crude example of this could be a seventeenth-century poem which begins with an invocation of Apollo. Surely no reader will object to the passage simply because Apollo was a mythical figure and therefore could not possibly help the poet. The invocation was a convention and Apollo, as the god of poetry, was a conventional figure to be invoked; both were parts of the frame of reference of the past. Furthermore, if the passage begins, "O Apollo, on the wings of morning . . ." the reader has reason to dislike the phrase but not to condemn it entirely, since it is again part of an established convention and it is compatible with the logic of invocation. However, if the poet were to begin "Hey, Apollo . . . ," then the diction is obviously not compatible with the logic of the poem (unless it is a burlesque) and deserves condemnation.

CONVENTIONS OF RHYTHM AND METER

We are all rhythmical creatures: our pulse beats to a rhythm, we breathe in rhythm, we brush our teeth in rhythm. The poet takes natural rhythm and conventionalizes it; that is, he builds it into different artificial rhythms that we call meter. As we have said before, he establishes a pattern of regularity and then breaks that pattern for emphasis.

The study of meter is called prosody. Different kinds of poetry use different prosodic systems. Most systems rest on the counting of recurring sounds or stresses. A few do not. Syllabic verse, for example, is built on similar line length, as in the haiku. Marianne Moore, the American poet, writes syllabic verse; you cannot hear one sound recurring regularly in a line nor can you count a recurring number of stresses in a line, but you can count a recurring number of syllables in the line. This prosodic system, however, is unusual.

A poet can employ many other rhythmic devices besides those already mentioned:

(1) Alliteration: the repetition of initial consonants to tie phrases and ideas together ("When to the sessions of sweet silent thought")

(2) Assonance: the repetition of vowel sounds ("Nor let the beetle nor the death-moth be")

(3) Consonance: the repetition of consonant patterns ("Loving and living, I could not leave")

Rhyme is also a rhythmic device, basically the repetition of a similar vowel sound at the end of successive lines. A great deal of poetry does not rhyme. Many poets have felt that rhyme restricts them or destroys a natural sentence effect; they have therefore turned to unrhymed forms such as blank verse (unrhymed iambic pentameter) or free verse (unrhymed verse, usually without regular foot patterns). On the other hand, rhyme has great advantages to offer the poet: It appeals to the rhythmic demand in each of us; it organizes a poem in that rhyme is the basis of stanza forms; it offers a frame for a poem in much the same way that a picture frame enhances a portrait; and it is an effective mnemonic device.

Furthermore, the poet can use various kinds of rhyme.

(1) Slant rhyme: repetition of a similar but not identical vowel and an identical consonant: heel/still

(2) Light rhyme: repetition of identical vowel sounds but with varying stress on the vowel: be/silly

(3) Eye rhyme: repetition of different vowel sounds that appear identical to the eye: sentry/comply

(4) Full rhyme: repetition of an identical vowel sound and identical following consonants: hope/scope

Rhyme and meter are the basis of stanza form. Like many formal conventions, stanza form can best be studied in the poems themselves.

The Modes of Poetry

Traditionally, poetry has been divided into three modes: (1) narrative; (2) dramatic; (3) lyric.

Narrative verse is used primarily to tell a story. It ranges in complexity from the simple folk ballad to the mock epic. Dramatic poetry may also tell a story, but it involves an identifiable speaker or speakers in a specific and identifiable situation that unfolds before the audience. Dramatic poetry, as generally defined today, includes plays in verse and the dramatic monologue, although one can argue that the dramatic monologue is as lyrical as it is dramatic. Lyric poetry, formally plotless, is the expression of feeling of a single speaker. It includes the sonnet, the ode, the elegy, and the song.

As we said, narrative poetry tells a story. Narratives can be extremely simple, as in some ballads, or they can be very complex. Lord Byron's *Don Juan*, for example, while it narrates the fictional adventures of a well-meaning but accident-prone young man, also comments, sometimes gently, sometimes savagely, on love, friendship, literature, politics, war, and morality. It is a kind of casebook of hypocrisy. Alexander Pope's *The Rape of the Lock*, a mock epic, tells the story of a flirtation but tells it ironically in the framework of the complicated conventions of heroic poetry. The *Iliad*, the *Odyssey*, *Paradise* Lost, all epics, are narrative poems.

Conventions of the Ballad

The simplest narratives are the folk ballads. These ballads are the popular music of bygone days. How they came to be composed, who composed them, under what circumstances—these things are not known. Theoretically, they could have been composed by a group gathered around a campfire; practically, they were probably composed by individual authors and then passed through many hands and many voices until they were finally written down and solidified. The same ballad has usually many variant forms: "Lord Randal" in England may become "John Randal" in New England, "Johnnie Randolph" in the South, and "Jamie Rambo" in the Southwest. The basic story line is usually the same in all versions, but the special events are changed to fit the region.

From some of the more obvious conventions in the ballads, one can make additional inferences about their development. Many ballads, for example, have a refrain, sometimes a nonsense refrain: "with a hey and ho/ and a hey-nonny-no!" At other times, the refrain changes slightly each time to make use of incremental repetition; that is, each time the refrain repeats, it adds a little more to the narrative as a kind of progress report. Simply changing one word in a refrain can accomplish this. For example, in a ballad about a young man who goes to his wedding only to find his bride has died in the night (a common ballad theme), a refrain might in successive stanzas go like this:

(1) And onward he did go, oh!

(2) And quickly he did go, oh!

(3) And gladly he did go, oh!

(4) And sadly he did go, oh!

(5) And madly he did go, oh!

The change in the adverb reflects the change of mind in the main character.

This habitual use of a refrain implies two things: First, the ballad is basically an oral form; the refrain is used as a summary to pull together divisions of the story in a fashion that would not be necessary if the ballad were a printed form. Second, many ballads probably were dance forms: The nonsense refrain suggests that it allowed the dancers to regroup for the next "set" or pattern.

It is easy to see why the ballad is defined as the popular music of bygone days. Like most popular forms, its appeal rests largely on using material and techniques familiar to the audience: familiar themes, images, characters, phrases, actions—in other words, conventional material and methods. Following is a list of conventional folk ballad elements:

(1) Stanza form: usually iambic quatrains (four-line stanza) with alternating lines of four feet and three feet—an abbreviated speech rhythm.

(2) Themes: the death of the young, the innocent, the beautiful, the good, often through no fault of their own.

(3) Images: stock figures, often connected by alliteration (hounds and hawks, dale and down, heath and hollow), sometimes alone (nut-brown maid, snow-white steed).

(4) Character: usually noble characters, either by birth or innate goodness. Kings, queens, princesses, lords, and ladies figure prominently in the ballads, as do folk heroes: Robin Hood, Jesse James, Allan-a-dale. Character itself is not developed; the hero or heroine is stereotyped.

(5) Phrasing: use of the refrain, stock comparisons (see also image); question and answer dialogue.

(6) Setting: very little attention to setting—the ballad is not nature poetry—because what matters is what happened, not where it happened.

(7) Point of view: the ballad is usually highly impersonal; the ballad signs itself. Usually there is no hint of the author's personality ("Jesse James" is a notable exception: the supposed originator, Billy Gashade, is clearly identified in the ballad itself). Part of the effect of the ballad comes from the starkly unemotional telling of an event that is fraught with strong emotion.

(8) Pace: ballads move very swiftly because of another very important convention. Although ballads deal more with action than with character, most of the action is not described but implied; that is, the real action occurs in the white spaces between the stanzas. Causes and effects get more attention than does the action itself.

Other Narratives

Except in the highly stylized ballad form, the narrative poet is his own master. He can choose his own stanzaic pattern, his own degree of subjectivity. He can make narrative verge on drama and incorporate lyrical elements. For example, remember the *Rime of the Ancient Mariner*. While it is ballad-like in form, it is a philosophical narrative.

DRAMATIC POETRY

Narrowly defined, a dramatic poem is a play in verse. But today the dramatic monologue is usually included in this category, because it is sometimes much like a condensed play. In the monologue, a single speaker, having reached a crucial point in his life, reveals his character by speaking to a listener or listeners whose presence and characteristics we know only through signs the speaker gives us. Every word in the poem belongs to the single speaker.

The monologue, then, is like a compressed play in that it requires a dramatic situation and an invented speaker who is not the poet. It differs from a play in that only one character speaks, and from a soliloquy in that the speaker in the monologue does address a specific audience.

The popularity of the dramatic monologue is attributed to its "reality," its concentration on a single, vivid, human character, and its complexity. The reader is able to see the character as he sees himself, as we see him, and by implication, as others, usually the listeners, see him. An example is Tennyson's *Ulysses*.

LYRIC POETRY

Lyric poetry is personal song. Many older lyrics were set to music; the convention has persisted to the extent that the lyric, although it now has no musical accompaniment, has become a highly personal expression of both thought and feeling, usually in musical meters.

That expression, however, can be in any tone, mood, metrical form, and level of formality, from the limerick to the ode. The most common of the fixed lyric forms is the sonnet.

Conventions of the Sonnet

A conventional sonnet is a fourteen-line poem dealing with a single subject, usually weighty in nature.

The convention of length varies. Some of the earliest sonnets in English (for example, Thomas Watson's "Hecatompathia" or "The Passionate Century of Love" [1582]) had eighteen lines; some more recent sonnets (George Meredith's "Modern Love" sequence) have sixteen lines. These exceptions are really not departures—basically, sonnet form is more a method of development than a stipulated length. Critics sometimes apply the term "sonnet structure" or "sonnet development" to a poem shorter or much longer than fourteen lines. They are referring, first, to the convention of the single weighty subject, and, second, to the pattern of discussion in the poem. This pattern may take either of two forms.

(1) Italian (or Petrarchan) form: a two-part development, consisting of an octave (eight lines) and a sestet (six lines). The octave of the Italian sonnet rhymes abba abba; the sestet may rhyme in almost any way (cde cde; cdc dcd, and so forth.)

(2) English (or Shakespearean) form: a four-part development, consisting of three quatrains (rhyming abab cdcd efef) and closing couplet (gg).

Spenserian form has the same development as the English form, except that the rhyme scheme is interlocked (for instance, abab bcbc cdcd ee). This form is sometimes regarded as having more continuity than the English form because of its interlocked rhymes, but it has never been used much by British and American poets. It can be considered simply a variant of the English form.

Conventions of the Pastoral

A pastoral is a poem dealing with country life as the "good life"; pastorals celebrate the virtues of the simple, uncomplicated, close-to-nature existence of carefree shepherds, swains, milkmaids. In other words, pastorals present country life in a highly idealized fashion. Pastorals are not rural poetry; they develop from a highly sophisticated society and are often a form of social criticism. They express the wish that human beings could exist so simply. Since life in the country was never like that described in pastorals, the implication in most pastorals is that the narrator longs for rest from the burdens of a complex society.

Conventions of the Ode

A conventional ode is an elaborate lyrical poem of praise, elevated in tone and intricate in form. Once popular, the form has been used very little during the past hundred years.

The Pindaric ode is characterized by sets of three stanzas (strophe, antistrophe, epode); the strophe and antistrophe are metrically identical and the epode different. It largely disappeared in the seventeenth century, perhaps partly because the original reason for the three-part division became meaningless: A Greek chorus moving to the left while chanting the strophe, to the right for the antistrophe, and then remaining still to recite the epode.

Since the seventeenth century, the most frequently used form has been the irregular ode, first written by Abraham Cowley. It retains the previous tone and form, but it abandons the three-part organization and metrical repetition. See, for an example of the irregular ode, Wordsworth's "Ode: Intimations of Immortality."

Finally, the Horatian ode, an irregular ode with a less elevated tone and less intricate form, has attracted the talents of many excellent English and American poets. For an example, see Keats's "Ode on a Grecian Urn."

The Elegy

The elegy is a lyrical, meditative poem lamenting the death of a loved or honored person. Most common in English is the "pastoral elegy," a highly conventionalized lament borrowed from the Greeks. The dead person and his associates are rendered as shepherds in the pastoral elegy. The poem generally begins with an invocation, moves to a description of how all nature mourns the dead one, describes a procession of mourners, philosophizes on the justice and injustice of death, and ends positively with despair changed to hope, grief to acceptance. Woven into the conventional fabric may be digressions of various kinds; indeed, the best-known parts of our better-known English elegies are often from digressive passages.

Pattern Poems

The following poem shows how some poets have gone far beyond the conventions of poetry as an oral form to approximate almost a sculptural form. We add no questions or comments, except to note that the Raleigh poem differs from the others in that it can be read horizontally or vertically without disturbing its form or content.

SIR WALTER RALEIGH

In the Grace of Wit, of Tongue and Face

Your face	Your tongue	Your wit
So fair	So sweet	So sharp
First bent	Then drew	So hit
Mine eye	Mine ear	My heart
Mine eye	Mine ear	My heart
To like	To learn	To love
Your face	Your tongue	Your wit
Doth lead	Doth teach	Doth move
Your face	Your tongue	Your wit
With beams	With sound	With art
Doth blind	Doth charm	Doth rule
Mine eye	Mine ear	My heart
Mine eye	My ear	My heart
With life	With hope	With skill
Your face	Your tongue	Your wit
Doth feed	Doth feast	Doth fill
Oh face	O tongue	O wit
With frowns	With checks	With smart
Wrong not	Vex not	Wound not
Mine eye	My ear	My heart
This eye	This ear	This heart
Shall joy	Shall bend	Shall swear
Your face	Your tongue	Your wit
To serve	To trust	To fear

ANSWERS TO PRACTICE SETS

Set 1
Fatigue

A. Introduction

B. Causes of Fatigue

C. Three Common Types of Fatigue

1. Normal Physical Fatigue
2. Psychological Fatigue
3. Disease Fatigue

D. Fatigue: A Major Problem Among College Students

Set 2

The Civil Rights of Citizens

A. Introduction

B. Our Bill of Rights
1. The Right to Protection
   a. Protection of Life
   b. Protection of Liberty
   c. Protection of Property
2. Freedom of Expression
   a. Freedom of Speech
   b. Freedom of the Press
   c. Freedom of Assembly
   d. Freedom of Religion
3. Fair Treatment Before the Law
   a. Protection Against Unjust Imprisonment
   b. Due Process of Law
   c. The Right to a Fair Trial
   d. Safeguards Against Injustice

C. Civil Rights in a Democracy

Set 3

Poetry

A. An Introduction
1. General Methods
2. Conventions of Diction
3. Conventions of Rhythm and Meter

B. The Modes of Poetry
1. Narrative Poetry
   a. Conventions of the Ballad
   b. Other Narratives
2. Dramatic Poetry
3. Lyric Poetry
   a. Conventions of the Sonnet
   b. Conventions of the Pastoral
   c. Conventions of the Ode
   d. Pattern Poems

12

Summarizing and
Note-Taking

ILLUSTRATION

These notes record a summary of information in the article about James
Van Der Zee. Look at how the summary is a summary by selection. It has
only that information bearing on two questions set down ahead of time.

Summarize the information bearing on these two questions. Write your
summary.

1. What did James Van Der Zee do?
2. Who honored him?

Summary and Notes

1. *What did James Van Der Zee do?*
   *Mr. Van Der Zee, a photographer, recorded 70 years of black
   life. His pictures have been collected in a volume, The
   World of James Van Der Zee.*

2. *Who has honored him?*
   *He has been honored by the American Society of Maga-
   zine Photographers, Who's Who in the East, and the
   Metropolitan Museum of Art in New York.*

THE "BEAUTIFUL PEOPLE" OF JAMES VAN DER ZEE[1]

87-year-old photographer captures more than 70 years of black N.Y. life on film.

Marcus Garvey glares from an open-air touring car, a brooding general in trusses and feathers. Children are shown at the door of a school against a lusterless background of grating and brick. In an elegant salon, beaded socialites relax among the sofas: poised, carefully placed, as on canvas.

The photos are the work of James Van Der Zee, whose sensitive studies of black Americana chronicle 70 years of black life. They are collected in a volume, *The World of James Van Der Zee*, described as capturing the "pride and fascinating beauty" of blacks, their humanity and "tremendous love for the children." Adds Reginald McGhee, who edited the work: "In this man I have found the same qualities of the masters—an eye for detail, composition, light, form and texture, and deep involvement with his subject matter."

The book, however, is just one expression of a belated discovery of the 87-year-old artist. He has been honored by the American Society of Magazine Photographers, selected for listing in *Who's Who in the East* and named lifetime fellow of the Metropolitan Museum of Art in New York, where his photos are a part of the permanent collection.

Yet the artist may well have died unknown had it not been for a series of singular events. In 1967, McGhee, a black photographer, was conducting research for an exhibit, "Harlem on My Mind." He found Van Der Zee in a Harlem studio along with possibly as many as 50,000 negatives. "It was amazing they had been kept in such condition," McGhee recalls. Van Der Zee thus became the exhibit's principal contributor. But real fame awaited a tragedy of sorts, part of a life of bad luck that has haunted the photographer.

Van Der Zee and his wife, Gaynell, were evicted from their longtime home in Harlem. (They had purchased the house but later lost possession on a mortgage foreclosure.) On the day of the eviction, the *New York Times* carried a picture story showing the saddened photographer in front of the home. Aroused friends found lodgings for the couple, but, more importantly, publishers with an eye for black subject matter suddenly became aware of the photographer's existence.

Fortunately, McGhee, in arranging the exhibit, had preserved most of Van Der Zee's negatives, saving the collection from almost certain destruction. Thus when Grove Press expressed interest in the work, the editors could draw upon an abundance of photographs.

---

[1] "The 'Beautiful People' of James Van Der Zee," *Ebony*, October 1970, pp. 85–86. Reprinted by permission of EBONY Magazine, copyright 1970 by Johnson Publishing Company, Inc.

Says Van Der Zee, remarking on the irony of it all: "It seems that my best days were my worst days and my worst days and hardest times have come in these days which should be my best. They say that when something happens, you should overlook it and look to the good that can come from it."

DESCRIPTION

What Are Summarizing and Note-taking? Summarizing is stating the writer's message in shorter form. There are two forms of summarizing.

1. Reducing information. Here you cover all of the information in a selection. You restate it in your own words in a briefer form.
2. Selecting information. Here you pull out some of the information in a selection to fit a purpose you have; for example, selecting just the main ideas and leaving the supporting ideas. You may use the writer's statements or you may restate the information in your own words.

Note-taking is recording the information you summarize. You may use various forms of note-taking: you may underline in your books, write in the margin, write on separate cards and paper, or record your notes on audio tape.

Note this important point. There are two stages in summarizing and note-taking when you are processing information for a project, problem, or question. The first stage is when you are dealing with a single selection—an article, chapter, or textbook. In this stage, you start by summarizing what the writer says within a selection; then you record your summary in notes. The second stage is when you combine material from several selections. In this stage, you start with your notes on each separate selection. Then you synthesize them, pull them together, and summarize them across selections. The next chapter (Chapter 13, *Synthesizing*) is about the second stage. The present chapter is about the first stage.

Why Are Summarizing and Note-Taking Valuable? Summarizing and note-taking are ways of keeping information you read so that it can be used at another time. No one can remember everything he reads, so you need to summarize and take notes to study later or to use in problem solving. A further benefit of summarizing and note-taking: they are recitation and recitation helps in both understanding and remembering material.

How Do You Summarize and Take Notes? Here are some of the main steps.

1. Be very clear about your purpose. How will you use the information you summarize and record? Your answer will influence what form of summary you use and how much detail you go into.

2. Find and mark the ideas you are going to put in your summary. Use all of the skills for checking relevance. (See Chapter 10.)

3. State the writer's information about these ideas. Copy the writer's statements, or paraphrase his ideas, stating them in your own words. The way you plan to use the material will help you decide whether to paraphrase or whether to copy material word for word.
   —If you are going to quote material, then you need to copy exactly the sentences, tables, figures, and other items.
   —If you are only going to use the writer's ideas, then you can paraphrase.

4. Document your notes. Put in the source of the selection, and note where in the selection you got the information for each of your summary statements. Be very sure to do this when you are paraphrasing as well as when you are quoting exactly.

5. Decide on the mechanics. Mechanics may seem silly to worry about, but don't be fooled. They can mean a lot of difference in time, energy, and understanding when you are using or storing your notes. Try different ways and decide which mechanics suit you best. Here are some examples.
   —You have several choices when you are making notes in a separate place, not in the book. Some people like cards of various sizes, others like regular paper. Some write only on one side; others use both sides. Some keep notes in envelopes, others in notebooks, and others in file folders. Some use abbreviations and key phrases, others don't. Some use ink or typewriters.
   —You also have several choices when you are marking the reading selection. One approach is to use a code like this. Put the topic paragraphs in brackets [   ]. Underline the main ideas. Put the key words of supporting ideas in boxes [   ]. Circle important details like dates. In the margin, write index words which indicate what the paragraph or segment is about, page numbers where additional information is located, questions about points you don't understand, and comments about points you agree with or disagree with.

In this book, our purpose is to deal with *reading* skills. And to keep relevant, we have so far considered summarizing and taking notes on written selections which you read. As a student, you also have to summarize and take notes in situations not involving reading; that is, in oral presentations like lectures. It is harder to summarize and take notes for oral presentations than for written presentations. For example, with written presentations, you have time to think, reread, make judgments, and write more complete statements. With oral presentations, you must adjust to the speaker's style, work under time pressure, share the speaker's attention with other students, and so on. *Practice Set 3* below has some details about taking notes on lectures.

PRACTICE

Use the form of summary named as you answer the questions. Write your notes in the space given.

Set 1

Form of Summary: Reducing information

Questions:

1. What was Socrates' main purpose? _____

_____

_____

2. Why did he seek that purpose? _____

_____

_____

SOCRATES[2]

In Athens in the late fifth century, B.C., there was a man named Socrates who attracted admiring crowds wherever he went. He was homely and shabbily dressed, but he had a noble heart and brilliant mind.

___

[2] Nathaniel Platt and Muriel Jean Drummond, *Our World Through the Ages,* 3rd ed., © 1967. By permission of Prentice-Hall, Inc., Englewood Cliffs, New Jersey.

He devoted his life to seeking truth and to teaching men to distinguish between right and wrong. For money and superstition, he had only contempt. Socrates believed that if any idea could not stand up under thorough examination, it should be rejected as untrue. He kept questioning his own thinking as well as others'. He was constantly asking people searching questions on their ideas of duty, justice, reason, and love. Clear thinking by all, Socrates believed, would strengthen the government. The great philosopher felt that false knowledge would prevent people from living the happiest and most honest lives that were possible. "Know thyself," he urged.

Set 2

Form of Summary: Selecting information.
Question: Name and define (with examples) each area of study in the

field of geography. _____

_____

_____

_____

_____

_____

_____

_____

_____

_____

_____

_____

_____

_____

GEOGRAPHY[3]

The field of geography is generally divided into several areas for the purpose of study. These include physical (natural) geography, cultural (human) geography, economic geography, regional geography, and systematic geography. The student may study one of these aspects exclusively, or he may concentrate on a combination of them.

Physical Geography

In the study of physical (natural) geography stress is laid upon the natural elements of man's environment. These include a study of topography, soils, earth materials, earth-sun relations, surface and underground water, weather and climate, and native animal and plant life. Physical geography, as an academic study, cannot be entirely free from the impact of man upon his environment. For example, the elements listed above have all been altered to some degree by man. Even climate, which is the element least subject to change, shows some definite modification by the work of man. Man's destruction of great areas of forest throughout the world has greatly accelerated soil erosion in those areas and has allowed the surface winds to blow at a greater speed. Similarly, man's quarrying of rocks and mining of ores have created minor landform features.

Cultural Geography

In cultural geography, emphasis is placed upon the study of observable features resulting from man's occupance of the earth. These features include population, buildings, roads, factories, farms and field patterns, mines, communications, and rural and urban settlement patterns. Cultural geography is one of the most rapidly expanding divisions of geography. The geographical study of cities (urban geography) becomes more and more important as the number of people living in cities increases. Additional aspects of regional settlement types, features, and patterns together with the sequential occupancy of the land provide the geographer with a field of investigation known as settlement geography.

[3] Arthur H. Doerr, J. L. Guernsey, and Eugene Van Cleef, *Principles of Geography* (Woodbury, N.Y.: Barron's Educational Series, 1959), pp. 4–6. Used with permission.

Economic Geography

In economic geography the relationships between man's efforts to gain a living and the earth's surface on which they are conducted are correlated. In order to study how man makes a living, the distribution of materials, productive activities, institutions, and human traits and customs are analyzed. Economic geography deals with the areal distribution of many widely varying activities, such as the production and distribution of a complex economic activity like the machine-tool industry of Northeastern United States or the simple grazing activities of the Asiatic nomads.

Regional Geography

In regional geography the basic concern is with the characteristics of areas. The principal emphasis is placed upon patterns and elements of the natural environment and human activities. By using the regional technique in studying geography, what otherwise might be a bewildering array of facts is brought into focus as an organized pattern. Regional geography is generally treated in terms of specific areas—such as the *Arctic*, the *Central Valley of Chile* or the *American Corn Belt*.

A geographic region is an area that has one or more dominant features. Since there may be a large number of regional characteristics, care must be taken in selecting criteria to emphasize the actual, meaningful, cohesive relations within a region such as landforms, climate, soils, crops, industries, and people. When emphasis is placed upon such static concepts as expressions of latitude and longitude, various political boundaries, detailed information concerning elevation, area, or other geographic features of less importance, the true character of the region may be obscured. Geographers find the regional concept an excellent device for comparing or contrasting different areas of the earth's surface.

Systematic Geography

It is also feasible to study topics (purposefully) concerning the geography of a small area or the entire surface of the earth in systematic fashion. By this method, settlements, climates, soils, landforms, minerals, water, and agricultural crops may be observed, described, analyzed, and explained. Research in systematic geography has proved to be quite successful in shedding light on the problems of the modern world. Whole new sub-divisions of systematic geography have come into existence as a result of ever-broadening investigations. *Biogeography,* for example, seeks to establish the geographical limit of plants and animals and points to the finding of additional areas for the production of new and useful crops and strains of livestock. *Medical-geography,* a newcomer in the field of systematic geography, is devoted to the investigation of the areal extent and the locational concentration of diseases as well as their environmental limits.

Set 3

Forms of Summary: Selecting *and* reducing information

Questions:

1. Cite three lecture-note forms.

   a. _____

   b. _____

   c. _____

2. Name eight suggested practices for taking lecture notes.

   a. _____

   b. _____

   c. _____

   d. _____

   e. _____

   f. _____

   g. _____

   h. _____

3. What is a good balance between adequacy and conciseness in lecture notes? _____

_____

_____

4. List four suggestions for effective use of notes.

a. _____

b. _____

c. _____

d. _____

TAKING LECTURE NOTES[4]

Students who take poor notes are often those who fail to perceive the nature and purpose of the lecture and its organizational plan. They look upon the talk as a catalogue of facts. Instead of thinking and abstracting, they try to take down everything, or they set down random items, too spotty and disconnected to serve a useful purpose.

Upon looking into the mind of such a student during a biology lecture, we might see something like this:

"Predators—I'll write that down. What are predators? Eagles? Wolves? Hawks? Mountain lions? Mountain lions are predators? I remember, that big fellow up on the rocks at camp last summer.—Let's see now, *Predators, eagles, hawks, spiders.* Spiders? Seed-eating birds? How come? Birds eat worms and little snakes. Helpful to man, he says. Destroy weed-seeds. Humming birds? They fly backward. Fastest of all birds, I heard somewhere. What's the difference between predators and scavengers? Parasites? Now I am lost, for sure. What's he getting at? I'll leave a space and come back. No—I'll stop work and just listen. It's more interesting that way. Then I'll borrow somebody's notes."

Perhaps another student in the group works differently. As soon as the topic is announced, he begins to think about it: *Animals Helpful to Man.* "What kinds of animals are helpful to man?" "What services, precisely, does each perform?" He waits to see how the topic will be developed, and listens for his answers.

March 12, 19__
Biology 141 A
Animals Helpful to Man
A. Predators
   1. Service: controlling the number of rats, other pests
   2. Examples:
      a. Large: mountain lion, eagle, hawk, coyote, skunk
      b. Small: bird, bat, snake, frog, toad, spider

[4] Doris Wilcox Gilbert, *Study in Depth,* © 1966, pp. 65–70. By permission of Prentice-Hall, Inc., Englewood Cliffs, New Jersey.

B. Seed-eaters
  1. Service: destroying weed-seeds
  2. Examples: wild mice, some birds
C. Scavengers
  1. Services
    a. Removing bodies of dead animals
    b. Keeping cycle of carbon and hydrogen in rotation
  2. Examples
    a. Large: bear, vulture
    b. Small: bacteria
D. Etc. . . .

Working in this way, the second student provides himself with a useful and convenient record for study and review. In addition, he gets to the heart of the discussion while the lecture is still in progress. Instead of wasting his time on idle reflections, he accomplishes an important part of his work in class. The most compelling force toward clear understanding is the search for key points and the effort to set them down in a suitable form for mastery. You learn by hard thinking.

It is not the purpose here to imply that good notes necessarily follow the outline form used by the second student. The sentence outline may be more suitable for some material, or the summary outline, or even running notes. There are several other useful forms.

EXAMPLES OF LECTURE NOTE FORMS

The Topic Outline

Here the main points and the contributing details are condensed into topic form.

1. Reasons for the poor outlook for the silk industry in the U.S.
    a. Poor suitability of Americans for silkworm care
    b. Recognition of the rights of other countries to this industry
    c. American preference for nylon for most purposes

The Topic-Sentence Outline

This form develops the subordinate ideas with complete sentences. Sometimes sentences are necessary to make the meaning clear. Sometimes the writing of the sentences is quicker than condensation into acceptable topic form.

1. General suggestions for studying a foreign language
    a. Study each day's lesson as it comes.
    b. Make an intensive effort right from the start to master pronunciation.

c. Where verbatim learning is required, work in short periods frequently repeated.

The Topic-Summary Outline

This form is particularly useful for certain lectures in philosophy, sociology, economics, and psychology—for example, where it is the purpose of the speaker to develop a point or a series of points through carefully planned analysis. He may provide a variety of examples to illustrate a principle or show how it might work out in a particular situation. For the note-taker, it is important to cut through the odds and ends so as to get the fundamental principle.

1. Price levels and the value of money
   A rise in the average level of all prices is a fall in the value of money. In effect, the average of money varies inversely with the general price level.
2. The impact on changing price levels
   Inflation is a rise in the price level—that is, a fall in the general purchasing value of the dollar. Deflation is a fall in "the" price level.
3. Inflation is full-employment economy
   Those whose incomes rise more rapidly than the average get bigger slices of the "national pie." Those whose incomes rise less rapidly get smaller slices.

There are also certain temporary expedients. For the novice, unused to taking lecture notes, or for the student unfamiliar with the lecturer's method of presentation, it may at first be necessary to resort to simple recording and then rewrite the notes later. The topics can be written as marginal headings. The amplifications are then set down in the words of the lecturer.

1. Normal fear
   It is instinctive and necessary for the preservation of life. It keeps us out of the path of a train or car, and from going too close to the edge of a cliff, or jumping into deep water when we can't swim. It represents the marshalling . . . .
2. Unreal fear
   Unreal fear, on the other hand, is senseless in that it doesn't accomplish anything. It is anxiety, dread, worry. Men and women, young and old, rich and poor, all feel some of this . . . .

To save time, the note-taker may sometimes substitute dashes for words.

Maize (Zea mays)—staff of life—aboriginal N. American Indian. One variety—Zuni corn—drought resistant—planted eighteen inches deep. Unique ability to reach surface due to elongation—mesocotyl up to 36 cm.

These days television is performing an invaluable service for higher education. Where the enrollment for required courses is large, lectures may be telecast to overflow groups in other rooms or other buildings. Also, the instruction in almost any course may be implemented and enriched by televised pictures and discussions—of far-away places, perhaps, of the distant past, of the biotic world of the jungle, of a laboratory experiment. Where the telecast calls for uninterrupted attention to the screen and where note-taking is not feasible, mimeographed "hand-outs" are often supplied.

It should not be assumed, however, that the day of the lecture is passing, and with it the need for note-taking skill. Invaluable as it is, television is but one of many media of instruction.

SUGGESTIONS FOR TAKING LECTURE NOTES

1. *Before the lecture, read any library references that have been assigned.* The more background you have, the better able you are to cope with the subject.

2. *Keep in mind the values to be realized from taking good notes* **IN CLASS.** Time is a critical factor in college and university work. In directing your attention to getting the meaning, you establish an active learning attitude and cover a part of your study during the lecture period. More than that, you provide a record for further study and review—a record of material that is probably not otherwise easily available.

3. *Space your notes so as to allow for memoranda from supplementary reading or from textbook study.* Many professors advise that you take lecture notes on alternate pages of your book.

4. *Begin each set of notes with the proper identification.* Give the date and the course number, and provide a suitable title.

5. *Listen actively and selectively with questions in mind.* "What is the main thought here?" "What are the major divisions?" "What details are essential in expanding or explaining the theme?"

   In order to make quick decisions, take advantage of full signals and half signals when they are given by the speaker. These are the sets of expressions like, "Three causes," . . . "First," . . . "Then second," . . . "Third," or "In England," . . . "In France," . . . "But in this country." . . .

6. *Mark out your page with signposts.* Make effective use of titles and

marginal headings so that you can see the organizational plan at a glance. Then provide as much elaboration as is necessary to give you the meaning. Use the note form most appropriate to the lecture material.

7. *Take down without change items that are to be used or learned exactly as they are given.* These may include reference lists, rules of grammar, formulas, quotations, directions for conducting an experiment. Where they are essential to the understanding of the discussion, copy diagrams, tables, maps, or charts from the blackboard.

8. *Meet the conventional requirements of good form.* Write neatly and space your notes for easy readability. Avoid either crowding or sprawling. Follow the rules for English usage in grammar, punctuation, and capitalization. If you use an outline form, observe the outline conventions.

STRIKING A BALANCE BETWEEN ADEQUACY
AND CONCISENESS

In abstracting, organizing, and condensing, you are attempting to set down the gist of the lecture without unnecessary examples, illustrations, and other forms of proliferation. You are working for conciseness so that you can keep the pace. But don't go beyond the point of diminishing returns. Make sure that your memoranda are full enough to serve the purpose for which they were taken. Once the lecture is concluded, it is gone forever.

How full is "full enough?"

Suppose for a moment that an experienced harbor-master wishes to instruct a group of new deputies regarding the rules and regulations governing the lighting of small boats. Before his talk, he writes out a plan. Since he is thoroughly familiar with the facts, he needs nothing more than a guide outline to keep him on course.

1. Lighting requirements
   a. Class A motorboats
   b. Class One motorboats
   c. Class Two motorboats
   d. Sailboats
   e. Motor sailboats
   f. Class Three motorboats
   g. Etc.

But for the deputies, notices like these would be utterly useless. Unlike the harbor master, they are new to the job and they need to learn the facts if they are to carry on their work effectively. Good notes for the deputies might look like this:

1. Lighting requirements
   a. Class A motorboats (less than 16 ft.)
      1. White light aft, sunset to sunrise, clearly visible around horizon
      2. Red-green lantern, bow, lower than stern light, green to star-board, red to port
   b. Class One motorboats (16 to 26 ft.)—same requirements
   c. Class Two motorboats (26 to 40 ft.)
      1. Bright, white light forward
      2. White light aft, visible around horizon and higher than for-ward light
      3. Starboard green light, with inboard screens
      4. Port red light, with inboard screens
   d. Etc. . . .

No matter what the topic of your lecture or the general form of your notes, the amount of detail you include must be determined by the an-swers to two questions: "What do you know about the topic?" and "What do you need?" Are you a harbor master or a deputy? The chances are good that you are not a harbor master. If you were, you would not be enrolled as a student in the course.

OUTLINE CONVENTIONS

1. When an outline requires a title (for example, in a full set of lecture notes), capitalize the first word and all others except the articles *a, an,* and *the,* and the conjunctions and prepositions.

2. Show the organizational plan through indentation, indicating the im-portance of each item, and its relationship to other items. Keep the items at each level of importance in sharp alignment.

Wrong	*Right*
1. Purposes of the bones	1. Purposes of the bones
a. To give shape to the body	a. To give shape to the body
b. To shield the vital organs	b. To shield the vital organs
c. To act as levers	c. To act as levers
d. To afford attachments for muscles	d. To afford attachments for muscles

3. In spacing and indenting, avoid both sprawling and crowding. Indent in such a way as to show the organizational plan at a glance.

4. In a formal outline, use a numbering-lettering system. Decide on one system, then keep to it consistently.

5. Follow each identifying number and letter with a period.

6. Be consistent in the use of capital letters. If the first word of an item

is capitalized, the first word of each of the other items in the set should be capitalized.

7. Avoid internal capitalization without reason.

Wrong	*Right*
1. Activities of termite workers a. Tending gardens and harvesting crops b. Tending and Milking insects c. Feeding and grooming other Termites d. Building Nests	1. Activities of termite workers a. Tending gardens and harvesting crops b. Tending and milking insects c. Feeding and grooming other termites d. Building nests

8. Avoid single subheadings.

9. When an item is too long to be completed on a single line, begin the second line even with the first. Be consistent in preserving sharp levels of indentation.

Wrong	*Right*
1. Reasons for the importance of the Louisiana Purchase a. It doubled the area of the United States. b. It opened up the mouth of the Mississippi River. c. It cost only about four cents an acre.	1. Reasons for the importance of the Louisiana Purchase a. It doubled the area of the United States. b. It opened up the mouth of the Mississippi River. c. It cost only about four cents an acre.

10. Use parallel grammatical structure in parallel parts of the outline.

Wrong	*Right*
1. Steps in making a time schedule a. List your activities and responsibilities. b. Discovering your best work hours. c. To plan a trial schedule in terms of a. and b. d. The schedule should be followed until habits are formed.	1. Steps in making a time schedule a. List your activities and responsibilities. b. Identify your best working hours. c. Make a trial schedule in terms of a. and b. d. Follow the schedule until it becomes habitual.

1. Soon after the lecture, the next hour if possible, reread your notes and make the necessary corrections and completions while your memory of the discussion is still fresh. Rewrite the entire set of notes only if you have an important reason for doing so. If you will need the material in your future professional work, it may be worth your while to type it out and add illustrations. But avoid wasting time on mechanical copying which has no purpose more serious than the general improvement of appearance.

2. Study your notes much as you would study a textbook assignment. Follow the general principles of learning. Lest you overlook the forest for the trees, think over the central idea of the lecture and try to put it into words. Then, with your marginal headings to guide you force yourself to recall the contributing points and explanations. Work from memory. Then check your performance and try once again.

   Where they are needed, make sure you can give precise definitions for technical terms or be ready to specify with names, dates, events, or statistics. Where rules, formulas, or quotations are to be learned verbatim use short practice periods, but repeat the practice often.

3. Opposite your notes in the spaces reserved for them, enter parallel notes from your text or your reference reading. Then think through a point-by-point comparison of the different treatments.

   When you do not understand a discussion, look up additional references or talk over the point with other students in the class. Upper division "honor students" who have taken the course are often available to help you.

4. In reviewing and trying to foresee questions that may be asked on quizzes and examinations, pay particular attention to differences in the treatments of topics in the lecture and in the text. The lecturer may be presenting evidence from research—possibly his own—too new to be included in even the most recent textbook on the subject.

   For obvious reasons, it is important to be alert to the lecturer's treatment of any subject. But don't be misled. Where a controversial point is at issue, the examination question may ask you to compare or contrast the theories of a number of thinkers or researchers in the field —and to document your statements.

ANSWERS FOR PRACTICE SETS

Set 1

1. Socrates' main purpose was to search for truth.
2. He thought that clear thinking and true knowledge would make the government stronger and help people personally to lead more honest and happy lives.

Set 2

1. *Physical geography*
   Study of natural elements of the environment: for example, typography, weather and climate, and nature and plant life.
2. *Cultural geography* .
   Study of features resulting from men's occupying earth: for example, population, buildings, settlement patterns.
3. *Economic geography*
   Study of relation between men's efforts to make a living and the earth's surface where these efforts take place: for example, industry in the Northeastern U.S. and grazing activities of Asiatic Nomads.
4. *Regional geography*
   Study of characteristics of certain areas; patterns and elements of the natural environment and human activities are brought together: for example, the Arctic, the American Corn Belt.
5. *Systematic geography*
   Study of particular problems of the modern world in relation to geographical areas and features: for example, one problem in *medical-geography* is to study how many areas a disease covers and where it occurs most heavily.

Set 3

1a. The topic outline.
 b. The topic-sentence outline.
 c. The topic-summary outline.
2a. Before the lecture read any library references that have been assigned.
 b. Keep in mind the values to be realized from taking good notes in class.
 c. Space your notes so as to allow for memoranda from supplementary reading or from textbook study.
 d. Begin each set of notes with the proper identification.
 e. Listen actively and selectively with questions in mind.
 f. Mark your page with signposts.

g. Take down without change items that are to be learned exactly as they are given.

h. Meet the conventional requirements of good form.

3. Set down the gist of the information without unnecessary details; but be sure the notes are full enough for the purpose they are to be used for.

4a. Soon after the lecture, reread your notes and make the necessary corrections and completions.

b. Study your notes much as you would study a textbook assignment.

c. Add to your notes parallel notes from your text or reference reading.

d. Pay particular attention to differences in the treatments of topics in the lecture and in the text.

13

Synthesizing

Here is a synthesis of information on a certain question about Hemingway and Wolfe, who were contemporary writers. Note how the array is used to pull together certain items in the chronologies in a way that shows relations more clearly.

Problem: To compare the output of books by Thomas Wolfe and Ernest Hemingway during the period that their careers overlapped.

Question: What were the men's publication records for books during the two decades, 1925–1944?

Array:

TITLES OF NOVELS

Time Period	Ernest Hemingway	Thomas Wolfe
	The Torrents of Spring	Look Homeward, Angel
1925	The Sun Also Rises	
through	Men Without Women	
1934	A Farewell to Arms	
	Death in the Afternoon	

TITLES OF NOVELS (Continued)

Time Period	Ernest Hemingway	Thomas Wolfe
	Green Hills of Africa	From Death to Morning
	For Whom the Bell Tolls	Of Time and the River
1935	Men at War	The Story of a Novel
through		The Web and the Rock
1944		You Can't Go Home Again
		The Hills Beyond

Summary Statements: During the 20-year period, they put out about the same number of books. Most of Hemingway's books were published during the first decade; most of Wolfe's, during the second.

CHRONOLOGY: ERNEST HEMINGWAY[1]

1899 Born in Oak Park, Illinois, second of six children of Clarence Edmunds Hemingway, M.D., and Grace Hall Hemingway.

1917 Graduates from Oak Park High School; rejected by Army because of eye injured in boxing; works as cub reporter on Kansas City *Star*.

1918 Goes to Italy as Red Cross ambulance driver. Legs severely injured by mortar fragments and heavy machine gun fire midnight July 8, two weeks before nineteenth birthday near Fossalta di Piave.

1920–24 Reporter and foreign correspondent for Toronto *Star* and *Star Weekly*.

1921 Marries Hadley Richardson; leaves for Europe.

1923 *Three Stories and Ten Poems* published in Paris. Contains "Up In Michigan," "Out of Season," and "My Old Man."

1924 *in our time*, thirty-two pages of miniatures published in Paris.

1925 *In Our Time*, U.S. edition, published by Boni & Liveright. Fourteen short stories plus miniatures of Paris edition, which are used as interchapters.

[1] Robert P. Weeks, "Chronology of Important Dates," in Robert P. Weeks, ed., *Hemingway: A Collection of Critical Essays* (Englewood Cliffs, N.J.: Prentice-Hall, Inc., 1962), pp. 175–76. Used with permission.

1926 *The Torrents of Spring* published in May by Charles Scribner's Sons, New York, publisher of all subsequent works. *The Sun Also Rises* published in October.

1927 Divorces Hadley Richardson; marries Pauline Pfeiffer. Publication of *Men Without Women*, fourteen short stories, ten of which had appeared in magazines.

1928–38 Lives mostly at Key West, Florida.

1929 *A Farewell to Arms*, Hemingway's first commercial success: 80,000 copies sold in first four months.

1932 *Death in the Afternoon*.

1933 *Winner Take Nothing*, fourteen stories. Publishes first of thirty-one articles and stories to appear in *Esquire* during next six years.

1935 *Green Hills of Africa*.

1936–37 Writes, speaks, and raises money for Loyalists in Spanish Civil War.

1937 In Spain covering Civil War for North American Newspaper Alliance. Appearance of *To Have and Have Not*, three interconnected stories, two of which had been published separately.

1938 *The Fifth Column* and the *First Forty-Nine Stories*. Contains the play, the short stories in the three previous collections, plus seven previously published stories.

1940 *For Whom the Bell Tolls*, Hemingway's best-selling book. Pauline Pfeiffer divorces him; he marries Martha Gellhorn.

1942 *Men at War*, a collection of war stories and accounts edited and with an introduction by Hemingway.

1942–45 Covers European theater of war as newspaper and magazine correspondent.

1944 Divorced from Martha Gellhorn; marries Mary Welsh.

1950 *Across the River and Into the Trees*.

1952 *The Old Man and the Sea* published in *Life*, September 1.

1954 Wins Nobel Prize. Cited for "forceful and style-making mastery of the art of modern narration."

1961 Dies of self-inflicted gunshot wound July 2 in his Ketchum, Idaho, home.

CHRONOLOGY: THOMAS WOLFE[2]

1900 Thomas Clayton Wolfe born October 3 at Asheville, a resort town in the Blue Ridge Mountains of North Carolina, son of a tombstone cutter from Pennsylvania. His mother was a native of the mountain area.

1904 Accompanied his mother at the St. Louis Exposition.

1905 Entered Orange Street Public School in Asheville.

1908 Moved with his mother to The Old Kentucky Home at 48 Spruce Street, which she had purchased two years before.

1912 Began four years at the North State Fitting School, a private institution operated by Mr. and Mrs. J. M. Roberts.

1916 Entered the University of North Carolina.

1917 Summer romance with Clara Paul. In November his first published writing, a poem, appeared in the university magazine.

1918 Worked at Langley Field, Virginia, in the summer. October 19 his favorite brother, Benjamin Harrison, died during the influenza epidemic.

1920 Graduated from the University at Chapel Hill and entered Harvard.

1922 Received an M.A. in English from Harvard. His father, William Oliver Wolfe, died June 20.

1923 Completed an extra year at Harvard, studying playwriting under Professor George P. Baker. Had no luck selling his plays to New York producers.

1924 Accepted an instructorship in English at New York University in January. In October sailed for Europe. On New Year's Eve, encountered his friend Kenneth Raisbeck in Paris.

1925 Traveled in Europe. On September 10, aboard ship returning to America, met Mrs. Aline Bernstein. Resumed teaching at New York University. Still found no producers for his plays.

1926 Second voyage to Europe began in June. During July, in England, began a novel tentatively called "The Building of a Wall."

1927 In January was back in New York; devoted his entire time to the novel instead of returning to teaching. Lived in an apartment in Greenwich Village, rented for him by Mrs. Bernstein. Completed the first draft of the novel and sailed for Europe in July. Taught again at New York University in the fall.

[2] From *Thomas Wolfe: An Introduction and Interpretation* by Richard Walser. Copyright © 1961 by Holt, Rinehart, and Winston, Inc. Reprinted by permission of Holt, Rinehart, and Winston, Inc.

1928 After several publishers rejected his novel, made a fourth trip to Europe in July. Attended "Oktoberfest" in Munich. "O Lost" accepted by Maxwell Perkins at Scribners.

1929 Returned to New York in January and taught part-time at the university. October 18 *Look Homeward, Angel* published, with violent reaction in Asheville.

1930 Finally gave up teaching in January, and at the same time made a break in his relations with Aline Bernstein. Sailed for Europe in May, after receiving a Guggenheim Fellowship.

1931 Returned to America and moved to Brooklyn to write.

1933 Completed draft of *Of Time and the River*.

1934 Worked with Maxwell Perkins on *Of Time and the River*.

1935 Went to Europe just before publication of *Of Time and the River* on March 8. Returned to New York on July 4. Settled in New York—now famous and successful. First trip to West Coast. *From Death to Morning* published November 14.

1936 Trip to New Orleans and Raleigh in March. *The Story of a Novel* published April 21. On seventh and last European trip, attended Olympic Games. Quarreled with Maxwell Perkins.

1937 In May, made first visit to Asheville since *Look Homeward, Angel*. Spent the summer at a nearby mountain cottage. Then lived in semi-seclusion at a New York hotel. In December, signed a contract with Harpers.

1938 Worked strenuously on new fiction. In May, spoke at Purdue University and continued on to the Far West to tour national parks. In July, hospitalized in Seattle. After two operations at Johns Hopkins Hospital, died in Baltimore on September 15. Buried in family plot at Asheville.

1939 *The Web and the Rock* published June 22.

1940 *You Can't Go Home Again* published September 18.

1941 *The Hills Beyond* published October 15.

1945 Julia Westall Wolfe, Wolfe's mother, died December 7.

DESCRIPTION

What Is Synthesizing? Synthesizing is the opposite of analyzing. It is putting together separate bits of information about a main idea and showing the relations among them. You use it in grouping and summarizing separate bits of information you read in building a new structure, a new whole, around a main idea.

Why Is Synthesizing Valuable? Synthesizing is a powerful tool for problem solving. When you are solving a problem, any one selection you read usually won't have all the information you need. When you read several selections, you still have separate bits of information. You have to put the bits together in a way to answer your question and solve your problem. Synthesizing skills can help you put together material quickly and clearly.

How Do You Synthesize Information? You group different sources of information around certain categories. Both your sources and categories can be any separate sets of information: writers, topics or supporting ideas, time periods, questions, and so on.

Here are the main steps in synthesizing:

1. State your problem and questions clearly. They are the main idea you are working on.

2. Decide what categories you need to carry out your main idea. State your categories clearly and briefly. You will use these categories two ways: in selecting information and in grouping or classifying information. There are endless ways to categorize materials: for example, by topics, by time periods, by analogous sets, by reasons, and so on. Be very careful here. This is probably the hardest part of the synthesizing process and the most crucial.

3. Set up an array, a structure with columns and rows.
   a. Head your columns with your sources and your rows with your categories. (Or you can do it the other way around.)
   b. Put in a place for summary statements.
      Here is a diagram of an array.

CATEGORIES   **SOURCES**

	#1	#2	#3
#1			
#2			
#3			

Summary statements: _____

4. From each source, select that information which relates to your categories. When you are selecting, use the rapid search skills to quickly find only that information which fits the supporting idea you are working on. (See Part Two.) For each bit of information, use the skills for checking relevance to be sure the information truly fits. Rule out any information that doesn't fit. (See Chapter 10.)

5. Classify your bits of information according to the array. For category #1, note what source #1 said, what source #2 said, and so on through all sources and supporting ideas. When you are listing information, use the skills for summarizing and note-taking. (See Chapter 12.)

6. As it fits in to do so, make a summary statement for each category and across categories. For example: "All sources agree that _____." "The sources don't agree. Source #1 holds that _____, on the other hand, Source #2 says _____ (and so on)."

Are There Different Ways to Lay Out the Material You Pull Together? By all means. The array shown above is the basic tool. It helps you see the whole picture. However, sometimes it's mechanically hard to use in practice. Why? Because it is hard to get everything on a page and in the little boxes. And so, when you do a synthesis, set up an array so you'll have a blueprint of what you are doing. Then use any way to lay out the material which suits you and the material you are working on. Here are some sample ways to lay out material.

1. Use the array as it stands.

2. Move to a checksheet. For example, you can mark yes or no showing whether a writer agrees or disagrees with certain supporting ideas. Look at Practice Set 1 below. It shows how a checksheet works.

3. Move to an outline. For example:
   —Category #1
      —what source #1 says
      —what source #2 says
      —what source #3 says
      —summary statement
   —Category #2
      —what source #1 says
      —what source #2 says
      —what source #3 says
      —summary statement

To repeat: You can lay out the material in any way that suits you and the material you are working on. And from problem to problem you may use different ways. But ***always set up your basic array showing sources and*** *categories.* You wouldn't try to build a house without a blueprint. And you shouldn't try to build a selection without an array, its blueprint.

PRACTICE

In each practice set, look at the problem and question, the array, and the selections. Finish the synthesis.

Set 1. The Good Life[3]

Problem: To get information about "The Good Life."

Question: Given five writers, what are agreements and differences in their ideas about "The Good Life?"

Array: If a writer mentions a feature as helping make the good life, write yes. If not, leave the space blank.

Selected List of Features	Oates	Dyan	King	Mannes	Sternhell
1. Having knowledge and wisdom					
2. Giving and receiving love					
3. Helping others reach a good life					
4. Enjoying present small pleasures					
5. Having freedom to make choices					
6. Ending war and reaching peace					
7. Having courage to do only what one believes in and to be nothing but loved					
8. Being able to see humor in situations					
9. Having gratitude and reverence for others					

Summary statements: _____

_____

[3] These selections were chosen from the larger set in the feature: "The Good Life on Earth," *McCalls,* January 1970, pp. 29–38, 95. (Oates, 31; Sternhell, 36; King, 37; Mannes, 38; Dayan, 95). Used with permission.

JOYCE CAROL OATES

(The acclaimed young novelist whose most recent book is *them*. She is now at work on her first book of poetry.)

in love
we are drawn in a long curve
like the rising of light
across the photographed globe
in love
we taste other mouths
indifferent
original
in every earthly touch
in love we repeat motions
we repeat love
we repeat our rising of love
like the fierce scanning of light
across the moving earth

There is no good "life" here on earth, but many good lives—the possibility of a galaxy of good lives, each holy. And certainly we know this: if there is a good life for us, it must be here on earth, in this historical, chaotic, tragic, all-too-worldly earth, and nowhere else. The good life for me is equal to love, to loving. What is there to say about the miraculous verb "to love" after so many centuries of loving?

Writing of love, ideally, as I do in the poem that has been inspired by this essay, I am thinking of any object outside ourselves that is worthy of our deepest commitment. I am thinking, it is true, of a man; but I am thinking also of the repetitive motions of love we make for many people, our families, our friends, even those stray, chancy, promising people we never quite meet but whom we might well love in some other dimension. I am thinking of the many ways of love: of creativity in all its forms, which is a generous and sometimes devastating love, whether it consists of the writing of poetry or novels or the production of works of visual art or the slow, careful cultivation of a family, the creation of anything that lifts us from ourselves, forcing us out of ourselves.

The good life exists, here on earth: it exists in the act of loving.

CAROL RUTH STERNHELL

(The managing editor of the "Harvard Crimson" is 20 years old and a junior at Radcliffe. She is majoring in English.)

I am not certain that I believe in the good life at all any more, just as I am no longer sure that I believe in "education" or "social justice." It's common knowledge that the world is over; it ended with neither a bang nor a whimper but with a cartoon, a caricature, perhaps a curse. And it doesn't really matter, of course, that I am losing my mind. I am not the only one. We are all tired of trying, too tired to blunder on through the garbage that keeps piling up. We can, if we like, wallpaper our minds with the *Village Voice* instead of the *Wall Street Journal*, but we won't be any happier. And it seems that somewhere in a discussion of the good life there should be some brief mention of happiness.

On why the world is over: We are tearing ourselves apart. With systems and countersystems, labels and logic, the right and the left and fear. I'm not talking about the bomb here. If we do blow it all up, then none of this matters. I'm talking about the end of the world as we know it, competition and nine-to-five idealism, and about why the brightest people I know don't want to do anything any more but sit around, and talk, and smoke dope.

(The hip culture is not an answer. It is too easily corruptible. But it may turn out a harbinger of what must come.)

Consider: In a Cambridge candy store a child buys "Blitzkrieg, a game of lightning warfare"; above his head an airplane draws a peace symbol in the sky. A million people demonstrate to end our endless war. Almost nobody goes to classes at Harvard; the biggest news is the rumor of Beatle Paul McCartney's death. A man is shot at Berkeley and we whisper about the cultural revolution. Someone has stolen my doorknob. Classified advertisement: "If you seek the good life in a bad world, come for talk and applesauce to First Church Graveyard."

Take it as one of the givens: The good life is not what we have now. It never was. What frightens us so now is the (suppressed) comprehension that we're not even on the right tightrope. A little more money, a little more justice, a little more culture—we can't believe that any more, not really. God yes, equality—political, social, and economic—is better than the terrible inequality that we have today. But only somewhat; the revolution begins with the recognition of total absurdity. The real revolution does not lie with those who think they can destroy the system; if those who are the system understood this, they would welcome student radicals who try to reject their structures while living by their fundamental definitions. It is not those who attempt to break the system on its own terms that are the threat (or hope) but those who slide from under.

The point is to get out of it all. To break away from all systems, accept and embrace the world as insane. To have the courage to do nothing but what we really believe in, and to be nothing but loved.

CORETTA SCOTT KING

(Since her husband's death, her singleminded dedication to peace and justice has made her a world figure.)

The good life for me in the 1970's would be the realization of my desire to be sufficiently zealous in the pursuit of the Good. The most serious failure, to my mind, of so many of the "good" people of the first two thirds of the twentieth century has been their detachment, their lack of active concern about the problems which have now grown in such magnitude that we, at the close of the '60's, are only one mistake away from extinction.

The twin of material comfort for a large segment of our society has been moral cowardice. In the '70's I would like to see increasing numbers of persons become involved in the struggle to share the material abundance of this great land with those who are now poor. My wish is to see moral cowardice turned into moral courage.

Too long have we been our brother's keeper; in the '70's, I would hope to become my brother's sister and my sister's sister. I would like to see a slowing down and perhaps a reversal of the present trends toward polarization—black and white, young and old, the rich becoming richer and the poor getting poorer. May we learn from the convulsions of the '60's the lesson needed for the '70's: that our youth are trying to show us our hypocrisy; that black people must know who they are before they can become equal participants in a society now dominated by whites; that violence and the mood it creates can destroy all of us; that the underprivileged, or differently privileged, want to share in the American Dream; and that our nation can endure during the last third of this century only as one nation.

I pray that the kinds of power we discovered in the '60's—the power of youth, the power of the ballot, the power of group solidarity, the power of unselfish giving—can be translated in the '70's into the good life for many, many more of us, a world full of compassion and concern.

MARYA MANNES

(Outspoken social critic, author, and television commentator. She is the author of *They* and *More in Anger*.)

The good life exists only when you stop wanting a better one. It is the condition of savoring what is, rather than longing for what might be.

This is, of course, heresy in a society where the words *Better, More,* and *Newer* support the entire economy and a plateau of existence higher than that of any other people's.

But the noble premise of more for all has in one profound way worked against the good life for many. Rising expectations in those who have been deprived of nearly all material and spiritual needs are one thing. But the virtually limitless escalation of material desire which has been sold to the more fortunate in the name of "the good life" is another. The itch for things—brilliantly injected by those who make them and sell them—is in effect a virus draining the soul of contentment. A man never earns enough, a woman is never beautiful enough, clothes are never new enough, the house is never furnished enough, the food is never fancy enough.

There is a point at which salvation lies in stepping off the escalator, of saying, "Enough: What I have will do, what I make of it is up to me."

Sometimes I am tempted to believe that this salvation can come to us as a people only through a catastrophe that makes us all equal in poverty. We might then, in common survival, in common humanity, learn the values of living.

As it is, what some of us consider essential to the good life costs more and more each day: a deadly spiral locked into "rising expectations." Privacy—quiet—access to unhampered nature—even the simplest food and drink and shelter and clothing and hospitality—are, by most of us, dearly won. And for those who earn it by work largely devoid of pleasure or meaning, the life is no longer good.

Neither, in my view, is a life without the commitment of chosen labor. That is why I have always believed the creative life to be the best of lives. Here at least the discontent is interior, the demands made of self, not circumstance. When you ask of this self More and Better, of what earthly importance is a new slipcover?

Or, say, the place where you live is dark much of the day because it is on a low floor in a city. Black dirt sifts through the windows, and they often shake with the blast of horns. But twice a day the sun wheels through them, makes abstract patterns on the wall, irradiates a bowl, warms old wood, and excites the heart. The good life, you believe, is also the ability to relish the small pleasures even if you are denied the great ones.

And even the great ones—love and freedom—can lie within the disciplines of craft and search for truth.

YAEL DAYAN

(At 19, the daughter of Israel's military hero fought in her father's army. At 29, she has a new baby and a new book.)

Dan, who is ten months old, started walking this week. On the desk rests the beginning of my new book. It is not too cold outside, and something good is cooking in the oven. I find family life is so exciting and novel that I do very few things out of duty rather than choice.

In a small, selfish sense, this is my good life. The Good Life, in capitals, has a remote quality for me now, its distance realized only when I hear a news broadcast or read a newspaper.

It then becomes the absence rather than the presence of things: Not to see names of 18-year-old boys framed in black . . . Not to lose sons, husbands, fathers in a war which is endless and yet inevitable . . . Not to breathe the tense, heavy air of an isolated country fighting for survival . . . Not to look at my son and wonder whether he too will have to fight for what elsewhere is taken for granted—the right to live on his land.

A family came from Russia to Israel after years of persecution. Five years later their only son, a medical student, was killed by terrorists.

In Kibbutz Ein Harod, a man was killed in the War of Liberation in 1948; his son was killed a month ago on the Suez Canal. In Rosh-Pina, we have friends who lost two sons within six months.

This is my microcosmos. This is why for us the Good Life is simply *life itself*. It is not having to pay the top price of one's life for the most elementary rights—the right to have a home and to bring up children without wondering whether they will reach their twentieth birthday.

But once there is peace, the Good Life will be the freedom to choose. Not the choice between one danger and another, between existence and exile, but the choice of the good things . . . To enjoy the sun or the shade, the mountains or the sea, to work and rest and work again. Not the absence of worries, but to worry about the things which one can solve. Not to be idle, but to be fulfilled at work, and to have total freedom, but self-imposed discipline.

I have glanced at the good life. When the Six-Day War ended and we were certain peace would follow . . . When my son uttered his first cry . . . When men touched the surface of the moon and I knew man is not a slave to nature . . . When the gold light of sunset engulfs Jerusalem.

(How tragic it is to think that most elements of the good life are nature-given, while all the obstacles on the way to it are man-imposed.)

Perhaps one day I will think differently. Perhaps one day my idea of the Good Life will read like the menu at Maxim's and the advertisements for cruises to sunny islands. But meanwhile I remain modest. Let us have life and peace, and the Good Life will follow.

Set 2. Reflexes

Problem: To write a paper on reflexes.

Question: What is the nature of reflexes?

Array:

SOURCES

Categories	Gramet & Mandel	Eisman & Tanzer
Definition		
Characteristics		
Examples		
Values		

Summary statements: _____

THE NATURE OF REFLEXES[4]

Unlearned Behavior

Slaves of stimuli! The leaves of a plant must turn toward light. The stem must turn away from gravity. A paramecium must move toward a weak acid solution. Truly, such organisms are slaves of stimuli. We know that such responses are called tropisms. We know further that these unlearned responses of organisms without a nervous system or with a very simple nervous system are *inborn* and *automatic*.

But what of the animals that have a complex nervous system? Are they too slaves of stimuli? Pet a cat and he will arch his back. Rub the side of a dog and his hind leg on that side will scratch. Place your finger in the hand of a newborn baby and he will grasp it. Shine a light in your friend's eye and watch the pupil become very small. These responses, too, are all examples of unlearned behavior. They are inborn and automatic— but they are not movements toward or away from stimuli as tropisms are. Such inborn and automatic responses of organisms with a complex nervous system are called *reflex acts*.

[4] Charles Gramet and James Mandel, *Biology Serving You* (Englewood Cliffs, N.J.: Prentice-Hall, Inc., 1958), pp. 354–57. Abridged. Used with permission.

In a reflex act, you will usually find: (1) a stimulus, (2) a sensory neuron, which carries an impulse to a nerve center (the spinal cord or brain), (3) connections in the nerve center (association neuron and synapses), (4) a motor neuron from the nerve center to a part of the body, (5) a response.

The pathway through the sensory, association, and motor neurons is called a *reflex arc*. In most cases, the reflex arc uses many sensory, association, and motor neurons. The reflex responses are inborn, automatic acts.

Many reflexes do not need the brain; they take place through the spinal cord. The brain, however, as we shall soon see, may also act as a center for some reflexes.

Human Reflexes. You can explain how your reflexes work. Try this typical reflex. Cross one leg over the other and let the crossed leg hang freely; do not "tighten up." Now strike the leg with the edge of your palm just below the kneecap. When you hit the right spot, your leg will jump and you will not be able to stop it. This is called the *knee jerk* reflex. Doctors use it to test for certain conditions of the spinal cord.

In the knee jerk reflex, the stimulus is the pressure on the tendon just below the knee. A sensory impulse is carried to the spinal cord by sensory neurons. Here association neurons make connections with motor neurons that carry the impulse to the leg muscles, which contract so that the leg is raised.

The brain may also act as a center for some reflex acts. You are familiar with the blinking reflex. Pass your hand suddenly in front of the eyes of a friend and watch him blink his eyelids. You do so yourself when something moves toward your eyes. Another common reflex that you know well is the watering of the mouth at the sight or smell or taste of appetizing food. In these examples, the sensory impulses go to the brain and not to the spinal cord. In the blinking reflex, the brain sends a motor impulse to the muscles of the eyelids. In the mouth-watering, or salivary reflex, the impulse from the brain is called a secretory (se-cre'to-ry) impulse. It is carried by nerves to the salivary glands, and stimulates them to secrete saliva.

Importance of Reflex Acts. You can see that reflex acts are necessary for your very life. Automatic control lets you do reflex acts with little energy, with efficiency, and in the same way each time. You do not have to think to do them. That is what we mean when we say that reflex acts are automatic.

Many reflexes protect you. Thus, the blinking of your eyelids protects the delicate tissues of the eye from harmful particles. Blinking helps, also, to wash the surface of the eyeball and keep it free from dust and bacteria. When you jerk your hand away from a hot object or when you jerk your foot away from something sharp, you are automatically protecting yourself through reflex acts. A reflex act covers your windpipe when you swallow food to prevent you from choking. Coughing removes any particles of food that might accidentally get into the windpipe. Sneezing removes irritating substances from the nose.

WHAT ARE REFLEXES?[5]

How did the world seem to you when you were a newborn baby? Of course you don't remember anything about your feelings at that time, but careful study by scientists has given us much information about the behavior of very small babies. Perhaps you can add some observations of your own by watching your baby brother or sister closely throughout the day's activities.

The Activities of the Newborn Baby

The very young baby has no control over his movements because his muscles are not developed and his nervous system is untrained. He cannot turn his body but he can throw his arms about and kick his legs. He cannot hold his head steady. He cannot even move his eyes properly, and at times his eyes may look in different directions. A very young baby cannot reach for any object nor can he put food in his mouth. In fact, a newborn baby is so helpless that he could not survive if he were not cared for constantly. However, if you study the very young baby more closely, you will soon find that there are certain things that he can do very well. If you put your finger in his open palm his hand will close around it with a surprisingly strong grip. You know, of course, that he can breathe, that his heart beats, and that his digestive system can operate quite well. By painful experience, you have learned that babies can cry very loudly. From the way babies act when they are treated in different ways, scientists have learned a good deal about them. For example, we know that although they cannot see or hear very well, they have a very good sense of taste and smell. Because of their thin skins babies are very sensitive to touch, pain, and temperature changes. So you see that even right after birth there are some things that a baby can do as well as you can.

[5] Louis Eisman and Charles Tanzer, *Biology and Human Progress* (4th ed.) (Englewood Cliffs, N.J.: Prentice-Hall, Inc., 1972), 180–84. Abridged. Used with permission.

Reflex Acts

Almost all of the actions a newborn baby performs, such as breathing, the beating of his heart, and sucking to get food, are actions over which he has no control. The baby is born with the ability to perform these acts, and they are necessary to enable him to remain alive. Many of your own daily activities are of this type. Such acts are known as reflexes (ree'-flex-es).

On your way to school on a windy day, you may have had a tiny speck of dust enter your eye. Immediately, tears began to flow in such quantities that they ran down your cheeks. Your eyelids kept fluttering, moving the particle about. In most cases, these two activities would be enough to wash the dust out of the eye. Like most reflexes, they were beyond your control. In fact, most of the time you do not even know when you are performing a reflex act. The event that starts the reflex going (in this case, the grain of dust entering the eye) is called a stimulus (stim'-you-lus). What your body does after the stimulus has acted is called the response (ree-sponse'). In this case, the response is the fluttering of the eyelids and the flow of tears.

Here are some reflexes that you perform every day:

Stimulus	*Reflex Response*

1. Drying of the eyeball
  Small object entering the eye
  Object coming near the eye
	1. Blinking of the eyelid

2. Sudden loud noise	2. Whole body jumps
3. Sharp or hot object on hand or foot	3. Quickly removing hand or foot
4. Food in mouth	4. Flow of saliva in the mouth
5. Danger of falling	5. Balancing yourself
6. Very bright light	6. Pupil of the eye gets smaller
7. Very weak light	7. Pupil of the eye gets larger
8. Food in back of mouth	8. Swallowing
9. Dust in the nose	9. Sneezing
10. Dust or smoke in windpipe	10. Coughing
11. Rise in room temperature	11. Sweating
12. Sudden chill	12. Goose pimples on skin

All Reflexes are Alike in These Ways

1. You are *born* with the ability to perform your reflex actions. A baby will sneeze if his nostrils are tickled with a feather. The same response takes place in an adult.

2. A reflex is a response that you *cannot control*. You cannot stop the flow of tears if you have a speck of dust in your eye, no matter how hard you try.

3. A reflex is completely *automatic*. It is performed in exactly the same way each time. There is no thinking on your part. In most cases, you do not even know that you have carried out a reflex response.

How Reflexes Help You to Stay Alive

Harry was on his way to school in a great hurry. As he ran along, he kept thinking of what would happen if he arrived late for his first class. His teacher had spoken to him very seriously the last time he was late. She had explained the importance of developing the habit of being on time. Suddenly he tripped over a curbstone and his books went flying in all directions as he fell heavily, face forward. After a moment, he was able to pick himself up off the ground. Fortunately he was not badly hurt. But then he looked at his hands. They were dirty, scratched, and bloody. As he picked up his books, Harry wondered how he had been able to throw up his hands quickly enough to save his face from serious injury. He had done this automatically, without thinking. It was another case of a reflex act being performed in time to protect him against harm.

Reflexes Protect You Against Injury

Perhaps you do not realize how many times you have been protected by your reflexes in a similar manner. Have you ever jumped out of the way just in time as an automobile horn sounded its warning? Have you ever pulled your hand away after touching a hot object unexpectedly? These are examples of how your reflexes saved you from injury or even from death. When a former heavyweight champion lost his last title fight, many of the experts said that he was beaten because his reflexes had become so slow that he had difficulty in avoiding the blows of his opponent.

Reflexes Control Your Internal Organs

Not only do reflexes protect us against injury, but many of them are so important that we could not stay alive for long without them. Most of our internal organs are controlled by reflexes. Although you may not be aware of your breathing or the beating of your heart, these functions are being carried on each minute of the day and night. The flow of our stomach juices is a reflex act. Food is carried through our intestines by muscles that contract as a result of reflexes. Think how busy you would be if you had no reflexes. You would have to make your heart beat, you would have to think about breathing, about making your digestive juices flow, about blinking your eyes, about controlling the muscles of your intestines, and about many other things. You could not sleep. You would not have time for study or play. Your food would probably not be digested properly. You could not stay alive for long without your reflexes.

Set 3. Themes About Literature

Problem: To understand two kinds of themes: character analysis and comparison and contrast.

Question: Do you do the two themes the same way or do you do them differently? That is, how much are the themes alike and how much are they different?

Array:

Type of Theme

Category	Character Analysis	Comparison and Contrast
Purpose of the Theme		
Problems of Writing the Theme		
Organization — Introduction		
Organization — Body		
Organization — Conclusion		

Summary statements: _____

_____

_____

WHAT IS A THEME?[6]

As you begin any of the following assignments, you should consider the following ideas about the nature of themes. A theme should be a

[6] These selections were chosen from Edgar V. Roberts, *Writing Themes About Literature* 2nd ed., © 1969. ("What Is a Theme?" pp. xxi–xxii; "The Theme of Character Analysis," pp. 10–20; "The Comparison-Contrast Theme," pp. 70–78. All were abridged.) By permission of Prentice-Hall, Inc., Englewood Cliffs, New Jersey.

short, accurate, and forceful presentation of ideas or descriptions, well contrived as a totality or unity. A theme should not ramble in any way, but should be clearly united around a dominating thought or *central idea*. A theme is a brief "mind's full" on any particular subject; that is, it presents and considers the subject in several of its various aspects. The theme cannot cover all aspects, as might a book or a long essay.

There are two basic needs that you must always remember: the first is for a *central idea* or *point*, and the second is for a *clearly ascertainable organization*.

THE CENTRAL IDEA OR POINT

Themes are so named because throughout the composition called a *theme* there runs a basic or central idea—a theme—that unifies the paper into a logical whole. On every subject you encounter there should be some dominating idea or mood that will suggest itself to you or one that you will derive from your own intensive concentration. For example, when you look at a room, you might feel that it is cheerful; when you listen to the latest news, you might decide that it is depressing. Were you to write a theme describing the room or another discussing the news, you would have to keep your central idea foremost in your reader's mind *throughout* your theme, or else you would not have a theme.

You should first bring out your central idea in the introduction. State your point clearly, for your reader must be left in no doubt about what you wish to assert. Your point might be that the story is well unified, or that it is about the folly of attempting what is beyond man's power, or about the necessity for dedication regardless of the consequences, and so on. Throughout your theme, you must constantly keep reminding your reader that your material is relevant to the point you have made; you must always emphasize the connection between your dominant idea and whatever you are saying at the moment. Anything not relevant to your point does not belong in the theme.

The need for a central idea will also make you aware of the need for paragraph transitions, because you are proving or showing *one* central idea, not a *number* of ideas. Transitions form bridges to connect one part of the theme with another; having a central idea always in mind makes continuity between paragraphs both essential and natural.

ORGANIZING YOUR THEME AROUND THE CENTRAL IDEA

Once you have thought of a central idea, you should make notes of materials that support it. You will need to treat these materials in order, and in your introduction you should write a sentence that describes this order. This sentence is called a *thesis sentence*. Thus the introduction is important for your whole theme: first because it announces the central idea, and second because it announces the pattern of the theme, through which the central idea should be carefully woven.

As the whole theme is organized around the thesis sentence, each paragraph should be organized around a *topic sentence.*

The Theme of Character Analysis

An extremely popular theme subject, particularly in courses in drama and novel, is the analysis of character.

If you recollect some of the novels and dramas you have read or seen, you will realize that they are about characters, their reactions to an extended series of actions, and their attempts, both successful and unsuccessful, to shape those events. The novel and the drama are similar because they show the interactions of character and action in rather full detail. To these genres one might add epic and narrative poetry, which also center on character and action. Short stories and poems do not aim at the broadness and fullness of the larger forms but concentrate on only the essential high points of human experience.

WHAT IS CHARACTER?

Although sometimes we use the word *character* synonymously with "person," "human being," and "literary figure," more often we use it in reference to an individual's personal qualities and characteristics. Both senses should be retained (we can speak about the "character" of a character), but the second sense will be amplified here.

Other words used as either equivalents or modifications of character are *psyche, soul, ego, consciousness, moral fiber, being,* and many others. What is probably meant by all these terms, however, is the sum total of typical qualities and propensities in any given individual that are controlled by that individual's drives, aims, ideals, morals, and ideas of conscience. These qualities are manifested in his behavior under any set of circumstances, and we make observations about his character by drawing inferences from this behavior. Always, the character we are talking about is something that exists somewhere and somehow *within* that individual, or simultaneously *with* him. It is the uniqueness or typicality of that something that concerns us as we discuss the character of the individual. Most persons desire to get ahead in the world, but what makes our friends John and Tom unique is that John works ten hours a day to get ahead while Tom works five. In discussing John and Tom, we would note this behavior (assuming that it results from choice) and attempt to make inferences about their character from it and from other behavior.

It is by such an inferential process that we learn about our fellow human beings, and if our inferences lead us to liking, this process (on both sides) leads us to form our friendships. We perceive the qualities of the person who is our friend by our contacts with him. We learn about his strengths and weaknesses by observing his speech and action and by listening to him as he communicates his thoughts and emotions to us. If we want to learn more about a particular quality, we ask him about it. With people who are not close to us, however, we are unable to acquire such information, and hence we have no very clear idea of their characters. This difficulty is even more pronounced when we, as voters, are asked to pass judgment on men who run for public office. These men therefore spend much time and energy, as do their campaign managers and aides, to project an "image" of themselves as men of fine, worthy character. The information we gain about them, however, must be supplemented with the comments of political analysts and opponents.

In studying character in literature, we approach a situation more like that of getting to know the public man than that of getting to know our friend. (Note this difference: the author usually attempts to describe every facet of the character, good and bad, not just those traits which create a one-sided view.) We can understand the qualities of a literary character only by interpreting what the author has written about him. All the character's actions, plus what he says and what is said about him, provide us with the only material from which we can make inferences, and we can expect no more than what the author has chosen to disclose.

HOW IS CHARACTER DISCLOSED IN LITERATURE?

Your first problem in character analysis is to find out how the writer chooses to disclose character. Here are four ways in which a writer usually shows character.

1. By what the personage himself says (and thinks, from the author's third person omniscient point of view).
2. By what the character does.
3. By what other characters say about him.
4. By what the author says about him, speaking as either the storyteller or an observer of the action.

These four points require amplification.

1. What a particular character says about himself may frequently be accepted at face value for truth, but just as often it may be only a reflection of his intellectual and emotional state at a given moment. If a character in deep despair says that life is worthless, for example, you

must balance that statement with what the same character says when he is happy. Then too, you must consider the situation in the literary work when a statement is made. If a character voices despair at the start, but is cheerful (or sad) at the end, there has been a development, or change, in that character's view of life. In *Crime and Punishment*, for example, Raskolnikov is convinced of his right to make judgments on the lives of other people, but at the end of the novel he doubts his right. A shift has taken place that any analysis of his qualities must consider. As you can see, you are free to interpret what a personage says in the light of the context in which it appears.

Most of the above applies to what a personage thinks as it is reported to us by the author acting as an omniscient narrator. If you detect differences between what the personage thinks and what he says, you may be sure that the author is demonstrating some quality of character, either (a) favorable, if the discrepancy is part of a worthwhile strategy, or (b) unfavorable, if the discrepancy is part of a worthless or ignoble one.

2. You have heard that what you do speaks louder than what you say. The same is true in literature, and sometimes actions illustrate important character traits. An author may create a character who professes honesty yet does dishonorable things. Uriah Heep in *David Copperfield* and Tartuffe in Molière's play *Le Tartuffe* have such characteristics. Iago in *Othello* is another case in point: he professes to be Othello's friend, but secretly behaves like a devil. In analyzing what characters do, you must ask whether the character's actions are consistent with his words. If not, why not? What does the author communicate by showing inconsistencies? In the three examples just cited, the authors succeed in showing the diabolical nature of hypocrisy.

Exposing hypocrisy, however, might not be the reason for showing gaps between statement and action. This technique may illustrate ideas like "Human beings have a great capacity for self-deception," or "Human beings are weak." An author may show characters behaving consistently with what they say as a mark of favor to these characters (or also as a mark of credit to a rogue who is honest with himself like Peachum in John Gay's play *The Beggar's Opera*).

3. In literature, as in life, people are always talking about other people. What they say of course raises the problem of *point of view*, because the character and motivation of a personage will condition whatever he says about someone else. You know, for example, that the word of a person's enemy is usually biased against that person. Therefore, an author may frequently give you a favorable impression of a character by having a bad character say bad things about him. Similarly, the word of a close friend or political manager may be biased in favor of a particular character. In short, you must always consider the context and source of all dramatic

remarks about a particular character. In Conrad's *Victory*, for example, an evil hotel manager named Schomberg always claims that the hero, Heyst, is a villain. The reader is to believe the opposite of what Schomberg says about Heyst, because Schomberg seems to be attributing his own evil motives to Heyst. By contrast, in *Macbeth*, when Macduff and Malcolm say that Macbeth and his rule in Scotland are bad, their statements should be accepted as truth because the two men are presented as honest, just, and good.

4. What the author says about a character is usually to be accepted as truth about that character. Naturally, the author must be accepted absolutely on matters of fact in the narrative or drama. But when in his own person he interprets the actions and characteristics of his characters, he himself assumes the role of critic, and his opinions are open to question. For this reason, authors frequently avoid making overt interpretations, and devote their skill instead to arranging events in the drama or narrative so that their own conclusions are obvious to the reader. If the author chooses to present an analysis of character, however, he might resort to a personage in the work who will then be bound by his own limitations as an observer. In this case, the dramatic commentator is like the characters discussed in paragraph 3.

JUDGING THE COMPLETENESS OF CHARACTER DEVELOPMENT

Literary characters should be "true to life under given conditions," and to this phrase should be added another one, "within certain literary specifications." Your second problem in your study of character should always be to discover if the character—whether intended by the author to be a full, complete, round, lifelike personage, a romantic hero, or an absurdist abstraction—is related to your concept of what human beings might reasonably be expected to do and say under the exact conditions presented by the author. Does the character ring true, or do the qualities of character presented in him ring true? In other words, does he come to life? Does he illustrate many qualities that add up to a really complete facsimile of a human being, or does he seem to be flat, one-sided, one-dimensional? Lola, a minor figure in Dreiser's *Sister Carrie*, is such a character; we see little in her beyond the fact that she is a wordly-wise working girl in a chorus line. On the other hand, Stephen Dedalus in Joyce's *Portrait of the Artist* is totally realized, because his thoughts, words, responses, and actions are described fully from earliest consciousness to young adulthood. The degree to which an author can make a character come alive is a mark of his skill; if you think that your author is successful in this regard, you should say so in your theme.

The Organization of Your Theme

As always, your theme should have a clearly stated central idea that runs throughout your entire character analysis. Your central idea here will be whatever general statement you make to describe the character you analyze. Your thesis sentence must be a brief statement of the main sections of the body of your theme.

Your organization is designed to illustrate and prove your central idea. You have much freedom in organizing your main points. Some possible methods are the following:

1. Organization around central characteristics, like "kindness, gentleness, generosity, firmness," or "resoluteness of will frustrated by inopportune moments for action, resulting in despondency, doubt, and melancholy." A body containing this sort of material would demonstrate how the literary work brings out each of these qualities.

2. Organization around central incidents that reveal primary characteristics (see, for example, the sample theme). Certain key incidents will stand out in a work, and you might create an effective body by using three or four of these as guides for your discussion, taking care to show in your topic sentences that your purpose in this arrangement is to illuminate the character you have selected, not the incidents. In other words, you would regard the incidents only as they bring out truths about character.

   Naturally, with this arrangement, you would have to show how the incidents bring out the characteristics and also how they serve to explain other things the character might do.

3. Organization around various sections of the work. This arrangement is particularly effective if you are demonstrating that a character is undergoing changes and developments. In analyzing the character of Iago, for example, you might say that up to Act II, Scene iii of *Othello* he behaves in a reasonably motivated way, that from there to Act V he behaves like a devil, and that in Act V he becomes an enigma.

The conclusion should contain your statements about how the characteristics you have brought out are related to the work as a whole. If the personage was good but came to a bad end, does this discrepancy elevate him to tragic stature? If he was a nobody and came to a bad end, does this fact cause you to draw any conclusion about the class or type of which he was a part? Or does it illustrate the author's view of human life? Or both? Do the characteristics explain why the personage helps or hinders other characters in the literary work? Does your analysis help you to clear up any misunderstanding that your first reading of the work produced? Questions like these should be raised and answered in your conclusion.

SAMPLE THEME

The Character of Jim in Conrad's *Lord Jim*

Jim is difficult to understand. He is seen mainly through the eyes of Marlow, who imparts his own values to much of the story. He is also the subject of much interpretation by other informants in the story, so that we receive many views of him. In addition, Jim is the principal figure in a richly symbolic tapestry, so that much of what he does and says is relevant to most people at most times. In this respect his individuality is sacrificed to his existence as a symbol. Despite these difficulties, however, Jim emerges as a fully developed individual, even though we do not hear of every detail that might ever have concerned him. *The key to understanding Jim's character is that he is a man capable of imagining the best in himself and in men generally—a man whose action at any given moment is controlled by an idea of the best.* (central idea) He is, in Stein's word, a "romantic," and I would add that he is an introspective dreamer. *His character is made clear by three incidents in the novel, all of which are connected with leaps, or jumps, that Jim either makes or does not make.* (thesis sentence)

When Jim has his first opportunity to leap, he does not take it. This failure to jump is symbolic of Jim's preference for mental over physical heroism. It hurts his own high evaluation of himself. Imbued with the British ideals of manhood and adventure in the days of the naval empire, he has been dreaming of his own "devotion to duty" in a way "as unflinching as a hero in a book." But when the opportunity comes to join in a rescue operation, he misses the boat. He does not jump. From this point Jim becomes a drifter, for this failure has given him a hint of the basic indecision (*cowardice* would be too strong a word at this point) which is worrying the bubble of his own self-esteem. This one incident, in short, explains the moral laziness which finally causes him to ship aboard the *Patna*.

The bubble of Jim's esteem is totally destroyed by his second jump—from the *Patna* when it is listing heavily and supposedly near sinking. This jump is the major incident in the novel, since it brings out the depths of Jim's being, that inner panic which destroys all his conscious dreams by causing a single cowardly act despite his good intentions. This jump brings out Jim's sense of shame, which must be overwhelming, since it causes him to wander all over the Indian Ocean, fleeing whenever anybody mentions the *Patna* episode. With his depths thus exposed, I believe that Jim feels morally naked, without the privacy that most of us have, since we know, or hope, that the depths of our own souls may never emerge to haunt us. Jim's emerges, and he runs from it, as run he must.

But the *Patna* jump also emphasizes Jim's good qualities. He has a high sense of justice and before he runs he therefore faces trial, which can end in nothing but his dishonor and disgrace. His conscious dream of what is right has enabled him to face the consequences of his real guilt. Perhaps this facing of the trial when all the other deserters flee is the start of Jim's awareness, acted upon but never clearly stated by him, that life constantly demands expiation for guilt that is caused not entirely by our own choice.

Jim's final leap results from his own choice, however, and as such it enables him finally to live out his dream. It is a kind of triumph. Leaping over the fence enclosing Rajah Allang's courtyard, he allies himself with Doramin, and proceeds quickly to justify the title *Lord Jim* by acting wisely, in concert with Doramin, in governing the forlorn outpost of Patusan. He is convinced of the value of his dream, and always behaves with justice, honor, and firmness, yet always with forgiveness. These are the conscious virtues, to which Jim adheres closely, since they are the embodiment of his character as a dreamer.

This adherence explains why he accepts the final responsibility for the death of Dain Waris. Beyond question, his third leap has enabled him to dedicate himself to the good life in Patusan as expiation for his guilt in the *Patna* episode. The personal quality of this dedication should be stressed, however, and contrasted with the quality of Jim's feelings after Gentleman Brown commits his treacherous act. In this affair Jim is responsible only for not having destroyed the Gentleman *before* the murder is committed. Yet, in Gentleman Brown, Jim apparently sees that the cowardly depths are common to all mankind, not just to himself. So Jim faces Doramin in expiation, just as he had earlier braved the court and the subsequent disgrace. But as Jim sacrifices himself, the best in him, his capacity to dream, triumphs over whatever it was that made him leap from the *Patna*. He is genuinely great at that moment of sacrifice, when he expiates for us all.

Admittedly, Jim is a puzzling character, since his characteristics show that human life is a mystery and since we never really get inside him. But Conrad uses him to demonstrate that, if life has its depths, it also has its high points. At the highest point, a human being willing to live out his dream, if this dream has value and ennobles mankind, can justify the claim that life is elevated and great. Jim, with all his frailty, is a truly great representation of a human being, since he has met and conquered life's greatest obstacle—the deflation of one's own high self-esteem.

The Comparison-Contrast Theme

A popular theme subject is the comparison of different authors, of two or more works by the same author, of different drafts of the same work, or of different characters, incidents, and ideas within the same work or in different works. Your instructor may assign this theme in many ways, such as "Compare X and Y" or "Discuss the idea of Z in such-and-such works." No matter how the assignment is made, your job is to write a comparison-contrast theme. This assignment requires detailed study and a thorough consideration of a much wider range of material than is needed to write a theme about a single work, idea, character, or author.

COMPARISON-CONTRAST AS A WAY TO KNOWLEDGE

Comparison and contrast are important means to the gaining of understanding. If you have ever looked at your hands together, for example, you probably just saw two hands, but if you put your hands next to someone else's you quickly were able to see salient characteristics of your own simply because of the contrast. You realize that hands are hands, with all their identical qualities, but you also perceive differences between yours and the other person's. In short, similarities between things are brought out by *comparison,* and differences are brought out by *contrast.* The essences of objects and artistic works can be quickly illustrated by use of the comparison-contrast method.

INTENTION

Do not begin to write this, or any theme, without a plan or intention. *Your first problem* is to decide your objective. You ought to relate the material of the assignment to the purposes of the course, for the comparison-contrast method can be focused on a number of points. One focal point may simply be the equal and mutual illumination of both (or more) subjects of comparison; thus, in a survey course, where your purpose is to gain a general understanding of all the writers in the course, a theme about Milton and Pope would serve to describe the methods of both poets without throwing primary attention on either.

THE NEED TO FIND COMMON GROUNDS FOR COMPARISON

Your second problem is to select the proper material—the grounds of your discussion. It is useless to compare essentially dissimilar things, for then your basic conclusions will be of limited value. Therefore, your task is to put the works or writers you are comparing onto common ground. Compare like with like; that is, style with style, subject with subject, idea with idea, structure with structure, characterization with characterization, prosody with prosody, milieu with milieu, evaluation with evaluation, and so on. Putting your subjects on common ground makes you arrive at a reasonable basis of comparison and therefore a legitimate occasion for contrast. Nothing can be learned, for example, from a comparison of "Pope's style and Milton's philosophy." But much can be learned from a comparison of "the influence of philosophy on style in Milton and Pope." The first promises little, whereas the second suggests common ground, with points of both comparison and divergence and with further implications about the ages in which the two poets lived.

In attempting to find common ground, seek possible similarities as you prepare yourself by reading and taking notes for the assignment. Here your generalizing powers will assist you, for apparently dissimilar materials may meet—if you are able to perceive the meeting place. Thus a comparison of *The House of Mirth* by Edith Wharton and *The Catcher in the Rye* by J. D. Salinger might put the works on the common ground of "The Treatment of the 'Outsider'" or "Corrosive Influences of an

Affluent Society on the Individual" or "The Basis of Social Criticism," even though the works are about different characters living in different ages. As you can see, what appears at first dissimilar can often be put into a frame of reference that permits analytical comparison and contrast. Much of your success in writing will depend on your ingenuity in finding a suitable basis for comparison.

METHODS OF COMPARISON

Let us assume that you have decided on your rhetorical purpose and on the basis or bases of your comparison: you have done your reading, taken your notes, and know what you want to say. The remaining problem is the treatment of your material. Here are two acceptable ways.

A common, but inferior, way is to make your points first about one work and then to do the same for the other. This method makes your paper seem like two big lumps, and it also involves much repetition because you must repeat the same points as you treat your second subject. The first method, in other words, is only satisfactory—it is no better than a C method.

The superior method is to treat your main idea in its major aspects and to make references to the two (or more) writers as the reference illustrates and illuminates your main idea. Thus you would be constantly referring to both writers, sometimes within the same sentence, and would be reminding your reader of the point of your discussion. There are reasons for the superiority of the second method: (a) you do not need to repeat your points unnecessarily, for you can document them as you raise them; (b) by referring to the two writers in relatively close juxtaposition in relation to a clearly stated basis of comparison, you can avoid making a reader with a poor memory reread previous sections.

The Organization of Your Theme

INTRODUCTION

State what works, authors, characters, and ideas are under consideration, then show how you have narrowed the basis of your comparison. Your central idea will be a brief statement of what can be learned from your paper: the general similarities and differences that you have observed from your comparison and/or the superiority of one work or author over another. Your thesis sentence should anticipate the body of your theme.

BODY

The body of your theme depends on the points you have chosen for comparison. You might be comparing two works on the basis of *structure*, *tone, style,* two authors on *ideas,* or two characters on *character traits.* In your discussion you would necessarily use the same methods that you would use in writing a theme about these terms in a single work, except that here (a) you are exemplifying your points by reference to more subjects than one, and (b) your ultimate rhetorical purpose is the illumination of the subjects on which your comparison is based. In this sense, the methods you use in talking about *structure* or *style* are not "pure" but are instead subordinate to your aims of comparison-contrast. Let us say that you are comparing the ideas in two different works. The first part of your theme might be devoted to the analysis and description of the similarities and dissimilarities of the ideas *as* ideas. Your interest here is not so much to explicate the ideas of either work separately as to explicate the ideas of both works in order to show points of agreement and disagreement. A second part might be given over to the influences of the ideas on the *structure* and *style* of the particular works, that is, how the ideas help make the works similar or dissimilar. Or, let us say that your subjects of comparison are two or more characters. Your points might be to show similarities and dissimilarities of mental and spiritual qualities and of activities in which the characters engage.

CONCLUSION

In this section you should bring out the conclusions that have emerged from your study. If your writers were part of a "school" or "period," you might show how your findings relate to these larger movements. You also should illustrate the limitations and implications of your treatment; you might show that more could be done along the same lines, and what might be the effects of pursuing the method further.

SAMPLE THEME

The Use of Westward in Wordsworth's "Stepping Westward"
and in Donne's "Good Friday, 1613, Riding Westward"

The reason for comparing these two poems is obvious from the titles, and the similarities become more obvious as a person reads the poems. Both employ "westward" as the direction in which the speakers move. As they move, they become aware of death, since the west—where the sun sets and the day dies—is the traditional direction symbolizing death. The reality of this situation causes the speakers to meditate on religion and philosophy. There is a difference in the ways in which the speakers move. Wordsworth's speaker is *stepping* westward, while Donne's is riding (*i.e.,* being carried). If these actions can be interpreted symbolically, Wordsworth may be suggesting that his speaker's will is governing him, whereas Donne may be suggesting that his speaker's will is subordinate to something external. The poems tend to bear out this distinction. My feeling is that the differences in these poems are more noteworthy than the similarities and that Donne's poem emerges as better, more forceful, and more realistic than

Wordsworth's. This superiority can be seen clearly in the ideas that both poets have about the forces that govern life.

The idea of moving westward prompts both poets to be concerned with the nature of life once the fact of death has been taken into account. Death is, in other words, the one unavoidable fact that causes everyone to pause and think. On the nature of life, Wordsworth seems to be raising a question that Donne has already answered. Wordsworth's poem asks whether we are governed by chance—the *"wildish destiny"*—or whether we are controlled by *"heavenly"* forces. Naturally, he opts for the "heavenly" destiny to guide him on his "end-less way." Donne does not raise this question, however, for there is no doubt in his mind that the heavenly destiny exists; his idea, instead, is that his speaker is riding *away* from his destiny, since God is in the East, and "Pleasure" and "businesse" are whirling his "Soule," like a "Spheare" westward away from God. On a nonparadoxical level, Donne uses this opposition of East and West to bring out a conflict between faith and human frailty—a conflict that is far different from the relative calm in Wordsworth's poem.

Donne's poem is not only more agitated than Wordsworth's, but it contains images demonstrating that Donne is out after bigger game than Wordsworth. The first image is described by the sentence "Let man's Soule be a Spheare." The individual soul, from this image, is a world in itself over which the forces of good and evil contend, and the loss of any individual is of cosmic significance to God. I have sought unsuccessfully for anything of comparable imaginative force in Wordsworth's poem. Donne's other image is that of Christ on the Cross, a symbol at once of both death and life, who, in Donne's paradoxical expression, by dying made death an entry way into life. The westward direction of travel therefore becomes not only the direction of death but also of life— heavenly life—since it ultimately is the direction in which one must travel in order to see God:

Hence is't, that I am carryed towards the West
This day, when my Soules forme bends towards the East.
There I should see a Sunne, by rising set,
And by that setting endlesse day beget;
But that Christ on this Crosse, did rise and fall,
Sinne had eternally benighted all.
—lines 9–14

This short passage, ending with the word *all*, demonstrates that man's soul is in the balance. The conflict is thus not just personal, it is typical of all men. On the one hand they see the good, but on the other they do not follow it, and so the conflict is cosmic. But as they avoid God, they move toward death, which is another and more permanent way to God.

Donne's world, in short, is much more complex and difficult than Words-worth's. I do not imply that Wordsworth interprets life as easy, for "In a strange Land and far from home" his speaker feels that "The dewy ground was dark and cold; / Behind, all gloomy to behold"; (4, 9, 10). But Wordsworth is simply not as forceful as Donne. As a result, after Wordsworth's speaker decides that his destiny is "heavenly," the dark, dewy ground is transformed into a "region bright" (16). This change seems a little too simple, a little too pat. By contrast, Donne's world (the soul) is constantly "Subject to forraigne motions," which drive it away from its heavenly destiny, corroding it and deforming it. His speaker therefore ends the poem in anguished prayer, asking God to purify his life so that he can withstand death:

O thinke mee worth thine anger, punish mee,
Burne off my rusts, and my deformity,
Restore thine Image, so much, by thy grace,
That thou mayst know mee, and I'll turne my face.
—lines 39–42

Thus, for Donne, the only salvation in this difficult life is God's love, which enabled endurance upon the Cross, where His flesh was "rag'd and torne" (28). Paradoxically again, God dying on the Cross is a sight on which the speaker "durst not looke"; consequently, his ride westward is an almost inevitable result of his own weakness, for which God is the only remedy. These are contorted, tortuous ideas, which are sharply in contrast with Wordsworth's emphasis on "human sweetness" and "The very sound of courtesy." Both ideas are in accord so far as they account for the individual's dependency for support on something external, but Donne's thought is full of pain, uncertainty, anguish, and paradox, whereas Wordsworth's is characterized by calm, certainty, and simplicity.

The principal difference between the two poems is that Donne's view of life is fuller, rounder than Wordsworth's. Wordsworth's problem ends where Donne's begins. This difference is perhaps the same one that exists between a fairy tale ending on the note that "They lived happily ever after" and a modern novel that treats the problems and anguish that frequently appear in adult life. This difference applies only to these two poems, for Wordsworth brings out personal conflicts elsewhere: poems like *The Prelude*, the "Ode to Duty," and the "Immortality" ode illustrate that life, to him, was not pure unruffled calm. Nor does he, presumably, have in his poem the idea of the Crucifixion before him, as Donne of course did on Good Friday. But even in these poems one does not find a view of life comparable in forcefulness to what Donne shows in his poem about the errant soul's westward departure from God hanging "upon the tree" (36).

ANSWERS FOR PRACTICE SETS

Set 1. The Good Life

Selected List of Features	Oates	Dayan	King	Mannes	Sternhell
1. Having knowledge and wisdom					
2. Giving and receiving love	yes				
3. Helping others reach a good life			yes		
4. Enjoying present small pleasures				yes	
5. Having freedom to make choices		yes			
6. Ending war and reaching peace		yes			
7. Having courage to do nothing but what one believes in and to be nothing but loved					yes

Selected List of Features	Oates	Dayan	King	Mannes	Sternhell
8. Being able to see humor in situations					
9. Having gratitude and reverence for others					

Summary statements: The five writers mention different features as helpful to the good life. Many things can help make a good life. And what is most important to one person may not be the most important to another. Here are the things these writers said were important to them: Oates, giving and receiving love; Dayan, having freedom to make choices and ending war and reaching peace; King, helping others reach a good life; Mannes, enjoying present small pleasures; Sternhell, having courage to do only what one believes in and to be nothing but loved.

Set 2. The Nature of Reflexes

1. Definition

(1) Gramet and Mandel

Reflexes are inborn and automatic responses of organisms with a complex nervous system.

(2) Eisman and Tanzer

Reflexes are actions you do not control, actions you are born with, actions that are automatic.

2. Characteristics

(1) Gramet and Mandel

A reflex act involves five things: a stimulus, a sensory nerve, connections in the nerve center, a motor nerve, and a response. The center for some reflexes is the spinal cord; for others, the brain.

(2) Eisman and Tanzer

The event that starts a reflex going is called a stimulus. What your body does after the stimulus has acted is called the response.

3. Examples

(1) Gramet and Mandel

Here are a few examples: a dog's scratching when you rub his side; the pupil getting smaller when you shine a light in the eye; the leg jumping when you strike the knee in the right place; the mouth watering at the sight of food.

(2) Eisman and Tanzer

Here are some examples: breathing; a baby's crying, palm grasp, and sucking; the blinking of an eyelid when an object comes near the eye; the jumping of the whole body at a sudden loud noise; coughing when something gets in the windpipe.

4. Values

   (1) Gramet and Mandel

  Reflexes protect you from injury and pain.

   (2) Eisman and Tanzer

  Reflexes protect you from injury. They keep you alive by controlling your internal organs.

5. Summary statements

  The two sets of writers give their information in slightly different ways. But they agree about the nature of reflexes.

Definition. Reflexes are inborn acts which are automatic and beyond our control.

Characteristics. Reflexes start with a stimulus; they go through the nervous system (a sensory nerve, either the brain or the spinal cord as a nerve center, and a motor nerve); and they end up with a response.

Examples. A few examples of reflexes are the knee-jerk response, the eye blink response, breathing, a baby's crying, and coughing when something gets in the windpipe.

Values. Reflexes help us to stay alive and to avoid injury and pain.

Set 3

1. Purpose of the Theme

   (1) Character analysis

  To understand the qualities of a literary character by interpreting what the author has written about him. That is, to make inferences on the basis of the character's actions, plus what he says and what is said about him.

   (2) Comparison-contrast

  To understand the characteristics of more than one writer, work, character, and so on by looking at their similarities and differences.

2. Problems

   (1) Character analysis

  To find out how the writer chooses to disclose character.

  To discover (and say so) if the character rings true, if he is related to your concept of what human beings might reasonably be expected to do and say under the exact conditions presented by the author.

   (2) Comparison-contrast

  To decide on your objectives, the points or elements you'll focus on.

  To select the common grounds you will discuss.

  To decide on the way you will treat the material.

3. Organization: Introduction
   (1) Character analysis
   The central idea will be a general statement describing what you found out about the character you analyzed.
   The thesis sentence must be a brief statement of the main sections of the body of the theme.
   (2) Comparison-contrast
   The central idea will be a statement of similarities and differences you observed in your comparison and/or the superiority of one work or author over another.
   The thesis sentence should anticipate the body of your theme.

4. Organization: Body
   (1) Character analysis
   To prove and illustrate your central idea, you can choose several ways to organize your main points, for example: around central characteristics like kindness, gentleness, generosity, firmness; around central incidents that reveal primary characteristics; around various sections of the work which reveal a character's qualities.
   (2) Comparison-contrast
   Methods depend on the points you chose to focus on. For example, you might be comparing two characters on the basis of character traits. You would use the same methods that you would use in writing about characters in a single work except that in comparison-contrast you are (a) proving and illustrating your points by looking at more than one subject; and (b) your final goal is to show something about the subjects you are comparing.
   If you focused on other topics like point of view, tone, or structure, then, you would first use the methods you do for a single work on that subject; next, you would go beyond to make a general statement about the relations between the things you are comparing.

5. Organization: Conclusion
   (1) Character analysis
   Your conclusion should show how the characteristics you brought out relate to the work as a whole. For example, what do the character's qualities show about the author's view of the nature of human life?
   (2) Comparison-contrast
   Your conclusion should show what you found out in your comparison-contrast; what your information means; and needs for further study.

6. Summary statements

Character analysis and comparison and contrast themes are a lot alike; their differences lie in what is covered. Comparison and contrast is broader in two ways: one, you use it with various literary elements: not only character but also writers, style, tone, and so on; two, within an element, you deal with more than one instance: *e.g.*, more than one character, more than one writer. The likenesses and differences in the two themes can be summarized most clearly by staying with comparison and contrast of character, the common ground between the two themes.

Purpose. Both themes are devoted to understanding character. With character analysis, your purpose is to analyze one character and use that analysis in your interpretation. With comparison and contrast, you go beyond to analyze more than one character, compare the results of the analyses to pinpoint likenesses and differences, and make your interpretations on the basis of these likenesses and differences.

Problems. In both themes, you have the problems for character analysis—figuring out how the writer shows character and seeing if the character rings true. You go beyond in comparison and contrast. First, to pick out the common grounds, the particular things you will compare the characters on. Second, to decide how you will treat your material.

Organization: Introduction. In both themes, your central idea is a general statement about what you found out about the character or characters. In both, the thesis sentence foreshadows the points you will make in the body of the theme.

Organization: Body. In both themes, you choose a way to organize your main points: *e.g.*, around sections of the works, and so on. With comparison and contrast, you deal with more than one character and go on to point out similarities and differences and what they show about the characters.

Organization: Conclusion. In both themes, your conclusion is your broad statement about what the results of your work mean.

V

LOCATION SKILLS

Three important location skills are using a book's structure, using the library, and using reference works. These skills help you find information you need. In a way, they are like an atlas or road map. They guide you to the spot where information you need is located. We have room here only to look at *using a book's structure;* Chapter 14 is about using parts of the book to find information in that book. For information on the other skills check with your librarians. They can guide you in using the library to find books, magazines, and other sources of the information you are seeking. Also, they can help you in using reference works to find collections of information on a problem area.

14

Using a Book's Structure

Take the problem about comparing Aretha Franklin and Dionne Warwick.
See how one part of the book's structure, the table of contents, helps you
quickly find information on the problem.

Problem: To compare Aretha Franklin and Dionne Warwick as modern
singers of soul music.

Question: What pages have the information you need?

*Answer: Pages 5–14 (Introduction); pages 39–45 (Aretha Franklin—
Lady Soul); pages 99–107 (Dionne Warwick—Songbird of Soul).*

SOUL MUSIC[1]

TABLE OF CONTENTS

---

[1] Rochelle Larkin, *Soul Music* (New York: Lancer, 1970), p. 3. Used with permission.

DESCRIPTION

What Is a Book's Structure? A book's structure is its parts and the relation among those parts. Textbooks and other non-fiction books have three big parts; in turn, each part has smaller parts. In the order they come in a book, the parts are front matter, body or text, and back matter. Here are the smaller parts in each big part.

—Front matter: page with title, subtitle, author, and publisher; page with copyright dates and editors, preface, foreword or introduction; table of contents.

—Body or text: sections, chapters, and so on; information about the book's topic.

—Back matter: appendices, glossary, bibliography, subject index, author index.

Why Is a Book's Structure Valuable in Locating Information? It saves you time and work. How? You can quickly use parts in the front matter and back matter to find out three things: whether the body or text has information about a main idea, a problem you are working on; if so, the pages where that information is located; and, other sources of information on that problem.

How Do You Use a Book's Structure in Locating Information? Here are the main steps:

1. As always, be sure you have a very clear idea about your purpose, the problem or main idea for which you are finding information.

2. Use the skills for skimming, scanning, and checking relevance. (See Chapters 6 and 10.) Use the skills in the various parts of the book as you look for information about your main idea.

   a. Title

   The title, of course, tells you the book's main idea, what it is about. The title may be specific enough that you can decide immediately whether the book has information about your problem, or it may be broad and only give you a possible lead which you must follow up in the other parts of the book.

   b. Preface, Foreword, or Introduction

   In the preface, the writer introduces you to the book. He tells you such things as what the book is about, his purpose in writing the book, the plan he followed, and so on.

   c. Table of Contents

   The table of contents lists two things: the major topics covered in the book; the pages where these topics are located.

   d. Body or Text

   The body or text has the book's information. It is divided in various ways depending on how long the book is. Usually there are parts, chapters, and sections within chapters. Headings tell what information is in the various divisions.

   e. Bibliography

   The bibliography is a list of references. It names the books, articles, and other sources which the writer used to get information he used in writing the book. References may be put at the ends of chapters, or references for all chapters may be combined at the end of the book.

   f. Glossary and Appendix

   The glossary and appendix have information that backs up information given in the book. They help you deal with the main ideas given in the book. Usually, the glossary lists special terms (words or formulas) and their definitions; these terms are usually in alphabetical order. The appendix may have any kind of supporting information the writer wants you to have close at hand: for example, maps, numerical information, original documents, and so on.

   g. Index

   Indexes are detailed guides to books. They are made of lists of items arranged in alphabetical order with page numbers. The *subject index* is a list of the specific units of information and the pages where they are located. The *index of names* lists each person referred to in the book and where that reference was made.

PRACTICE

Look at the problem and the directions for locating information. Use the part of the book's structure given to carry out the directions. Check the materials to find the answers.

Set 1: Preface/Introduction

Problem: To find information to answer certain questions about tests.

Directions: This book will help with some questions but not all. Check the book's introduction. Write the code number of the questions it will

help you with. _____

---

1. How does intelligence develop in children?
2. What are weapons for doing better on tests?
3. Which costs most: achievement tests, intelligence tests, personality tests, or interest tests?
4. What are good defenses against character, interest, and aptitude tests?
5. Is a good vocabulary related to IQ?

THE STRATEGY OF TAKING TESTS[2]

Introduction: How to Use this Book

Of the things we want, a frighteningly large and expanding number are dependent upon the showing we make in one kind of formal test or another.

The reason for all these tests lies in the growing complexity of things. Someone had to provide a basis for the many decisions about who is best suited to do a job, handle a promotion, get into a crowded college, or make use of scholarship assistance. The psychologists stepped in and took this responsibility. Their tool for fitting square pegs into square holes is tests.

---

[2] Darrell Huff, *Score: The Strategy of Taking Tests* (New York: Appleton-Century-Crofts, 1961), pp. vii–ix. Used with permission.

This situation puts an unprecedented premium on testmanship, the art of doing better on an examination without actually cheating. Conversely, it means that to lack skill or sophistication in the art of taking tests is to handicap yourself at the critical moment of facing an examination.

The purpose of the book you are now holding is to wipe out that handicap and to replace it with a degree of skill. Its aim, quite simply, is to help you take tests and examinations of all kinds more successfully.

Why does anyone need skill in test-taking? Isn't it enough to have the qualities needed for the work in question—and to let the test simply and automatically reveal this fact? Unfortunately not. For lack of test-taking technique it is possible to do badly on a test for a job for which you are well-qualified. You need test-taking skill to do yourself justice.

Otherwise you may find yourself in the position of the Eskimos in a wry tale told by one Alaskan worker. Before being hired for a job on the Distant Early Warning (DEW) line, he took—and passed—a test designed to find out in advance whether he would be able to adapt to arctic conditions. On the job he met a number of Eskimos who had also taken the test—and failed.

Because the importance of your attitude toward a test is so great, this book will aim first of all to develop your confidence. It will take some of the mystery out of tests, show how they are put together and what they are all about.

It will go on to give you an armory of test-tested weapons-systems, methods, devices, background, techniques, and specific tips—for attacking efficiently and briskly any test you may meet. Then it will narrow the subject down to the specific tests you are likely to encounter in a variety of fields. A chapter made up of representative test items will give you material for practice and warmup.

Finally this book will zero in on the increasingly important psychological tests. These are the probing inventories that delve into your character and interests and aptitudes, often at the expense of your privacy. This book will supply you with what has been proved to be an effective defense against them.

Set 2: Table of Contents

Problem: To find and read 10 particular *prose* selections.

Directions: Check the book's table of contents. Is the selection in the book? Write yes or no. If yes, write the page number where it is located.

Selection Number	Author	Title	Selection in Book?	Page Number
1.	Alfred Kazin	*A Brownsville Kitchen*	_____	_____
2.	Marcia Davenport	*Of Lena Geyer*	_____	_____
3.	Eric Segal	*Love Story*	_____	_____
4.	William C. Williams	*The Use of Force*	_____	_____
5.	Robert Benchley	*What College Did to Me*	_____	_____
6.	Walter Kerr	*Tragedy and Comedy*	_____	_____
7.	Stephen Crane	*The Open Boat*	_____	_____
8.	Joyce Carol Oates	*Them*	_____	_____
9.	Elizabeth Drew	*Poetry and Meaning*	_____	_____
10.	Joan Didion	*Play It As It Lays*	_____	_____

THE COMPLETE READER[3]

TABLE OF CONTENTS

[3] Richard S. Beal and Jacob Korg, eds., *The Complete Reader* (Englewood Cliffs, N.J.: Prentice-Hall, Inc., 1961), pp. v–x. Used with permission.

Set 3: Bibliography

Problem: To check Jersild's book on Child Psychology to see whether he cited materials on topics in testing or studying children.

Directions: Use the selection from the book's bibliography. See if Jersild cited works on the topics listed. If no, write no after the topic. If yes, write the work's citation—title, place of publication, publisher, and publication date.

1. The use of easel painting to study children's personality._____

2. The use of the broad jump, push-up, 50-yard dash, and quarter-mile run to study children's motor development and endurance. _____

3. The use of arithmetic achievement tests to study children's progress in school. _____

4. The effects of speaking two languages (bilingualism) on children's intelligence test performance. _____

CHILD PSYCHOLOGY[4]

Bibliography

Abel, H., and R. Sahinkaya, 1962, "Emergence of Sex and Race Friendship Preferences," *Child Development*, 33, 939–943.

Abt, L. E., and L. Bellak, 1950, *Projective Psychology*. N.Y.: Knopf.

Adler, A., 1931, *What Life Should Mean to You*. N.Y.: Blue Ribbon Books, Inc., 1937, "The Significance of Early Childhood Recollections," *International Journal of Individual Psychology*, 6, 484–493.

Adler, R., 1957, "Effects of Early Experience on Emotionality," *American Psychologist*, 12, 410.

Adorno, T. W., E. Frenkel-Brunswik, D. J. Levinson, and R. N. Sanford, 1950, *The Authoritarian Personality*. N.Y.: Harper.

Albee, C. W., 1950, "Pattern of Aggression in Psychopathology," *Journal of Consulting Psychology*, 14, 465–468.

Allen, F., 1942, *Psychotherapy with Children*. N.Y.: Norton.

Allinsmith, W., 1960, "The Learning of Moral Standards," in *Inner Conflict and Defense*, edited by D. R. Miller and G. E. Swanson, pp. 141–176, N.Y.: Holt.

[4] Arthur T. Jersild, *Child Psychology*, 6th ed. © 1968, pp. 554–55. By permission of Prentice-Hall, Inc., Englewood Cliffs, New Jersey.

Allport, G. W., 1937, *Personality*. N.Y.: Holt; 1950, "Foreword," in M. G. Ross, *Religious Beliefs of Youth*, N.Y.: Association Press.

Almy, M. C., 1967, *Ways of Studying Children*. N.Y.: Teacher's College, Columbia University.

Almy, M. C., E. Chittenden, and P. Miller, 1966, *Young Children's Thinking*. N.Y.: Teacher's College, Columbia University.

Alschuler, R. H., and L. A. Hardwick, 1943, "Easel Painting as an Index of Personality in Preschool Children," *American Journal of Orthopsychiatry*, 13, 616–626.

Amatora, M., 1954, "Similarity in Teacher and Pupil Personality," *Journal of Psychology*, 37, 45–50.

Ames, L. B., 1940, "The Constancy of Psycho-Motor Tempo in Individual Infants," *Journal of Genetic Psychology*, 57, 445–450; 1946, "The Development of the Sense of Time in the Young Child," *Journal of Genetic Psychology*, 68, 97–125; 1952, "The Sense of Self of Nursery School Children as Manifested by Their Verbal Behavior," *Journal of Genetic Psychology*, 81, 193–232; 1965, "Changes in the Experience-Balance Score on the Rorschach at Different Ages in the Life Span," *Journal of Genetic Psychology*, 106, 279–286.

Ames, L. B., and J. Learned, 1946, "Imaginary Companions and Related Phenomena," *Journal of Genetic Psychology*, 69, 147–167.

Ames, L. B., J. Learned, R. W. Metraux, and R. N. Walker, 1952, *Child Rorschach Responses, Development Trends from Two to Ten Years*. N.Y.: Hoeber.

Ammons, R. B., 1950, "Reactions in a Projective Doll-Play Interview of White Males Two to Six Years of Age to Differences in Skin Color and Facial Features," *Journal of Genetic Psychology*, 76, 323–341.

Anastasi, A., and F. A. Cordova, 1953, "Some Effects of Bilingualism Upon the Intelligence Test Performance of Puerto Rican Children in New York City," *Journal of Educational Psychology*, 44, 1–19.

Anderson, H. H., 1937a, "Domination and Integration in the Social Behavior of Young Children in an Experimental Play Situation," *Genetic Psychology Monographs*, 19, 343–408; 1937b, "An Experimental Study of Dominative and Integrative Behavior in Children of Preschool Age," *Journal of Social Psychology*, 8, 335–345.

Anderson, H. H., and G. L. Anderson, 1951, eds., *An Introduction to Projective Techniques and Other Devices for Understanding the Dynamics of Human Behavior*. N.J.: Prentice-Hall; 1954, "Social Development," in *Manual of Child Psychology*, 2nd ed., edited by L. Carmichael, pp. 1162–1215, N.Y.: Wiley.

Anderson, H. H., G. L. Anderson, A. I. Rabin, A. S. Elonen, T. M. Abel, and R. Diaz Guerrero, 1960, "Culture Components as a Significant Factor in Child Development: Symposium," *American Journal of Orthopsychiatry*, 31, 481–520.

Anderson, H. H., and H. M. Brewer, 1945, "Studies of Teachers' Classroom Personalities: I. Dominative and Socially Integrative Behavior of Kindergarten Teachers," *Applied Psychology Monographs*, No. 6, Stanford, California: Stanford University Press.

Anderson, H. H., J. E. Brewer, and M. F. Reed, 1946, "Studies of Teachers' Classroom Personalities: II. Follow-up Studies of the Effects of Dominative and Integrative Contacts on Children's Behavior," *Applied Psychology Monographs*, No. 11, Stanford, California: Stanford University Press.

Set 4: Appendix

Problem: To check Cain's ideas about certain errors in writing.

Directions: If Cain deals with the error, write yes. If he does not, write no.

Type of Error	*Is Error Cited?*
1. double negatives	_____
2. exclamation points for emphasis	_____
3. failure to illustrate	_____
4. wrong words used for the intended meaning	_____
5. mixed metaphor	_____
6. spelling error	_____
7. cliches	_____
8. incorrect division of words	_____
9. misuse of homonyms	_____
10. inflated and repetitious writing	_____

COMMON SENSE ABOUT WRITING[5]

Key to the Error Lists of Chapter One

"and/or." This clumsy and unpleasant device is fortunately never necessary. The writer needs only "or." If French 15 and/or French 20 is

---

[5] Thomas H. Cain, *Common Sense About Writing*, © 1967, pp. 138–40. By permission of Prentice-Hall, Inc., Englewood Cliffs, New Jersey.

required for entrance to the major . . . , then anyone who has French 15 or French 20 will be admitted. Anyone who has both simply has more than the minimum requirements. If you see some special reason for writing "and/or," write instead "French 15 or French 20 or both." This is a little longer but avoids barbarity.

Anticlimax in Organization. Whether you end with a special final paragraph or not (see valid final paragraphs, pp. 85–89), make sure you end with a good firm point. Anticlimax occurs when the writer has obviously finished his paper, then thinks of a minor point or qualification or bit of detail—anything not centrally important to the argument of the paper—and sticks it on at the end.

"as." This is inelegant used causally. When "as" means "because" and occurs late in the sentence, it sounds unpleasant.

We went home, as it was late.

Most readers would accept

As it was late, we went home.

But in either case there is no need for "as," which is used much too freely in bad writing, has the other and more essential meaning of "while" or "during," and can always be profitably replaced by "because," which has only one meaning. So when "as" means "because," always use "because."

cliches. See *cliches and other weary words*, pp. 116–17.

conclusion, unjustified. See *final paragraph*, pp. 85–89, especially *do you need a special final paragraph?* p. 85, and *proof established*, pp. 86–87.

copyread. See *and last, copyread*, pp. 136–37.

detail, excessive. See also *illustrate* and *generalization*, both below. Occasionally a paper suffocates in detail, although more often it expires in the oxygen-poor air of generalization. The right amount of details is the amount that particularizes the point, that roots an air-borne generalization in solid ground. To say

Hemingway became a disappointing writer as he grew older.

is mere unconvincing opinion. But if you can add details, like

In late novels like *The Old Man and the Sea*, for instance, he substitutes telling for showing, in an attempt to make us feel heroism and pathos through rhetoric and not through spectacle. The image of the disciplined contest against nature, basic to the early works, has become blurred.

then the generalization begins to have body. But remember that enough is enough. If details proliferate unnecessarily, the reader may lose contact with the larger idea they embody.

digressions. When you have developed a flexible outline (see *a more flexible technique for disposition*, pp. 46–48), you should stick to it. When you feel an urge to digress into material not on your outline, ask yourself if it is a true digression or new and relevant information. If the latter, rearrange your outline to accommodate it. See *the outline as catalyst*, pp. 60–61.

exclamation points for emphasis. The writer who uses this mechanical form of emphasis readily soon finds himself doubling and even tripling it to indicate degrees of emphasis.

Raskolnikov finds himself trapped! At the top of the stairs he sees Porfiry Petrovich, the image of the law, but at the bottom he sees Sonia, the image of his conscience!!!

This writer is using exclamation points to bludgeon ordinary sentences into inarticulate pulp. The exclamation point is seldom necessary in expository writing (its main use is in fictional dialogue). Use it only when your statement is truly remarkable. Otherwise, the exclamation point will suggest that you can't manage the words of your sentence to achieve proper emphasis. See *common sense about emphasis*, pp. 105–7.

"firstly." See p. 49.

generalization, too much. See *detail* above, and *illustrate* below. The ideal in writing is a balance of general statement against detail or illustration. An excess of generalization quickly renders the reader's mind blank. Statements like

There are some activities of thought that prepare the mind for ultimate engagement.

should not predominate in your writing lest your reader's mind becomes as transparent as glass and no more retentive. Too much generalization means that he will begin to pay less and less attention and so miss your real meaning.

illustrate, failure to. The well-known Chinese saying that a picture is worth a thousand words applies neatly to writing. Say it, then let us see it; keep this principle in mind as you compose. Some of us find it much too easy to deal in abstractions and generalizations that seem clear to us. But if you put yourself in the reader's place, as you should when you write and especially when you revise, you will begin to appreciate the Chinese saying. If one illustration clarifies the point, however, that is enough and better than three poor or tangential illustrations.

inflated and repetitious. See *how many words?* pp. 118–20, and *cut away the fat*, p. 153.

Set 5: Subject and Author Index

Problem: To check what DeCecco wrote about certain topics and writers. *Directions*: The topics and writers are listed below. If he did not cite them, write no. If he did cite them, write the page number.

Topic/Author	Page Numbers
1. Boredom and curiosity	
2. Anger and hostility	
3. John A. Brownell	
4. Achievement tests	
5. Carelessness and frustration	
6. Anxiety and IQ	
7. Thomas M. Bakerin	
8. Apparent retardation	
9. Aspiration level, and motivation	
10. Benefits of practice	

THE PSYCHOLOGY OF LEARNING AND INSTRUCTION[6]

INDEX

[6] John P. DeCecco, *The Psychology of Learning and Instruction* (Englewood Cliffs, N.J.: Prentice-Hall, Inc., 1968), pp. 789–90. Used with permission.

ANSWERS FOR PRACTICE SETS

Set 1

The book has information on Questions 2 and 4. It has none on Questions 1, 3, and 5.

Set 2

The book has Selection 1 (p. 7), Selection 4 (p. 253), Selection 5 (p. 55), Selection 7 (p. 266), and Selection 9 (p. 146). It does not have nos. 2, 3, 6, 8, and 10.

Set 3

Jersild did not cite works on Topics 2 and 3. He cited the following for Topics 1 and 4:

1. *Alschuler, R. H., and L. A. Hardwick, 1943, "Easel Painting as an Index of Personality in Preschool Children,"* American Journal of Orthopsychiatry, 13, 616–626.

4. *Anastasi, D., and F. A. Cordova, 1953, "Some Effects of Bilingualism upon the Intelligence Test Performance of Puerto Rican Children in New York City,"* Journal of Educational Psychology, 44, 1–9.

Set 4

Cain takes up these errors: #2 exclamation points for emphasis, #3 failure to illustrate, #7 cliches, and #10 inflated and repetitious writing. Cain did not mention these errors in the pages selected here: #1 double negatives, #4 wrong words used for intended meaning, #5 mixed metaphor, #6 spelling error, #8 incorrect division of words, #9 misuse of homonyms.

Set 5

DeCecco cited the following: #1 Boredom and curiosity (pp. 138–39), #3 John A. Brownell (p. 545), #4 Achievement Tests (pp. 666–70), #6 Anxiety and IQ (pp. 200–1), #9 Aspiration level, and Motivation (pp. 166–67). He did not cite the following: #2 Anger and hostility, #5 Carelessness and frustration, #7 Thomas M. Bakerin, #8 Apparent retardation, and #10 Benefits of practice.

VI

VOCABULARY SKILLS

Part Six concerns the vocabulary meaning skills. These are the skills you use to figure out what words mean. In turn, figuring out what words mean is a key to using all the other reading skills. Chapter 15, *dealing with homonyms*, looks at sets of words which are identical in sound but different in spelling and meaning. Chapter 16 concerns *dealing with synonyms and antonyms*, synonyms being words that mean the same thing and antonyms being words that mean the opposite. Chapter 17, *dealing with figurative language*, is about language that describes the feeling and sense of events. Chapter 18, *dealing with verbal analogies*, is about discovering a special relation between word meanings and using that relationship with other sets of words. Chapter 19, *using context analysis*, covers figuring out what a word means by the way it fits into its surroundings.

15

Dealing with Homonyms

Here is a situation where you must deal with homonyms.

Teachers very often *counsel* their students to study harder.

What does *counsel* mean? By phonetic analysis, we know that it is pronounced *koun' sel*. That sounds like two other words: *consul* and *council*. Here is what all three mean.

counsel	advise	John will *counsel* James when he buys the car.
consul	government officer in another country	He visited the American *consul* in Panama.
council	governing or advisory group	The college *council* meets twice monthly.

Which meaning fits the sentence? We can try all three meanings. *Advise* fits the sentence. *Counsel* means *advise*.

DESCRIPTION

What Are Homonyms? Homonyms are words that are both alike and different. They sound alike when they are pronounced but they have different spellings and different meanings. Often, the differences in spelling are quite small—one or two letters.

How Is Dealing with Homonyms Important in Reading? Homonyms are important when you deal with word meanings. In fact, they can cause you trouble in reading if you get their meanings mixed up. When you pronounce a word, you may mix up its meaning with the meaning of a word it sounds like. Or if you don't notice small differences in spelling, you may think you are reading one word in a homonym set rather than another.

How Do You Deal with Homonyms? There are two ways to deal with homonyms.

1. Use context clues and the dictionary. Use context analysis to try out meanings of the homonyms in the set. Keep trying until you find a meaning that fits. If you don't know other homonyms in the set, check the dictionary for the definition.

2. Learn often-used homonyms by studying. Note the small differences in the way the words are spelled, and learn the relation between each spelling–meaning pair. Some often-used homonyms are listed in the last section, *Core Homonyms*.

You need both methods to deal with homonyms. You can learn a lot of homonyms but not all, because there are too many. You can figure out a lot of meanings with context analysis and dictionary work; however, you should not depend on context analysis and dictionary work alone; they cause you to stop and break your chain of thought and thus cut down on your reading comprehension and speed.

How Do You Learn Homonyms? You learn homonyms by studying. Practice Sets 1 and 2 below show you good models for reciting. Use these models as you study the core of often-used homonyms in the last section, *Core Homonyms*. Remember: learning homonyms takes a good bit of practice; use the practice models as often as you need to to master the homonym sets given and others like them.

PRACTICE

Use these homonym sets as you carry out directions for the practice sets below.

1. affect
   effect

2. all ready
   already

3. cite
   site
   sight

4. complement
   compliment

5. descent
   dissent

6. dual
   duel

7. elicit
   illicit

8. lead
   led

9. principal
   principle

10. stationary
    stationery

11. their
    there
    they're

12. who's
    whose

Set 1. Learning Homonyms

Compare the words' spelling. Underline the letters where they differ. Check the word meanings in the dictionary. Write each word meaning and a sentence using that meaning.

Homonyms	Word Meanings	Sentences
Ex. beach	_waterfront_	_He left the books on the beach._
beech	_tree_	_He planted a beech tree._
1. affect	_____	_____
effect	_____	_____
2. all ready	_____	_____
already	_____	_____
3. cite	_____	_____
site	_____	_____
sight	_____	_____

Homonyms	Word Meanings	Sentences
4. complement	_____	_____
compliment	_____	_____
5. descent	_____	_____
dissent	_____	_____
6. dual	_____	_____
duel	_____	_____
7. elicit	_____	_____
illicit	_____	_____
8. lead	_____	_____
led	_____	_____
9. principal	_____	_____
principle	_____	_____
10. stationary	_____	_____
stationery	_____	_____
11. there	_____	_____
their	_____	_____
they're	_____	_____
12. who's	_____	_____
whose	_____	_____

Set 2. Checking Context

Look at the homonyms in parentheses. Think about their meanings. Choose the one that makes sense in the sentence. Write your choice. As you need to, look back at your work in Set 1.

Example:
The children walked on the (beech/beach) looking for driftwood.

Choice: ___*beach*___

1. The people's (dissent/descent) led to reform of the tax laws. *Choice:* _____

2. The cold front is still (stationary/stationery). *Choice:* _____

3. The wrecks during the Labor Day weekend were not a pleasant (cite/sight/site) to see. *Choice:* _____

4. The U.N. tried to decide (whose/who's) fault the trouble was. *Choice:* _____

5. The (principal/principle) causes of wars are economic. *Choice:* _____

6. The summer session has (all ready/already) started. *Choice:* _____

7. His (illicit/elicit) tricks led him to trouble with the law. *Choice:* _____

8. Students should plan (there/they're/their) time carefully. *Choice:* _____

9. His classmates were happy to (compliment/complement) his beautiful drawings. *Choice:* _____

10. We have to deal with the (dual/duel) problems of ignorance and poor health. *Choice:* _____

11. The (led/lead) pipe was very heavy. *Choice:* _____

12. Interest rates on borrowed money directly (effect/affect) housing sales. *Choice:* _____

ANSWERS FOR PRACTICE SETS

Set 1

Homonyms	Word Meanings	Sample Sentences
1. *af*fect	to influence	Amount of practice does *af-fect* learning.
effect	result of an influence	Sleep loss has a bad *effect* on attention span.
2. *all* ready	each part prepared	The players were *all ready* for the game.
*al*ready	happened by or before a given time	By 9:00 P.M., the votes were *already* counted.
3. cite	refer to, summon	Be sure to *cite* your references on your paper.
site	location	The building *site* is outside the city limits.
sight	view, to see, aim	The mountains at sunset were a lovely *sight*.
4. complement	complete	The two right angles *complement* each other.
compliment	praise	The *compliment* helped her feelings.
5. descent	act of going down	The mountain climbers found the *descent* dangerous.
dissent	disagreement	*Dissent* may lead to trouble and physical fighting.
6. dual	double, two-part	The car had a *dual* exhaust.
duel	fight between two people	The two congressmen had a verbal *duel* over the new housing law.
7. elicit	to bring out	The questionnaire was built to *elicit* attitudes about child-rearing practices.
illicit	not lawful or acceptable	They looked for the *illicit* sources of drugs.
8. lead	heavy metal	The atomic scientists stood behind the *lead* shield.
led	directed, guided	The president *led* the party through the close election.

Homonyms	Word Meanings	Sample Sentences
9. princip*al*	main one, head	The supply shortage was the *principal* reason for their defeat.
princip*le*	general rule	The math *principle* applied widely.
10. station*a*ry	standing fixed	The bolts kept the engine *stationary*.
station*e*ry	paper writing materials	The young girl liked the pink *stationery* best.
11. the*re*	in the place	We were just standing *there*.
the*ir*	possessive form of they	It's *their* house; they bought it.
they*'re*	contraction for they are	*They're* coming later.
12. who's	contraction for who is	*Who's* covering the south goal?
whose	possessive form of who	*Whose* car is over-parked at the meter?

Set 2

1. dissent
2. stationary
3. sight
4. whose
5. principal
6. already
7. illicit
8. their
9. compliment
10. dual
11. lead
12. affect

CORE HOMONYMS

Here are some often-used homonyms and some near-homonyms which are enough alike to cause you trouble in reading. When you learn these, you will have a solid core to add to as you go along in your reading. When you recite, use the models for practice in Practice Sets 1 and 2 above. That is, underline the small differences in spelling, find the meanings in the dictionary, use each word in a sentence, and then practice checking the meaning in context.

1. affect effect	16. bridal bridle	30. discreet discrete	44. knead need
2. aisle isle	17. buy by	31. emigrate immigrate	45. peace piece
3. aloud allowed	18. canvas canvass	32. eminent imminent	46. pedal peddle
4. all together altogether	19. capital capitol	33. fare fair	47. plain plane
5. altar alter	20. cede seed	34. flour flower	48. pole poll
6. ascent assent	21. ceiling sealing	35. foreword forward	49. presence presents
7. bail bale	22. cell sell	36. forth fourth	50. reign rein rain
8. baring bearing	23. cent sent scent	37. gilt guilt	51. raise rays raze
9. beet beat	24. cite site sight	38. guessed guest	52. rap wrap
10. berth birth	25. coarse course	39. hangar hanger	53. right rite wright write
11. blew blue	26. complacent complaisant	40. hear here	
12. board bored	27. core corps	41. hoard horde	54. ring wring
13. boarder border	28. deer dear	42. idle idol idyl	55. road rode rowed
14. bolder boulder	29. dew due	43. its it's	
15. brake break			

56. rung
    wrung

57. sail
    sale

58. scene
    seen

59. seam
    seem

60. serf
    surf

61. serge
    surge

62. sore
    soar

63. stair
    stare

64. stake
    steak

65. steal
    steel

66. straight
    strait

67. suite
    sweet

68. their
    there
    they're

69. threw
    through

70. to
    too
    two

71. timber
    timbre

72. troop
    troupe

73. vain
    vane
    vein

74. wade
    weighed

75. wait
    weight

76. waist
    waste

77. waive
    wave

78. weak
    week

79. won
    one

80. you're
    your

16

Dealing with Synonyms
and Antonyms

Here are two kinds of situations where you must deal with synonyms and antonyms.

—Pick the word that is a synonym for the underlined word in the sentence.

That lady is just plain *penurious*. She won't even buy enough to eat.

thoughtful   nice   Choice: *stingy*
stingy   happy

—*Probity* is the antonym of _____.

goodness   dishonesty   Choice: *dishonesty*
privilege   practical

What Are Synonyms and Antonyms? Synonyms are words that are generally alike in meaning—words that can be exchanged for one another in most places. Antonyms are words that are opposite in meaning.

How Is Dealing with Synonyms and Antonyms Valuable? The main value of synonyms and antonyms is that they enable you to use various words in speaking or writing in a clear and interesting way. However, they are also valuable in reading and test-taking.

—As you learn more synonyms and antonyms for a word, you gain a richness and depth of meaning about the event the word stands for. Therefore, knowing synonyms and antonyms helps you understand more.

—Knowledge of synonyms and antonyms is very important in using context clues.

—Knowledge of vocabulary is considered to be one of the best signs of ability to learn and achieve. Thus, most aptitude and achievement tests look at your knowledge of synonyms and antonyms.

What Are Some Problems in Using Synonyms? We have synonyms mostly because words have come from other languages into English. Having several words for an event has values. But the various languages are not the same, therefore synonyms may differ sometimes in shades of meaning even though they have the same general meaning. As an example, look at this set of synonyms. Generally, all mean *bearing on the matter at hand*. However, each has a slightly different shade of meaning which you need to watch out for.

—*relevant*: implies close logical relationship with, and importance to, the matter under consideration (*relevant* testimony).

—*germane*: implies such close natural connection as to be highly appropriate or fit. (Your experiences are truly *germane* to the problems.)

—*pertinent*: implies an immediate and direct bearing on the matter in hand (a *pertinent* suggestion).

—*apposite*: applies to that which is both relevant and happily suitable or appropriate (an *apposite* example).

—*applicable*: refers to that which can be brought to bear upon a particular matter or problem. (Your description is *applicable* to several situations.)

—*apropos*: applies to that which is opportune as well as relevant. (That remark was not *apropos*.)

How Do You Deal with Synonyms and Antonyms? There are two basic ways:

1. Use the dictionary and context analysis.
   Check the dictionary for synonyms and antonyms and their various shades of meaning. Choose the word with the shade of meaning that best fits the context. In checking fit, watch the form-class (the part of speech). It will help you decide because synonyms have to be the same form class; so do antonyms.

2. Learn some often-used synonyms and antonyms by studying. The last section in this chapter, *Core Words*, has a basic set of words for which to learn synonyms and antonyms.

As with homonyms, you need both methods. There are too many words to learn synonyms and antonyms for. Thus, you need a core. If you keep stopping for dictionary work or context analysis, you will break your chain of thought and cut down on your reading speed and comprehension.

How Do You Learn Synonyms and Antonyms? By studying. There are many to learn. For your reciting, use the models given in Practice Sets 1–4 below. Use the skills and models with the core of words given in the last section, *Core Words*, and words like them.

PRACTICE

Use these words as you carry out the directions for the practice sets below.

1. acquiesce	8. disparate	15. persiflage
2. adamant	9. gaunt	16. prolix
3. alacrity	10. halcyon	17. seemly
4. brazen	11. impeccable	18. superfluous
5. censure	12. languid	19. surreptitious
6. cognizant	13. nefarious	20. tacit
7. deleterious	14. obstreperous	

Set 1. Finding Synonyms and Antonyms

Check your dictionary. Find at least two synonyms and antonyms for each word.

Word	Synonyms	Antonyms
Ex. sedate	*quiet, serious*	*wild, lively*
1. acquiesce		
2. adamant		
3. alacrity		

Word	Synonyms	Antonyms
4. brazen	_____	_____
5. censure	_____	_____
6. cognizant	_____	_____
7. deleterious	_____	_____
8. disparate	_____	_____
9. gaunt	_____	_____
10. halcyon	_____	_____
11. impeccable	_____	_____
12. languid	_____	_____
13. nefarious	_____	_____
14. obstreperous	_____	_____
15. persiflage	_____	_____
16. prolix	_____	_____
17. seemly	_____	_____
18. superfluous	_____	_____
19. surreptitious	_____	_____
20. tacit	_____	_____

Set 2. Checking Context

Read the sentence and look at the underlined word. In the blank space, supply the synonym or antonym that best fits the sentence.

Example:
The *sedate* man spent a lot of time studying. He was very _____.

lively   high   separate   quiet

Choice: ___*quiet*___

1. When you write a paper, keep checking until you are *cognizant* of all relevant information—until you are _____ all the data.

   agreeable to   aware of   unknowing of   leader of

   Choice: _____

2. She was so _____ that she could not be *brazen* about the mistake.

shameless   speed   fry   sensitive

Choice: _____

3. Sadly, the *prolix* textbook was too _____ to read and understand.

brief   mark   wordy   blame

Choice: _____

4. Come now. Let's cut out the *persiflage* and get down to _____.

harmful   serious talk   polled   joking

Choice: _____

5. When the weather gets hot and humid, they are too *languid* or _____ to do much of anything.

lively   wrong   listless   remark

Choice: _____

6. He can't say so in public but the action has his *tacit* approval. Are you saying that his approval is _____?

scraggly   chair   stated   understood but not stated

Choice: _____

7. Unless you give me good reasons for the plan, I will not *acquiesce*. I will _____ to go along.

virtuous   agree   better   refuse

Choice: _____

8. He did not do his duty and he was not honest. We should *censure* him rather than _____ him.

criticize   praise   somberness   natural

Choice: _____

9. The *halcyon* days of May are a better time for vacation than the _____ days of September.

vague   fair   stormy   straight

Choice: _____

10. The two debate teams gave *disparate* points on the subject instead of
    _____ ones.

    lessen   disorder   different   like

    Choice: _____

11. The sailor was in the lifeboat for twelve days after the shipwreck.
    When they found him, he was *gaunt*, very _____.

    stout   fitting   tall   thin

    Choice: _____

12. We finally changed the *obstreperous* children into _____
    children with the aid of the TV set.

    noisy   quiet   expert   sign

    Choice: _____

13. After a large dinner, dessert seems *superfluous*, just _____.

    red   too much   secret   not enough

    Choice: _____

14. The coach is *adamant*. He is quite _____ in his rule that
    to be on the team you have to practice and carry out all other train-
    ing rules.

    recent   wishy-washy   bashful   firm

    Choice: _____

15. Losing too much sleep can be *deleterious* to your health. It is not
    _____ at all.

    helpful   firm   hurtful   present

    Choice: _____

16. When they went to the big party, they dressed with *impeccable*
    taste. We all agreed that their sense of style was not _____.

    perfect   stormy   faulty   stare

    Choice: _____

17. He wrote me from jail. His nefarious, or _____, activities
    finally caught up with him.

    explain   unlawful   permit   legal

    Choice: _____

18. His laughing during church was just not very *seemly*, not _____ at all.

careful   forestall   first   fitting

Choice: _____

19. The spy was very *surreptitious* when he entered the country. In view of the danger, he needed to be _____.

touch   brief   secret   above-board

Choice: _____

20. When I have a chance to go sailing, I can move with *alacrity*. I don't show any _____ at all.

speed   slowness   noisy   finish

Choice: _____

Set 3. Choosing Synonyms

Find the synonym and write your choice. As you need to, look back at your work in Set 1.

Example:
sedate: _____*quiet*_____

lively   separate   quiet   high

1. nefarious _____

good   unlawful   accept   quick

2. deleterious _____

hurtful   quickness   helpful   trivial

3. cognizant _____

unknowing   crude   criticize   aware

4. gaunt _____

harmful   stout   very thin   plant

5. obstreperous _____

approved   scraggly   quiet   noisy

6. impeccable _____

minimum   faulty   faultless   wicked

7. surreptitious _____
secret   perfect   open   spoken loudly

8. brazen _____
bashful   shameless   raillery   drench

9. seemly _____
fitting   hidden   imitate   not proper

10. languid _____
waver   lively   becoming   listless

11. acquiesce _____
refuse   stubborn   agree   urge

12. prolix _____
impudent   wordy   strict   brief

13. disparate _____
different   reckless   like   aware

14. tacit _____
unlike   stolid   understood—not stated   empty

15. alacrity _____
slowness   pleasantness   calm   speed

16. superfluous _____
spiritless   not enough   confuse   too much

17. adamant _____
firm   boisterous   wishy-washy   incite

18. persiflage _____
depart   joking   long-winded   quick

19. censure _____
praise   unneeded   blame   caution

20. halcyon _____
weakness   fair   implicit   disturbed

Set 4. Choosing Antonyms

Find the antonyms and write your choice. As you need to, look back at your work in Set 1.

Example:
sedate _*lively*_

high   quiet   lively   separate

1. brazen _____
sensitive   handmade   shameless   firm

2. seemly _____
becoming   insensitive   not proper   tiny

3. deleterious _____
round   helpful   ignorant   harmful

4. persiflage _____
fortunate   raillery   unlike   serious talk

5. languid _____
spiritless   lively   stormy   affable

6. adamant _____
spiritless   stubborn   yielding   recent

7. surreptitious _____
above-board   awkward   hidden   terse

8. disparate _____
unlike   similar   noisy   repair

9. impeccable _____
faulty   too much   perfect   young

10. nefarious _____
reject   merge   legal   wicked

11. acquiesce _____
accept   refuse   explicit   strong

12. gaunt _____
turning   slowness   very thin   stout

13. prolix _____

long-winded   brief   follow   criticize

14. cognizant _____

beneficial   waver   unknowing   aware

15. obstreperous _____

husky   noisy   simple   quiet

16. alacrity _____

slowness   quickness   faulty   careless

17. halcyon _____

foreign   wicked   calm   disturbed

18. superfluous _____

somberness   not enough   risky   unneeded

19. tacit _____

stated   implicit   becoming   free

20. censure _____

lower   open   praise   criticize

ANSWERS FOR PRACTICE SETS

Set 1

Word	Sample Synonyms	Sample Antonyms
1. acquiesce	agree accept	refuse reject
2. adamant	firm stubborn	wishy-washy yielding
3. alacrity	speed quickness	slowness sluggishness
4. brazen	shameless insensitive	bashful sensitive
5. censure	blame criticize	praise compliment

Word	*Sample Synonyms*	*Sample Antonyms*
6. cognizant	aware knowing	ignorant unknowing
7. deleterious	hurtful harmful	helpful beneficial
8. disparate	different unlike	like similar
9. gaunt	very thin scraggly	stout husky
10. halcyon	fair calm	disturbed stormy
11. impeccable	perfect faultless	wrong faulty
12. languid	listless spiritless	lively eager
13. nefarious	unlawful wicked	legal virtuous
14. obstreperous	noisy boisterous	quiet restrained
15. persiflage	joking raillery	serious talk somberness
16. prolix	wordy long-winded	brief terse
17. seemly	fitting becoming	not proper indecent
18. superfluous	too much unneeded	not enough necessary
19. surreptitious	secret hidden	open above-board
20. tacit	understood—not stated implicit	stated explicit

Set 2

1. aware of	8. like	15. secret
2. sensitive	9. thin	16. understood—not stated
3. wordy	10. quiet	17. refuse
4. serious talk	11. helpful	18. too much
5. listless	12. faulty	19. firm
6. praise	13. unlawful	20. slowness
7. stormy	14. fitting	

Set 3

1. unlawful	8. shameless	15. speed
2. hurtful	9. fitting	16. too much
3. aware	10. listless	17. firm
4. very thin	11. agree	18. joking
5. noisy	12. wordy	19. blame
6. faultless	13. different	20. fair
7. secret	14. understood—not stated	

Set 4

1. sensitive	8. similar	15. quiet
2. not proper	9. faulty	16. slowness
3. helpful	10. legal	17. disturbed
4. serious talk	11. refuse	18. not enough
5. lively	12. stout	19. stated
6. yielding	13. brief	20. praise
7. above-board	14. unknowing	

CORE WORDS

Here are some words to learn synonyms and antonyms for. They will give you a core you can add to as you read. Recite, using the models in Practice Sets 1–4 above: that is, use the dictionary to find synonyms and antonyms for each word, practice with the word–synonym or word–antonym pairs, and then work with the synonyms or antonyms in the context of sentences.

abstruse	glib	predilection
ameliorate	gullible	prolific
attrition	habitable	propitiate
auspicious	heterogeneous	qualm
authentic	hinder	quandary
axiomatic	impassioned	quiescent
banal	incessant	recalcitrant
bountiful	inexorable	recant
burly	inimical	reminisce
circuitous	jeopardize	retroactive
concomitant	kinetic	sagacious
concur	laconic	salient
contiguous	latent	solicitous
copious	lethargic	sporadic
curtail	lucid	stringent
deplete	magnanimous	superficial
diminution	meticulous	temerity
discernible	mitigate	tenacious
discursive	mollify	transient
dulcet	momentous	trenchant
efficacious	nadir	unwitting
elucidate	novice	ubiquitous
encroach	obtuse	vacillate
equivocal	officious	veracious
erudite	optimism	verbatim
exacerbate	ostensible	vitiate
facetious	paucity	wan
finite	pervade	wary
fortuitous	plausible	wrangle
germane	pragmatic	zealous

17

Dealing with
Figurative Language

Here are two examples of figurative language and their interpretations:

—"It's raining cats and dogs." This sentence gives you a feeling or sense of the information: "It's raining very hard."
—"The fog came in on cat's feet." Sandburg's famous line gives you a feeling or sense of how the fog came in.

What Is Figurative Language? Figurative language is language that carries a meaning different from the literal or "real" meaning of the words. We use figurative language for special effects: to show the sense or feeling of a situation, to add interest, variety, beauty, humor, and so on.

What Are Some Values of Dealing with Figurative Language? Being able to deal with figurative language helps you get more meaning out of what you read. It helps you go beyond the facts to get the feeling or sense of what the writer is trying to show. Also, it makes reading more interesting and fun for you.

What Are Some of the Problems in Dealing with Figurative Language? Figurative language can mix you up if you try to use some of the literal or real meanings. For example, take the expression, "It's raining cats and dogs." A person would be confused if he looked for four-footed animals all over the place. That's an easy example, but some figurative language gets pretty hard to interpret.

How Do You Deal with Figurative Language? There are three main steps:

1. Identify the figurative expression. It may be one word, a phrase, a sentence, or a longer passage. It is the expression whose literal meaning does not make sense in the context.

2. If you have heard the figurative expression before, recall its meaning. If you have not heard it, try to figure out its meaning.

3. Take the meaning you decide on and try it out in context to see if it fits the sense of the material you are reading. If not, work out another meaning.

What Are Some Types of Figurative Language? Here are nine types which cover most cases you see in reading. These types overlap some but they show the many possibilities. In most cases, you can interpret the figurative expression without labeling the type too closely.

1. *Idiom*
An idiom is an expression that has come to have a figurative meaning through long usage. The expression's meaning is not readily understandable from its grammatical structure or from the meanings of its parts.

It was *raining cats and dogs.*
She was *bright eyed and bushy-tailed.*

2. *Simile*
In a simile, two unlike things are compared using *like* or *as*.

After running around the track, he was *as hot as fire.*
Her skin felt *like velvet.*

3. *Metaphor*
In a metaphor, two unlike things are compared. The words *like* and *as* are not stated. One thing is spoken of as if it were another.

When he plays football, Joe is a *tiger.*
In June, the clouds are *cushions* in the midday sky.

4. *Metonym*
A metonym is the name of one thing used for another thing which is associated with it or suggested by it.

The *college* requires these courses.

College here means the people in charge of the college.

The lawyers were waiting for a decision from the *bench*.

The *bench* here means the judge in charge of the law court; he sits on the bench.

5. Synecdoche

Synecdoche is an expression in which the name of a part is used to mean the whole; or the opposite, the whole is used to mean the part.

The farmer sold twenty *head* of cattle.

The farmer, of course, sold all of each cow.

The captain commanded 100 *hands*.

The captain commanded 100 people.

6. Personification

In personification, something non-human is given human characteristics.

Father Time waits for no one.
The waves *nibbled hungrily* at his feet.

7. Irony

In irony, an expression is used in a humorous or sarcastic way to mean exactly the opposite of what it says.

Your plan is *really tricky*. The other team will figure it out in about one play.
What a fine day I've had. Everything I did went wrong.

8. Understatement

In understatement, the language is deliberately gentler, milder, weaker or less sensational than the situation requires.

He was a *bit put-out* when the dogs tore up his newly planted garden.
When the other team gets after me, I *amble* on down the field without wasting time.

9. Hyperbole

Hyperbole is just the opposite of understatement. It is overstatement or exaggeration.

I'm so hungry I could *eat everything in the kitchen*.
I'm so tired I could *sleep for a week*.

PRACTICE

The figurative expressions are in italics. Figure out their meanings. Check to see if their meanings make sense in the sentence. Then, write them in the space given.

Examples:
That sentence is as *clear as mud.*

Meaning: *not clear at all*
She talked *a mile a minute.*

Meaning: *very fast*

1. When he finally gets going, Jack is *a streak of lightning.*

Meaning: _____

2. Louise was so late that Mac was really *climbing the wall* by the time she finally got there.

Meaning: _____

3. I found the 52 pounds of books you left for me to carry. *Your kindness really moves me.*

Meaning: _____

4. When you take that course, plan to study *thirty hours a day.*

Meaning: _____

5. The wind *howled angrily* around the house all night.

Meaning: _____

6. When *the White House* called, the ambassador went at once.

Meaning: _____

7. George was *rather pleased* when he won the new car in the contest.

Meaning: _____

8. Man does not live by *bread* alone.

Meaning: _____

9. Lee was *as sharp as a tack* this morning. He answered every question as soon as it was asked.

Meaning: _____

Set 2

1. If you are not happy with the service, go talk to *City Hall*.

Meaning: _____

2. The river *ate away* the bank.

Meaning: _____

3. Keep overeating like that and pretty soon you'll *weigh 1000 pounds*.

Meaning: _____

4. After she heard the good news, she was grinning *like a mule eating briars*.

Meaning: _____

5. The captain was in charge of *100 horses*.

Meaning: _____

6. Joe *cried a little* when he lost the thousand dollars.

Meaning: _____

7. I was wrong and I'm ready *to eat crow* when I see them.

Meaning: _____

8. You can depend on Mary, she's *a rock* when trouble comes.

Meaning: _____

9. *Your wit is only exceeded by your charm and good looks.*

Meaning: _____

Set 3

1. The driver let the *pit* know that he was stopping for repairs on the next lap.

Meaning: _____

2. *With friends like you*, who needs enemies?

Meaning: _____

3. He *is the army*.

Meaning: _____

4. He's so *hardheaded* that he won't listen to anyone.

Meaning: _____

5. *Research says* that these methods are best.

Meaning: _____

6. Right this minute, I could drink *a barrel of water* without stopping.

Meaning: _____

7. Alice came in *gently like a May breeze*.

Meaning: _____

8. You came in 37 minutes after the 50-minute class started. You were *a bit late*.

Meaning: _____

9. Little Susie is *a picture of loveliness* in her new dress.

Meaning: _____

ANSWERS FOR PRACTICE SETS

Set 1

1. (metaphor) very fast
2. (idiom) nervous and upset
3. (irony) You are not very kind
4. (hyperbole) a long time each day
5. (personification) caused loud noises
6. (metonym) the President of the United States
7. (understatement) very pleased
8. (synecdoche) material things
9. (simile) very alert

Set 2

1. (metonym) the people who run the city's business
2. (personification) eroded or washed away

3. (hyperbole) be very overweight
4. (simile) grinning widely or broadly
5. (synecdoche) 100 men
6. (understatement) was very sad
7. (idiom) humbly say I'm sorry
8. (metaphor) steady and strong
9. (irony) You're not very witty

Set 3

1. (metonym) group of mechanics who took care of his car
2. (irony) You're not a very good friend
3. (synecdoche) stands for all the soldiers
4. (idiom) stubborn
5. (personification) information collected by researchers shows
6. (hyperbole) a lot of water
7. (simile) very gently
8. (understatement) very late
9. (metaphor) very lovely

18

Dealing with
Verbal Analogies

These are verbal analogies. Note how they are worked out.

> knife : cut : : shovel : _____
> hoe   wood
> dig   metal

You read the sentence this way: Knife is related to cut the same way as shovel is related to _____.

> The answer is _____ dig _____.

The first part of the sentence sets the relationship. It is one of purpose. The purpose of a *knife* is to *cut*. The second part of the sentence is where you use that relationship with a new set of words. What is the purpose of a shovel? To *dig*.

> Head : hair : : wheel : _____
> car   tire
> engine   round

The answer is *tire*. The relation between the first set of words is whole—part. When you apply this relation to the second set of words, you get *tire* which is part of the whole, *wheel*.

Vehicles : car : : birds ——————

robin   cat

fly   animal

The answer is *robin*. The relation in the first set is class—member; a car is a member of the category *vehicle*. Similarly, in the second set, a robin is a member of the category *birds*.

DESCRIPTION

What Are Verbal Analogies? Verbal analogies involve relations among words. In the first set of words, a relation is set up. In the second set, that same relation is applied to pick a new word which is related in the same way. That is, you figure out the relation between the words in the first set, then you use it to pick out the word needed to finish the second set.

Why Is It Valuable to Be Able to Deal with Verbal Analogies? Being able to deal with verbal analogies has two main values: it is a very important part of using context analysis to find word meanings; verbal analogies are one of the most-often used types of questions on reading achievement tests and scholastic aptitude tests.

How Do You Figure Out Verbal Analogies? There are two main steps:

1. Look at the first set of words. Figure out the relationship between them. There is an almost endless number of possible relationships. However, some happen more often than others. (Some of these more common relationships are shown below.)

2. Use the relationship with the new set of words. Try it out with the possible choices. Take the choice that bears the same relationship as the first set of words.

What Will Help You in Dealing with Verbal Analogies? Four things help you in dealing with analogies: knowing word meanings, knowing word functions, being able to deal with various forms of analogy problems, being able to see and use various types of relations.

1. Knowing word meanings is a must. It's quite direct. If you don't know the word meanings, you can't do the analogy. You can't figure out the relation between a known and an unknown or between two unknowns. Also, you need to be alert to fine shades of meaning.

2. Knowing word functions (parts of speech or form classes) helps. The first members of each set must be the same form class. So must the second members. By looking at word functions, you can rule out words that do not fit the analogy. However, you still have work to do because usually several of your choices are of the same form class.

3. You must be able to deal with various forms of analogy problems. Different people set up analogy problems in various ways. You need to be able to deal with all of them.

   a. The sentence may be in symbols or it may be spelled out. For example, knife : cut : : shovel : _____
   Knife is to cut as shovel is to _____.

   b. The first word in the second set may be given to you and you only have to choose one word. Or, you may have to choose the entire second set. For example:

   knife : cut : : shovel : _____
   hoe   dig   wood
   knife : cut : : _____
   wood : burn
   hoe : tool
   shovel : dig

4. You must be able to figure out and apply relations. Being able to see and use the relations also is a must. It takes some careful thinking. It will help if you know some common relations to look for. It also will help if you practice a lot and get used to seeing relations among words. Being good with analogies takes a lot of practice. Some models for practice are given in Practice Sets 1, 2, and 3. Use these models as often as necessary to become skilled with the often-used relations given below and with others like them.

What Relations Are Often Used in Verbal Analogies? Here are ten relations which are often involved in verbal analogies: purpose, whole —part, part—part, class—member, cause—effect, synonym, antonym, place, sequence, and numerical relations.

These are some of the many types of relations that can be used in verbal analogies. In your reading, you will see other types of relations. Add them to this basic list. One note: Most of the relations below can appear in the reversed form. That is, analogies can be set up for the relations: part to whole, effect to cause, and so on.

1. *Purpose Relation*
   The second member in the set shows the first member's purpose— what it's used for.

car : ride : : fork : _____

run   spoon

eat   table   *Choice:*   eat

2. *Whole—Part Relation*
The second member is a part of the first member.

hand : finger : : foot : _____

tree   jump

walk   toe   *Choice:*   toe

3. *Part—Part Relation*
Both members are parts of some whole. The whole is not given directly.

stairs : window : : wings : _____

feathers   man

bird   fly   *Choice:*   feathers

4. *Concept Class—Members Relation*
The first word in the set stands for a class; the second, for a member of that class.

furniture : chair : : animal : _____

grass   dog

wood   table   *Choice:*   dog

5. *Cause-—Effect Relation*
The first word in the set stands for an action; the second, for the result of that action.

run : tired : : not eat : _____

dish   bread

hungry   hope   *Choice:*   hungry

6. *Synonym Relation*
The two words in the set mean the same.

big : large : : little : _____

circle   small

high   size   *Choice:*   small

7. *Antonym Relation*
   The two words in the set mean the opposite.

   hot : cold : : high : _____

   low   warm

   tall   cool   *Choice*:   low
   _____   _____

8. *Place Relation*
   The words name a place.

   Philadelphia : Pennsylvania : : Los Angeles : _____

   Oregon   Utah

   California   Florida   *Choice*:   California
   _____   _____

9. *Sequence Relation*
   The two words in the set show a certain sequence.

   Fall : Winter : : May : _____

   Spring   July

   June   Summer   *Choice*:   June
   _____   _____

10. *Numerical Relation*
    The two members of the set are in a certain numerical relation.
    The members may be in numerals or in words.

    2 : 8 : : 10 : _____

    12   40

    20   5   *Choice*:   40
    _____   _____

PRACTICE

These practice sets have activities used in the two steps in dealing with verbal analogies: finding a relation and applying the relations. The sets are built on the often-used analogies listed above. Look back at that material as often as you need to.

Set 1: Finding the Relation

A set of words is given to you. Figure out what the relation between the words is. Take one of the choices given and write it in the blank space.

Example:

asleep : awake   *Relation:* antonym

Synonym   Cause—Effect

Antonym   Place

1. car : tire   *Relation:* _____

    Whole—Part   Numerical

    Antonym   Part—Part

2. plane : fly   *Relation:* _____

    Sequence   Purpose

    Synonym   Place

3. study : learn   *Relation:* _____

    Whole—Part   Numerical

    Cause—Effect   Purpose

4. 3 : 6   *Relation:* _____

    Class—Member   Place

    Cause—Effect   Numerical

5. fruit : apple   *Relation:* _____

    Synonym   Class—Member

    Sequence   Whole—Part

6. Chicago : Illinois   *Relation:* _____

    Place   Class—Member

    Purpose   Numerical

7. leaf : blossom   *Relation:* _____

    Whole—Part   Antonym

    Part—Part   Cause—Effect

8. pretty : beautiful   *Relation:* _____

    Synonym   Antonym

    Place   Sequence

9. first : third   *Relation*: _____

   Part—Part   Sequence

   Class—Member   Whole—Part

10. fall : rise   *Relation*: _____

    Numerical   Cause—Effect

    Synonym   Antonym

Set 2: Applying the Relation

The relation is named for you. Find the set of words that carries out that relation. Write it in the space given.

Example:

Antonym *asleep : awake*

furniture : chair   asleep : awake

coat : pants   tie : knot

1. Numerical _____

   Columbus : Ohio   6 : 5

   tree : pine   rod & reel : fish

2. Cause—Effect _____

   sleep : rest   hand : soft

   similar : like   cat : claws

3. Place _____

   5 : 25   September : October

   Portland : Maine   stumble : fall

4. Part—Part _____

   run : get tired   glasses : see

   pretty : lovely   deck : keel

5. Class—Member _____

   moon : stars   3 : 30

   flowers : rose   Kansas City : Missouri

6. Synonym _____
   Friday : Saturday   nice : kind
   black : white   ocean : waves

7. Sequence _____
   spring : summer   magazine : *Hot Rod*
   clothes : keep warm   driver : mirror

8. Purpose _____
   6 : 12   Arizona : United States
   practice : learn   pencil : write

9. Antonym _____
   bright : smart.   fast : slow
   Daytona : Florida   fish : trout

10. Whole—Part _____
    eraser : lead   Wednesday : Thursday
    friendly : affable   coat : button

Set 3: Finding and Applying the Relation

Do the analogy. Find the relation between the words in the first set. Use it in choosing the word to finish the second set. Be careful—sometimes the often-used analogies are reversed.

Example:
asleep : awake : : hungry : _____
table   hot
full   red   *Choice*: __*full*__

1. fingers : toes : : sole : _____
   mouth   run
   bottom   shoelace   *Choice*: _____

2. play : fun : : win : _____
   lose   green
   happiness try   *Choice*: _____

3. take off : land : : start : _____
    stop   train
    fly   water   *Choice*: _____

4. bed : sleep : : stove : _____
    white   cook
    blanket   wood   *Choice*: _____

5. sad : unhappy : : through : _____
    map   go
    finished   paper   *Choice*: _____

6. Denver : Colorado : : New York City : _____
    Wyoming   New York
    Vermont   Virginia   *Choice*: _____

7. tree : root : : house : _____
    white   grow
    roof   grass   *Choice*: _____

8. 14 : 7 : : 24 : _____
    20   8
    12   16   *Choice*: _____

9. insect : bee : : sport : _____
    fly   read
    like   basketball   *Choice*: _____

10. Monday : Tuesday : : January : _____
    March   February
    Wednesday   December   *Choice*: _____

11. star : solar system : : preface : _____
    book   address
    read   interesting   *Choice*: _____

12. pound : hammer : : play : _____
    sport   round
    fun   bat and ball   *Choice*: _____

13. oak : tree : : airplane : _____

    furniture   fast

    transportation   go   *Choice*: _____

14. Thanksgiving : Halloween : : Mother's Day : _____

    New Year's Day   Labor Day

    Independence Day   Father's Day   *Choice*: _____

15. angry : mad : : adamant : _____

    wishy-washy   firm

    quick   lively   *Choice*: _____

16. lead point : eraser : : blade : _____

    handle   sharp

    hard   wood   *Choice*: _____

17. Greece : Athens : : England : _____

    Paris   Washington

    Bonn   London   *Choice*: _____

18. 5 : 25 : : 10 : _____

    20   15

    100   5   *Choice*: _____

19. throw : hold : : stand : _____

    play   fall

    down   firm   *Choice*: _____

20. destroy : burn : : hunger : _____

    abstain   food

    eat   good   *Choice*: _____

ANSWERS FOR PRACTICE SETS

Set 1

1. Whole—Part
2. Purpose
3. Cause—Effect
4. Numerical
5. Class—Member
6. Place
7. Part—Part
8. Synonym
9. Sequence
10. Antonym

Set 2

1. 6 : 5
2. sleep : rest
3. Portland : Maine
4. deck : keel
5. flowers : rose
6. nice : kind
7. spring : summer
8. pencil : write
9. fast : slow
10. coat : button

Set 3

1. shoelace
2. happiness
3. stop
4. cook
5. finished
6. New York
7. roof
8. 12
9. basketball
10. February
11. book
12. bat and ball
13. transportation
14. New Year's Day
15. firm
16. handle
17. London
18. 100
19. fall
20. abstain

19

Using Context Analysis

Context analysis was used to figure out the meaning of the italicized word in the sentence below. See if you can figure out the meaning. Then look at the analysis.

> We had fun watching the new musical group. They were just *scintillating*, just sparkling, twinkling, and shimmering all over.

> *Scintillating* is an adjective. The relationship is word: synonyms. What was the group like? Sparkling, twinkling, and shimmering. *Scintillating* must mean sparkling, twinkling, and shimmering.

DESCRIPTION

What Is Context Analysis? A word's context is its setting, the way it fits in with the other words and phrases around it. Context analysis, then, is figuring out what a word means by seeing how it fits in with the other words and phrases around it.

Why Is Context Analysis Valuable? Context analysis can help you mainly in two ways. First, it can help you figure out the meaning of a word when no other word-study skill except the dictionary will help you. And context analysis may be better than the dictionary. You may not have a dictionary with you. You may not have time to use the dictionary. You may not want to break your train of thought to stop and use the dictionary. Second, context analysis can help you *check* the word meanings you have worked out by other vocabulary skills:

—Phonetic analysis skills: When you have figured out how to say a word and it sounds like one you know.

—Structural analysis skills: When you have studied the word parts and have figured out a possible meaning.

—Dictionary skills: When a word you find in the dictionary has several meanings and you have to decide which meaning to use.

—Semantics: When you must deal with homonyms and homographs or interpret the special meanings of figurative language.

How Do You Use Context Analysis? You use three steps in context analysis:

1. Get an idea of the function an unknown word has in a sentence. Does it act as a noun, verb, adjective, adverb, or connective? When you know the part a word plays in a sentence, you cut down the number of possible words and meanings you have to choose from.

2. Decide what the word probably means by using the context clues. Look at the other words and sentences surrounding the word. See if one of the types of context clues is present. Figure out the relation of the unknown word to the known words. Use the procedures for dealing with verbal analogies.

3. Check the meaning you decide on. Put the new word meaning in the sentence as you read the sentence again to see if it sounds right, to see if it makes sense with the new word meaning in it.

What Are the Types of Context Clues? There are several types of context clues.

1. *Elaboration with details or explanation*
Sometimes the writer gives you clues about the word meanings when he tells you more about something. He may give details or he may tell you how something works.

Mary did *satisfactory* work. Mr. Jones told her how pleased he was. The other girls decided she was the best in the office. At the end of the month, the boss gave her a pay raise.

Satisfactory is an adjective; the relation is cause—effect. Good things happened to Mary because of her work. *Satisfactory* must mean good enough or pleasing.

They gave the car much *publicity*. They talked about it on the radio. They showed pictures on the TV. They wrote about it in the paper and they had billboards all over town.

Publicity is a noun. The relation is whole—part. They told about the car in many places where people would notice. *Publicity* must mean methods for getting public notice or the act of getting public notice.

2. Examples

The writer may use examples to be sure you get the meaning he intends for a word. These examples may be members of the conceptual class—the word family—which the new word names.

The boys like different kinds of *vehicles*. Bill likes a car. Fred likes a bicycle. Jim says that he really would rather have a dog sled.

Vehicles is a noun. The relation is class—member. A car, a bicycle, and a dog sled all are ways of going places or carrying things on land. One meaning of vehicles, then, must be a form of land transportation.

Bob had to use a different *alias* in every state. For example, in New York, he called himself John; in Virginia, he called himself Michael; and in Florida, he called himself Arthur.

Alias is a noun. The relationship is class—member. Bob called himself by different names in different states. *Alias* must mean a false name one gives oneself.

3. Comparison

The writer may show word meanings by comparison, by similes or metaphors. Remember, similes are tipped off by the words *like* or *as*; metaphors don't have tip-off words.

He was as *spry* as a kitten.

Spry is an adjective. The relation is thing—characteristic. Kittens are active and nimble. *Spry* must mean active and nimble.

The stick was *brittle* like glass.

Brittle is an adjective. The relation is thing—characteristic. Glass breaks easily. *Brittle* must mean apt to break easily.

4. Contrast

The writer sometimes gives a clue to word meaning by telling you what something is not like. He shows you the contrast, the opposite. The contrast word may be a single word or a phrase. Watch for tip-off words like *not, instead, rather than,* and *nevertheless,* although these kinds of words are not always used.

George was *cautious*, not careless, with the gun.

Cautious is an adjective. The relation is word—antonym. Careless means failing to take care. Since George was not careless, he did take care, he was careful. *Cautious* must mean careful.

Mary decided to go *abroad* this summer rather than to stay in the United States.

Abroad is an adverb. The relation is word—antonym. If Mary were not going to stay in the U.S., she must be going outside of the country. *Abroad* must mean outside one's own country.

5. Experience

Sometimes you can figure out a word meaning by recalling a similar experience you had. You read the rest of the sentence and remember something you did, something that happened to you, or something you can imagine.

He was in *agony* when he cut off the end of his finger.

Agony is a noun. An association relation is used. You've cut yourself before. Imagine how it would feel to cut off the end of your finger. *Agony* must mean very bad pain.

John smiled *cordially* at Mrs. Jones. He liked her and he was glad to see her.

Cordially is an adverb. An association relation is used. Think how you smile when you see someone you like and are glad to see. *Cordially* must mean pleasantly or in a friendly way.

6. Definition

The writer often will tell you the meaning of a new word right in the sentence. He may use a synonym or a phrase to define the word.

Mary wanted a *circular*, or round, driveway.

Circular is an adjective. The relation is word—synonym. What kind of driveway did Mary want? A round one. *Circular* must mean round.

Sam's job was to *hoist* the flag, to run it up the flag pole.

Hoist is a verb. The relation is object—action. What did Sam do? He put the flag up the pole. *Hoist* must mean raise.

PRACTICE

These exercises are built on the six types of context clues above. There are two exercises for each type clue. Look at the underlined word in each sentence. Use context analysis to figure out its meaning. Pick one of the choices given. Write your choice in the blank space.

Example:

Fallen trees *obstruct* a road almost as badly as fallen bridges.

help   .   sandy

block   highway   *Meaning:* _*block*_

Set 1

1. The president's speech was the *climax*, the best and most interesting part of the whole meeting.

   low point   high point

   hopefully   jumping   *Meaning:* _____

2. The *rural* area was pretty. Cows and horses were in the fields, flowers grew beside the road, and birds sang in the trees.

   country   therefore

   burning   city   *Meaning:* _____

3. The flowers will *flourish* when the sun gets warmer and the soft rain falls more often.

   certain   and

   die   grow   *Meaning:* _____

4. On a busy highway, a car going too slowly is as big a *hazard* as a car going too fast.

   help   safe

   danger   pretty   *Meaning:* _____

5. The costs of toys do not stay steady; in fact, they *fluctuate* quite a bit.

   change   teach

   sometimes   house   *Meaning:* _____

6. Cousin Bill's coming *prematurely* for supper caused trouble. Mother had not finished cooking. Father had not come home from work. And the children's toys were all over the floor.

   too late   too early

   certainly   dinner   *Meaning:* _____

7. Books, like teachers, can *instruct* you in ways to get right answers to problems.

   read   green

   able   teach   *Meaning:* _____

8. His *resentment* at losing was easy to see. He did not smile at anyone. He hit a little boy. He shouted when someone spoke to him.

   chair   anger

   hope   sweetness   *Meaning:* _____

9. The barn was burning fast and the rats soon *emerged*. They ran through the door two or three at a time.

   came out   went in

   house   cat   *Meaning:* _____

10. The family all wanted a *beverage*. Mary asked for water; Mike, for milk; Susie, for Coke; Father, for coffee; and Mother, for tea.

    apple   hot

    please   drink   *Meaning:* _____

11. Martha bought a *remnant* of cloth; that's all she needed to make the doll's dress.

    a lot   small bit

    big red   something   *Meaning:* _____

12. He was a *valiant* soldier. He never stopped in the face of danger.

    captain   battle

    brave   weak   *Meaning:* _____

Set 2

1. The cup was perfect; they could not find a single *flaw*.

   good   print

   set   crack   *Meaning:* _____

2. The movie was a *horrid* one, really awful, and it seemed to last forever.

   right   very bad

   light   health   *Meaning:* _____

3. He *accumulated* money quickly by working overtime, calling his friends, going to the bank, and selling his house.

   got together   boyish

   familiar   spent   *Meaning:* _____

4. Mary's actions were *random*. She was going to the kitchen to wash dishes. But she stopped in the living room and then she went out to the yard. Finally, she went to her bedroom and lay down.

   mountain   curve

   direct   unplanned   *Meaning:* _____

5. Jim was *exceedingly* hungry, more hungry than he had ever been before.

   hard   not very

   unusually   worry   *Meaning:* _____

6. Paul's good grades in spelling and reading showed that he was as *proficient* in spelling as he was in reading.

   skilled   hard

   new   failing   *Meaning:* _____

7. Mae spoke softly and used nice words. She wanted to answer him *tactfully*.

   taste   roughly

   politely   wild   *Meaning:* _____

8. He is a *bachelor*; he has never had a wife.

   unmarried male   uncle

   every   porch   *Meaning:* _____

9. Look at the *alterations* in this dress. Mrs. Jones made it longer and bigger and she added buttons down the side.

   colors   cage

   blueprint   changes   *Meaning:* _____

10. Instead of closing slowly, the movie ended *abruptly*.

    gold   quickly

    something   needle   *Meaning:* _____

11. When his breakfast was late, he felt as *ferocious* as a hungry lion.

    play   full

    mean   book   *Meaning:* _____

12. The Pilgrims started and used Thanksgiving Day to show their *gratitude*.

    thankfulness   dull

    clear   troubles   *Meaning:* _____

ANSWERS FOR PRACTICE SETS

Set 1

1. high point
2. country
3. grow
4. danger
5. change
6. too early

7. teach
8. anger
9. came out
10. drink
11. small bit
12. brave

Set 2

1. crack
2. very bad
3. got together
4. unplanned
5. unusually
6. skilled

7. politely
8. unmarried male
9. changes
10. quickly
11. mean
12. thankfulness